6 Nightmares

"Lake's examination of nuclear and biological weapons, electronic crimes, and ambiguous warfare is so spirited that anyone could see the exposed underbelly of the world's security."
— Sam Omatseye, *Denver Rocky Mountain News*

"Lake does an excellent job of providing an easily digestible narrative that clearly illuminates the problem for the foreign policy novice. . . . The issue Lake seems most passionate about is peacekeeping."
— Robert A. Manning, *Far Eastern Economic Review*

"*6 Nightmares* helps to explain Washington's failure to prioritize threats and devise appropriate responses over the past decade. . . . Recommended for libraries specializing in international relations."
— James R. Holmes, *Library Journal*

"Refreshing insight into the American security network and the personalities who make the tough decisions. . . . Lake has provided, in a surprisingly readable form, a western expert's analysis of the global dangers that lie ahead."
— *Publishers Weekly*

"Lake is an informing guide to the recent past, and he calls eloquent attention to possible shipwrecks in the near future. . . . I welcome and applaud Tony Lake's book."
— Karl E. Meyer, *World Policy Journal*

"An insider's account of truly important issues . . . a brilliant book. The narrative is compelling and told by a profound foreign policy expert."
— John Deutsch, former Deputy Secretary of Defense and Director of Central Intelligence

"*6 Nightmares* is a vital examination of our national security that reads like a thriller."
— George Mitchell, former Senate Majority Leader

Also by Anthony Lake

Legacy of Vietnam (contributing editor)
The "Tar Baby" Option
Our Own Worst Enemy (with I. M. Destler and Leslie H. Gelb)
Somoza Falling
Third World Radical Regimes
After the Wars (editor)

Nightmares

REAL THREATS IN A DANGEROUS WORLD AND HOW AMERICA CAN MEET THEM

ANTHONY LAKE

BACK BAY BOOKS

LITTLE, BROWN AND COMPANY
Boston   New York   London

Originally published in hardcover by Little, Brown and Company, October 2000
First Back Bay paperback edition, January 2002

For information on Time Warner Trade Publishing's online publishing program, visit www.ipublish.com.

Library of Congress Cataloging-in-Publication Data
Lake, Anthony.
  6 nightmares / by Anthony Lake.—1st ed.
      p. cm.
  Includes bibliographical references.
  ISBN 0-316-55976-8 (hc) / 0-316-56147-9 (pb)
    1. Terrorism—United States—Case studies. 2. Terrorism—
  Government policy—United States—Case studies. 3. United States—
  Social conditions—Case studies. I. Title.
  HV6432 .L34 2000
  363.3'2'0973—dc21   00-042849

10   9   8   7   6   5   4   3

Q-FF

Designed by Stratford Publishing Services

Printed in the United States of America

For Alexander, Galen, and
the NSC staff, 1993–1997

CONTENTS

The Locusts Munching

The White House Situation Room, scene of so many intense meetings on the most dangerous crises facing our nation over the years, is surprisingly small. The conference table almost fills the room. One of the wooden panels on the wall can be opened to reveal a television screen and camera for videoconferencing. But the Situation Room has no computer-generated maps or other twenty-first-century briefing devices.

One day in 1996 the President's national security team (I was his national security advisor) met for a discussion of chemical and biological terrorism. I found the low-tech setting symbolic of our position in addressing such new threats to our nation's security. We are embarking on a new century with the mental furnishings of the century past. We can see some of its dangers. We are starting to act on them. But we have a very long way to go.

The meeting took place before the Atlanta Olympics. Military briefers came to the Situation Room to show us their preparations for any chemical or biological terrorist incident. A Marine appeared in a suit that looked like something to be worn by an astronaut. It would allow him to approach a suspicious device safely, communicating by radio with a team of experts in order to identify and begin to deal with the chemical or biological agent. It was all quite impressive. It added to our confidence that all our agencies were doing what could be done to prepare for unconventional attacks in Atlanta. But then I asked: What would happen if such an incident took place in the next few years in Toledo, say, or Spokane? When would we be able to react quickly to such incidents on a nationwide basis? The answer was the functional equivalent of silence.

This was one small moment that illuminated a big problem. We face a number of new threats, by no means limited to biological and chemical terrorism, that challenge the clarity of our thinking at least as much as our ability to act. America's military might dwarfs that of any foe. We spend more on national security every year than *all* our potential enemies and non-allies put together.[1] America's annual military expenditures are greater than all our NATO allies, Japan, Israel, and South Korea combined. (All this without impoverishing ourselves: In 1998 our military budget represented a smaller fraction of our gross national product than at any time since 1940 — yes, 1940 — an extraordinary tribute to the strength of our economy.) As with the productivity of our economy, our military's strength is expanded by its extraordinary use of new technologies. It should and will continue to grow.

But our military and diplomatic strategy has not kept pace with our hardware. It is not easy to adapt our national security mindset to a rapidly changing world. For example, when we think about national security and the safety of our people, the first thing we think of is the strength of America's enemies — both real and potential. But in a world grown closer, the *weakness* of other nations can harm the lives of our citizens as much as, or more than, the military strength of potential foes. When markets quake in Indonesia or Mexico, they send tremors from Wall Street to Main Street. When political unrest racks Central America, southern California's social services feel the aftershock. When our allies are struggling with economic recession, they are unwilling or unable to pull their weight on the global stage — leaving us to shoulder more of the burdens. When new democracies lack the means or experience to enforce their domestic laws, international criminals can set up shop — and stretch their tentacles beyond our doorstep.

We still face many threats from abroad. But we are thinking too much along traditional lines in our national security discussions. This was true in many of the decision meetings we held while I was in the White House in the mid-1990s; it has been true in most of the stories you read in our press and in most of our congressional debates since. We need to think more clearly about the changing nature of the threats we face. Most of these threats are based in the new reality of "globalization." To meet them we must anticipate, and help to shape, a world of change.

We live in a revolutionary time. With America's technological edge and culture of innovation, globalization in some ways offers our people more security as well as tremendous opportunities. Our military is using new information technologies to expand its qualitative edge. Economically, globalization brings consumers greater choice and lower costs. It stimulates trade and fosters the worldwide growth on which our rising prosperity depends.

But the winds of globalization carry clouds of danger as well. The electronic commerce that permits small companies to expand their sales also helps organized criminal gangs to launder dirty money. The same Internet that allows a doctor in Bucharest to consult a hospital in Baltimore can also be used by terrorists to hatch their plans and hide their tracks. Even as greater openness and mobility are promoting social progress, porous borders can be exploited by those who smuggle the drugs and guns that terrorize our communities. Consider: Only about one in twenty of the container shipments that enter the United States is inspected at the border.

And ironically, at a time when, thanks to the spread of democracy, more people than ever before in human history have a chance to influence their governments, globalization is eroding government's ability to act on their behalf.

Some see the effects of globalization as a blessing; others as the devil's work. In truth, globalization is like the weather: It simply *is*. We can try to understand it better. We can work to predict its course. But if we don't make the best of these forces of change, and seek to harness them, they will get the best of us.

There is a natural reaction in times of change to seek refuge within the familiar: within our own nations or our own ethnic groups or even within our own hatreds and fears. But the natural reaction is not always the smartest. And in our global age, it's downright dangerous. You can see the same struggle in nations on every continent. On one side are those who view change as inevitable; who see the opportunities of a world grown closer; who believe the solution is to compete, not retreat; who think the best way to stay strong within their borders is to band with countries beyond them. On the other are those who view change as an enemy; who think that the discipline and challenges of a new world can be avoided; who believe that it's better to go it alone than share an ounce of authority with others.

In the 1940s, America's great postwar leaders — Truman, Marshall, Acheson, Vandenberg — laid the foundation for half a century of unparalleled peace and prosperity. They knew that American leadership in the world was the only way to prevent another catastrophe. So they forged new instruments of international cooperation, such as the Marshall Plan, the United

Nations, NATO, the Bretton Woods institutions, and made the investments to sustain them. At the start of the twenty-first century, America is still reaping the returns of their farsighted vision.

Now, we have a chance to make the turn of the century another period of construction. We can forge and adapt the institutions and arrangements that will strengthen security, prosperity, and peace for those who work to sustain them, while raising the costs of isolation for those who defy their norms. At the turn of the century, the United States stands at the height of its power. If we want to retain that power tomorrow, we should use it to build today.

Much more can and should be done to enhance our security and promote our prosperity well into the twenty-first century. And much more can and *must* be done to deal with some new national security threats. Shaped by this period of rapid change, they are tests of our ability to think anew as well as to act.

Make no mistake: These threats are upon us. We can't be sure of their exact consequences, but we *can* be sure they are there. That is why I wrote this book — to help sound the alarm. Now, during a time of relative calm, we can and need to think and act strategically in addressing the challenges posed by globalization.

These are the questions that seem to me vital to our continued security:

- Are we doing everything we can to protect the American people from nuclear, chemical, and biological weapons? Could tomorrow's Timothy McVeigh gain access to a weapon of mass destruction?
- Could a foreign terrorist or international criminal gang use the computer to wreak terrible harm on us?
- Have we accurately anticipated the military battlefields of the future? How does a superpower fight a war against a state that responds through ambiguous acts of terrorism?

- When the next Rwanda, Bosnia, Haiti, or Kosovo teeters on the brink, will we step in early enough to pull it back before it falls into the abyss? In the age of CNN, can we say no? Are our purposes in our peacekeeping efforts clear enough, or are these operations Band-Aids that we will never dare remove?
- Are we looking at our geostrategic challenges through the right prism? In a new era, classic great-power relations still matter. But they cannot be understood only in classic ways.
- And, finally, will a Washington obsessed with political gamesmanship fritter away America's future through its own irresponsibility?

Each of these questions, left unanswered, or answered badly, could in the near future lead to an actual nightmare.*

The present danger is only compounded by a sense of complacency. These are good times. There are few challenges that cannot, seemingly, be deferred. So Washington can do what it likes to do best: indulge in its central pastime, partisan politics. Historians will record that Washington was unusually bizarre at the turn of the twenty-first century. We were conducting our politics through our courts; conducting our court business through

---

*Of course, there are other serious threats, in particular the risk of global economic collapse and the danger of global warming. I have chosen not to cover the former because it could happen at any time, and the focus of this book is the medium term — a few years; the latter, because the time line is longer and the science still debated. But both are real, and both could have an enormous adverse impact on our daily lives. The consequences of global economic depression are obvious. Consider also the danger and effects of global warming. The last century was the warmest in six hundred years; 1997 and 1998 set new temperature records. One study in 1999 concluded that Arctic sea ice is shrinking by 14,000 square miles a year. As the ice cap melts, the 50 percent of the world's population that lives in coastal areas is at risk. As a new homeowner living near sea level in Annapolis, Maryland, I have ample opportunity to contemplate this very practical danger.

the press; and, periodically, the press was examining itself, concluding it was making matters worse — and then continuing to do precisely what it had just condemned. Can we blame so many of our citizens for turning from healthy, democratic skepticism about our leaders to a dangerous, deep cynicism? There is nothing wrong, and much right, with politics — so long as its final purpose is serious governance.

With great power — and no nation has ever had more — comes great responsibility. Previous generations spent trillions of dollars to protect us during the Cold War. Now, Washington is squandering a historic opportunity to safeguard and strengthen our future. John F. Kennedy, writing in *Why England Slept,* cited a former British prime minister's description of the 1930s as the "years the locusts have eaten." Look around you. Listen. You can hear the locusts munching.

6 Nightmares

CHAPTER ONE

New Tools for New Terrorists

Thursday, April 22, 2003; Washington, D.C.

7:30 P.M.: Ed was not a basketball fan, but he did enjoy the hum of the gathering crowd in the MCI Center. And he most certainly enjoyed any time he could spend with his daughter, Samantha.

They were both overdressed for the indoor heat being pumped from a vent nearby. As Sam pulled her sweater over her head, static electricity caused her fine hair to float delicately toward the ceiling. Almost like a halo, Ed thought to himself, like an angel. He thought, for a moment, of the day he and Sarah brought Sam home from the hospital, remembering how impossibly tiny she looked in the brand-new crib. Nine years — of diapers, day care, finger paint, birthday cakes, bicycles — and now braces.

Sam spread the souvenir program on her lap and expertly thumbed the pages. Finding the Washington Mystics' photo, she launched into a practiced monologue. "Colleen, she runs really fast. Sharon's almost seven feet tall! Oh, and this one — Tamika Lewis — she has a daughter, too."

1

Ed draped an arm around his beautiful little girl and waited for the game to begin.

■ ■ ■

7:40 P.M.: Percy L. Bysshe had always thought of himself as a good man. So why was he here, approaching the seedy street that led to the arena, about to infect the thousands of people inside? And why was he still questioning himself, even at this moment?

Why, Percy wondered with irritation that bordered on revulsion, could he not act without observing himself, without analyzing every move? Did men of action, did heroes, simply act without hesitation? Was this unceasing self-examination, what he privately called the eye in the sky that judged his every move, a result of his Blanche DuBois of a mother — his clinging, complaining, goddamn poetry-reading mother who had chosen his curse of a first name? Wasn't the last bad enough? "Percy Piss," the children had chanted in the sunny heat of the Alabama playground. He saw himself as an adolescent, painfully skinny and shy, alone in the lab after school — a miserable, friendless, frightened boy seeking refuge in the solitude of science. Did heroes just act? Well, this wasn't heroism. It was hatred. Screw them all.

G Street seemed remarkably empty, even for a Tuesday night. The gaudy facades of the Chinatown shops looked even more pathetic than usual. Not that Percy spent time here, of course. Not when he could help it. He noticed a street sign had Chinese characters. Even here! In "Our Nation's Capital." *Our* nation's capital. Jesus.

The sound of their footsteps was like a ticking clock, Percy thought with satisfaction. A ticking clock, to mark the moment his life would change for good. He and the Russian and Lawrence were like the horsemen of the apocalypse. He knew it should be four horsemen. This night, three would be enough. More than enough.

Percy felt the rage welling up again, and he encouraged it, embraced it, drew strength from it as they neared the enormous arena with its fanciful columns, waves, and lines — some over-paid architect's dream. Giant signs read "MCI Center" in English and Japanese neon.

What was this country coming to? No, where had it gone? Obscene taxation, overregulation, bloated bureaucracies, fake politics, and a government taking away our rights while black and brown thugs ruled the streets. Just like we let the United Nations run roughshod over America. And when foreigners weren't running things through the UN, they were coming to live here.

He flashed back, bitterly, to the memory of Dr. Sen in his office doorway, swimming in an ill-fitting lab coat, nervously twisting his small dark hands. It was years ago, but he could remember every moment. Sen awkwardly telling him about the grant (did he think Percy hadn't heard?); Sen acting so sorry to learn Percy's own had been denied. Yeah, right.

It seemed like more and more of his colleagues had foreign names and accents. Chao and Lee and Lin and Chin. Hernandez. Gutierrez. Andropoulou. Dark-haired, nearsighted scholars who spoke a funny, precise, accented English that drove him crazy. Yes, they worked hard. No wonder the Institute hired them. He imagined them plotting, with Sen at the helm, to ride on the American taxpayer's back to their own professional success.

And what was the point of being a real American himself if he never got a piece of the action? Why should he be expected to help every freeloading foreigner who crossed the border? Why? Because the politicians, the reporters, the bureaucrats, the regu-lators had decided. The kind of jerks who were inside there, watching the game after screwing up the country all day.

What America needs is a wake-up call, he thought. No warning. No demands. A silent assault so stealthy that even its victims won't know for days. An act that will force the public to see how powerless they have become. An act of violence whose purity pulls this country back to its senses.

A dilapidated Diamond cab trundled past, snapping Percy out of his reverie. Its headlights made their shadows loom before them like silent companions. Percy wondered, not for the first time, about the men beside him. Yuri was easy to read — a mercenary Russian, trading terrorist skills for the money. But Lawrence was trickier. Whom did he work for, and what made him tick?

Percy suspected Lawrence had some connection to an embassy or organization of some kind in Washington. How else to explain the funding or the knowledge of the MCI Center and how to attack it? Percy had dared to ask only once, as the project was getting started. They were standing outside at the Georgetown harbor, where they sometimes met to talk. Lawrence had neither removed his sunglasses nor bothered to respond; just given Percy a humorless smile that chilled him to the bone. He'd never been sure if Lawrence's silence had meant "I won't tell you" or "I don't know."

■ ■ ■

7:48 P.M.: "Go Tamika! Yes! Go!" Samantha shrieked, and in spite of himself, Ed found himself swept up in her enthusiasm. He'd never been much of an athlete, but his daughter, by some miracle, was a natural, her love of playing matched only by her love of her Mystics — and they were on a roll tonight, against all expectations. Ed rose from his seat as number four sank an impossible 3-point shot. "Way to go, Colleen!" he roared, hoping Sam would notice he'd learned the player's name.

■ ■ ■

7:58 P.M.: "It's only a block away," Lawrence said quietly. "Are you ready?" Percy knew that he was, yet could only nod in assent. His dry mouth tasted as if he had sucked on a piece of copper. Was Yuri nervous? Percy thought not. Lawrence, as always, was cool and controlled. "Soon they'll be like us," Lawrence murmured. "No power. No hope. Dead."

It all began the day he learned his grant had been refused, that six and a half years of devoted research — long nights, lonely weekends, with only the animals and plates of bacteria for company — had taken a backseat to Dr. Sen and his goddamn miracle microbe. He downed most of a bottle of gin that night, then logged on to his desktop computer in search of electronic relief.

In seconds, Percy found his way to one of his secret hangouts — a home page of right-wing diatribes and extremist propaganda. Icons next to hyperlinks looked like little twinkling Molotov cocktails. "Pow!" they read when you clicked on "The Anarchist's Cookbook" or "Silent Death." The page was managed by someone called "Raz" and sponsored by someone named "Ebenezer."

He stumbled on the link to the "Rant and Rave" — a message board with the subtitle "Save Our Homeland — Share the Hate." Normally, he wouldn't have gone to a site where his presence would be recorded. But gin and fury clouded his judgment. He was lonely and wanted to let go. Hastily, furiously, Percy typed out the saga of Sen, the way that Indian had stolen his grant and rubbed it in his face. He said how sick it made him feel to have to turn to the government he hated, the government that restricted our rights and made us beg for the money the government had taken away from us in the first place. He described the work he would have done with the dollars that should have been his. He railed at immigrants — leeches sucking America's blood. And though he knew better, he clicked the mouse and let the message fly.

The next morning, he woke with a splitting headache and waves of roiling nausea. As he staggered to the bathroom, he remembered Raz and Ebenezer and the home page. Curiously, Percy felt little regret at having posted the message. No one he knew would ever find out. It was an oddly empowering feeling. Still, he resolved to stay away from Raz's page for a while. By the time the phone call came from Lawrence, Percy had almost forgotten the incident.

"Is this Percy Bysshe, from Maryland Bio-Ag Institute? Is this Dr. Bysshe, who is doing such interesting work on large animal pathogens?"

"It is," he replied, curiosity piqued. "And who are you?"

"I am a great admirer of your work," a cool voice responded. It offered a name — a string of syllables Percy had not understood — before suggesting the simple name of Lawrence. Lawrence was interested, he said, in bioagricultural science, and then spoke credibly of new developments in pathogenic research. It wasn't until he mentioned Sen that Percy grew alarmed.

"How do you know Dr. Sen?" he demanded, pacing the kitchen floor with his hand-held phone. Was this some spy dispatched by Sen to steal more of his ideas? Was he being paranoid to think so?

"Ebenezer," purred the voice in the phone, "told me all about that bastard."

Percy sank mutely into a chair as Lawrence proposed they meet. He knew he could end the phone call then and there, but something compelled him to listen. Was it fear? Or was it the unexpected thrill of the strange connection? Had he sent that message in the unconscious hope that someone would respond?

And so they had met. First Percy and Lawrence, then Yuri, the Russian, joined them as well. Of course, Percy was wary, but even so, their interest in him was exciting. At first, all they wanted to do was talk about his research. Week by week, they drew him out with deferential, admiring questions — probing hypothetically at first, and then with increasing precision — on what it would take to build a lab for manufacturing disease.

Percy understood, of course, the irony of the situation. He, who loathed and resented outsiders, was treating these two like colleagues, when one was a foreigner and the other was both colored and maybe a foreigner, too. Maybe Lawrence and Yuri were different because they weren't his rivals, because they weren't trying to take away what was his by birth. Maybe they made him feel special, respected. Or maybe it was the future they offered: the money, the lab, the revenge.

"We want you to help us," Lawrence said from behind his impenetrable sunglasses. "And we want to help you. We want you, Percy, to have what you deserve. Imagine a lab with new equipment, built to your specifications. A place where you and Yuri can work together. Percy, you won't ever have to ask for money again. All we ask is for you to work with us, with Yuri, in growing a bug. He knew a lot about it in Russia. The two of you can do this. All we need is some work in the lab." All they ask, Percy realized with a start, is for me to help them kill.

Lawrence leaned forward and lowered his voice. Somehow, it became more intense. "Help us. Show them how so many of us feel. No power. No hope. Dead."

It seemed to Percy as though time had stopped. He was about to decide not only what to do, but who he was. And he could do that by acting on his hate to overcome a life of humiliation. He would do this thing. "Okay."

Yuri explained the logic for building a biological weapon. It might be possible to acquire some nuclear waste from some people who knew some people in Russia, but using it in a conventional explosive was too complex and expensive. Chemical weapons were relatively cheap and easier to prepare, but releasing them at the target put the messenger at too much risk. You wouldn't know a bioassault had taken place until symptoms later appeared, so it would be harder to detect, investigate, and deal with. And ounce for ounce, bioweapons were far deadlier.

The challenge of a biological agent, he went on, was how to ensure its delivery. Poisoning the water supply was not an option; few germs could survive the chlorine. Dispersing the agent from an airplane or helicopter imposed too many constraints; they would have to attack under cover of darkness, because bacteria are susceptible to sunlight; and too much wind would risk disrupting the necessary concentrations. "That is why," Yuri informed him grimly, "we will carry them to the target ourselves."

Percy was not surprised to learn that anthrax was their chosen bacteria. While not contagious, it is highly lethal and relatively easy to make. And you wouldn't even know you were a victim until days later, when symptoms set in. The challenge of anthrax would be in transforming it from a liquid slurry to a powder. They'd need to be sure the dried particles were exactly .001 to .005 millimeters in diameter — small enough not to sink to the ground, yet big enough to be retained in their victims' lungs, where the anthrax spores would enter the bloodstream and begin the deadly process of replication.

Lawrence told Percy to make up a list of all the equipment he'd need. He would locate a space and foot the bill for setting up the lab. Then Percy was to steal a sample of anthrax from the Institute. Percy and Yuri would grow the bacteria, which Yuri and Lawrence would disperse.

Most of what they needed for the lab was easily accessible — equipment and solutions with commercial uses for products from pesticides to beer. Internet sites and mail-order catalogs presented a wide selection. Scores of scientists across the country ordered products like these every day. Percy prepared a shopping list of the biggest-ticket items: computer-controlled fermenter, centrifugal separator, freeze-dryer, high-efficiency particulate air filter. "And don't forget," he told Lawrence with a forced smile, "we'll need good surgical masks. At least until we can inoculate ourselves." Soon, Yuri sent word that the lab would be built in a "safe house" in Gaithersburg, Maryland. "Friends of Lawrence's," the Russian assured him. "Totally discreet."

Stealing the seed agent from the Institute proved much easier than expected. As in many labs, tough security standards were weakened by human carelessness. In Percy's department, where radioactivity, pathogenic bacteria, and biohazardous waste were part of the work environment, even the best scientists sometimes slipped in observing security protocols.

Percy knew that one of his colleagues was working with bacillus anthrax. He'd seen the delivery of the glass ampules from U.S. Bio Culture Source. But pocketing a vial was far too risky; it would be missed right away. Instead, Percy waited for Dr. Lin to start culturing the bacteria, carefully noting the time each day that he left the Bio-Containment Facility. This Bio-Containment Facility, ranked P-3, was for highly toxic materials. The doors were meant to be locked at all times, except to authorized users. But one afternoon, as Percy lingered nonchalantly in the hall, Dr. Lin exited the facility for a phone call and left the door ajar. Quickly, Percy slipped inside. The fermenter was right in front of him. Using a pipette, he transferred 1 milliliter of the culture to a plastic test tube. The entire procedure took a matter of seconds. Nobody noticed a thing.

Working evenings and weekends in the makeshift lab, Percy and Yuri were soon able to culture several kilos of concentrated anthrax slurry. At this stage, the surgical masks they wore were enough to protect themselves.

The second phase of the project was more difficult and more risky. They had to concentrate the slurry in the continuous-flow centrifuge, reduce it to a solid by careful freeze-drying, and mill the dried cake into dispersible powder — an extremely sophisticated procedure. Everything would need to be completely contained to avoid contamination, with hoods over the machines and arm-length gloves to guard against infection. Grinding the microscopic, amber-colored particles could take months to achieve the right size. Fifty to one hundred bioparticles in a row would be just the width of a human hair. Even after they had immunized themselves, they were very, very careful.

Percy was relieved, if a little jealous, when Yuri produced a detailed protocol. "I arranged a little 'gift' for a friend," the Russian told him with a shrug. "He used to work at Biopreparat. Now he makes pesticide in Ukraine. Do you think the Soviet Union wasn't building bioweapons? There are thousands of Russian scientists with this knowledge."

Within weeks, the powder was ready to be loaded into spraying devices. Lawrence resurfaced to check on their progress and fill Yuri in on the plan.

Percy felt an odd pang of regret that the project was almost over. His mouth was dry behind his mask as he looked around the lab. Was he a coward, to have worked only on manufacturing the microbe? Was this enough to be a man of action? What would it feel like to take another's life with his own hands? Remember, a small inner voice reassured him, no one will ever know. That's right. No one would ever know. Like the anthrax spores, unseen, unnoticed, yet filled with the power of death over life, he would reverse his pathetic life and strike an invisible blow. He would help the other two in the delivery, if they would let him. And they did.

■ ■ ■

8:02 P.M.: Halftime. Ed held Sam's hand as they made their way down the stands and out to the corridor. Her face was red with pleasure but also hot with sweat. The cooler air was refreshing after the heat being pumped inside. Throngs of cheerful Mystics fans paraded through the hallways as music blared from the loudspeakers and spirited vendors hawked their wares. "One beer and one large ginger ale," Ed said when they reached the counter. "Oh, yeah," he added as Sam tugged his hand. "Lots of ice in the ginger ale."

"Thanks, Daddy." His daughter had a mischievous look. She belched after the first sip. He was proud even of that.

■ ■ ■

8:03 P.M.: Down Ninth Street to a vacant lot just north of the MCI Center. A fence topped with barbed wire guarded the lot, but the gates at the ends of the fence nearest the Center were carelessly left open, as Lawrence had said. Crossing the lot, looking as natural as possible. Reaching the air intake at the darkened northeast corner of the building. Percy and Yuri standing on either side of Lawrence, watching the streets a few dozen yards away, blocking the vision of any passersby. Lawrence putting on a mask . . . taking the small container from his pocket . . . releasing the amber-colored powder, finer than talc. Percy glancing down behind him to see and experience the exact moment, disappointed he couldn't see his powder as it was sucked into the intake on its invisible, deadly voyage.

Walking away, now, across to Seventh Street and turning left back toward G Street, Chinatown, and the car. Looking natural. Two days, then, in which to get away. Where would the others go? He didn't want to know and hadn't told them his own plans. He hoped, but didn't really believe, they would never find him again.

Sunday, April 25, 2003; Washington, D.C.

4:17 A.M.: Ed woke up with a start and a groan. What time was it? He rubbed his temples. It felt like his head was burning up. His lungs constricted painfully. Maybe this was a heart attack. No. He was only thirty-seven. Why did it hurt so much to breathe? My God, he felt terrible.

Sarah was deep in sleep at his side. Whatever he had, she hadn't caught it. That was good — she was already stressed about the speech she was giving tomorrow. He brushed a hand over her fine blond hair, so similar to their daughter's. He wouldn't wake Sarah up just yet. No need for her to worry.

With effort, Ed pulled himself out of bed and made his way into the hallway. His T-shirt was soaked with sweat. Could it be an allergic reaction? Wheezing a little, he entered the den and picked up the phone. Dr. Murphy would know what to do. Now, where did they keep his number?

It was only when Ed went back into the hall that he heard Sam's labored breathing. "Sweetie . . . ?" he asked, pushing open her door.

"Daddy," she gasped, "I don't feel so good."

■ ■ ■

1.

Biological, Chemical, and Nuclear Weapons: The Tool Kit of Tomorrow's Terrorists?

In case you are wondering, there is no ventilation duct within reach of the ground at the MCI Center. But federal and state authorities did hold an exercise on dealing with a chemical attack there. And yes, the production and effects of anthrax are as described.

The particles of a bioweapon are invisible to the human eye. Each is just 1 to 5 microns in diameter — a micron equaling $\frac{1}{1000}$ of a millimeter, or one-fiftieth the width of a human hair.

There is no smell to alert you, no taste, no sight to warn an attack is under way. The first signal comes a few days later, as the symptoms begin to emerge.

These are the effects of inhaling a mere eight thousand spores of anthrax, a dose smaller than one of the dots of this colon: After entering your lungs, the spores travel to your lymph nodes, where they multiply and spread throughout your body. Within two to five days, you develop a high fever. Difficulty breathing. Chest pain. Vomiting. This progresses to acute respiratory distress, blood poisoning, and shock. Antibiotics can only delay the disease process. If you stop taking the antibiotics, anthrax may reappear. Your only hope of cure is to be immunized during the antibiotic treatment and pray your body is able to mount a protective immune response.[1]

What are your chances of surviving such a tiny dose of inhaled, weapons-grade anthrax? Maybe 50 percent. That's why the Congressional Office of Technology Assessment concluded in a 1993 study that a single airplane delivering only 100 kilograms of anthrax — a mere .2562 cubic yards — over Washington, D.C., after dusk on a calm night could kill many hundreds of thousands of people.

Even worse could be the product of "black biology," such as a genetically engineered, antibiotic-resistant strain of anthrax, as reportedly developed by Russian scientists at the Soviet bio-weapons conglomerate Biopreparat. Or a wildly contagious disease like smallpox, which can pass from person to person in a murderous microbial chain. (Only about 10 percent of our population is now inoculated against the disease.) Or incurable Ebola and pneumonic plague. Or bubonic plague, cholera, or botulism.[2] Not to mention the nightmarish notion of chimeras — viruses that, like their mythological namesake, are monsters made up of different parts. Scientists dispute whether chimera viruses already have been developed, such as an Ebola-smallpox hybrid that combines the worst aspects of both. But as genetic engineering continues to advance, so does the frightening likelihood that someone, somewhere will try to create them.

Terrorists who lack the scientific expertise to develop biological agents could turn more easily to chemical weapons, including nerve agents like sarin or VX. Sarin, also known as GB, was discovered in 1938 by a German company doing research on new pesticides. Inhalation of sarin's colorless, odorless fumes leads to difficulty breathing, headache, chest pain, choking cough, vomiting, impaired hand-eye coordination, and loss of control over body functions. Within minutes, it can result in convulsions and death by respiratory paralysis.

VX entered popular culture in the 1996 movie *The Rock*, in which a disgruntled brigadier general leads a team of renegade commandos in stealing VX from a military compound, taking tourists hostage on Alcatraz, and threatening to launch the VX on missiles aimed for San Francisco. (I liked the movie, but found its missile scenario more credible than its portrayal of instant communications in our government, even at high levels. In fact, during a number of crises, we had trouble reaching each other at all, much less instantly — and were never able satisfactorily to fix the problem.)

VX has never been used since it was first developed by the United States in the 1950s — and this is a merciful thing. VX, which is ten times more lethal than sarin, can kill either by being inhaled or by contact with skin. With its mineral oil–like consistency, it can persist on the ground for a period of several weeks, posing a longer-term contamination hazard than more volatile chemical substances. As with sarin, VX attacks the nervous system and causes an ugly death by suffocation.

The most familiar weapons of mass destruction (WMD) are nuclear devices. We like to think that nuclear weapons are the exclusive property of a few governments. But if terrorists choose the nuclear course, they need not rely on possession of sophisticated nuclear devices — though such a prospect is by no means impossible. Former Director of Central Intelligence John Deutch has warned of the terrible damage that a mixture of radioactive waste and conventional explosives could do in one of our cities.

HOW REAL IS THE THREAT?

Why would such terrible weapons appeal to terrorists? Aren't terrorists traditionally drawn to the bomb and the gun — weapons that are more "heroic" than a stealthy, silent killer like anthrax? Wouldn't it be easier to use such familiar means? Wouldn't the use of a weapon of mass destruction so revolt the public that the cause for which the terrorists had acted would be undermined, not advanced? Wouldn't any government supporting such an attack be subject to overwhelming retaliation? And, in any case, isn't the number of terrorist attacks in decline?

The good news is that it is apparently possible both to deter some state sponsorship of terrorism and to lessen the likelihood that such a state would use a weapon of mass destruction. In 1991, President Bush's warnings seem to have dissuaded Saddam Hussein from using Iraq's arsenal of chemical and biological weapons during the Gulf War. Similarly, Saddam's use of terror beyond Iraq's borders has apparently subsided since President Clinton launched military strikes against targets in Baghdad in 1993. We cannot know with certainty that the strikes deterred him. But it is better to be uncertain about why he has refrained than to be investigating why he has not. It may be instructive briefly to tell the story of this exercise in punishment and deterrence.

Some have written that we had insufficient reason for the attack. That, I believe, is nonsense.

On April 14, 1993, the same day that former President Bush arrived in Kuwait for a visit to the country he was primarily responsible for saving from the Iraqis, police there arrested a group of Iraqi terrorists and their Kuwaiti collaborators. The ten Iraqis had infiltrated across the border the night before with plans for three different ways of killing Bush on the fifteenth — and the explosives and weapons with which to carry them out. Their bomb, which contained approximately 80 kilograms of explosives, would have killed not only our former leader. It had the power to murder anyone standing within 400 yards, or farther than Tiger Woods can drive a golf ball.

On April 27, the Kuwaiti government announced that two of the Iraqis had confessed to the plot. Our own CIA was convinced that the Iraqi government was implicated. If so, it was clear to all of the President's senior national security advisors, and to the President, that an American response was required. To make sure that the Kuwaiti case for the plot was solid, we asked the Justice Department, which had the technical resources to best evaluate the evidence, to work with the Kuwaitis, and give the President their judgment. While it did so, the Joint Chiefs of Staff developed their plans for a retaliatory strike. The planning soon focused on the headquarters in Baghdad of the Iraqi Intelligence Service, a large, six-story building with three wings. As my deputy and friend Sandy Berger and I met with Secretary of Defense Les Aspin and the chairman of the Joint Chiefs, Colin Powell, and their planners, it became clear to us that it was the right target. It would send a clear message to the Iraqi officials actually involved in conducting the plot and disrupt their ability to act in the future.

I soon came to regret that the Justice Department was given more than a technical role in deciding the issue. While we needed their expert help, they brought to their recommendation a standard of proof that would later hold up in an American court — and on this and other foreign terrorist incidents, especially when the government with whom we are working may not be completely forthcoming, gaining such evidence is no easy task. Finally, in early June, the trial of the accused began in Kuwait City. Two weeks or so later, the Justice Department joined the CIA in concluding that Baghdad was behind the plot.

On the evening of June 24, in the President's family quarters, the President and Vice President heard from the President's senior advisors on the issue: Aspin, Powell, Secretary of State Warren Christopher, Director of Central Intelligence James Woolsey, Attorney General Janet Reno, Berger, and me. The President, who had followed the planning during the previous weeks, gave his final approval to the target. His major concern was the possibility — indeed, likelihood — that there would be civilian casualties from the Tomahawk missiles that might miss the building and land in the adjacent neighborhood. Once assured by Powell that they would be kept to a minimum, the President gave his approval for an attack — to take place after sunset following the Muslim Sabbath.

After the meeting broke up, the President and I walked down the corridor toward the exit from the family quarters. I told him that I admired the way he had frontally addressed the question of casualties. This takes more courage than shying away from the human reality of such decisions. It is all too easy for government officials in Washington to numb themselves to the fact that they are forced to recommend or issue orders that will result in the deaths of American and foreign human beings. Government memoranda are replete with the abstractions designed to allow such numbing. In such language, the President in this case was concerned about "collateral damage." In fact, he was concerned about innocent human beings.

When I think of President Clinton, this very human figure, I often recall his hands as they pulled apart his morning bagel at the national security briefings that began his working days. They are surprisingly delicate hands for such a substantial figure, with long fingers most suited to a concert pianist. But as with his surprising hands, he is an immensely complicated as well as talented person who defies simple description. A very tough politician, he hates to offend even his enemies. Genuinely warm and capable of extraordinary friendship, he has not always rewarded the loyalty of his subordinates (although I never had any complaints on that score). Extremely intelligent, his thinking is as much intuitive as linear. He loves jokes but can miss irony. He is one of the most generous and empathetic people I have ever known, but, like so many of his predecessors, also self-absorbed. Yes, he cares about himself. But he also cares, as much as any leader we have seen in generations, about the welfare of the people he has led. It is one reason I have retained a genuine affection for him.

The charge that President Clinton is a cynic who believes in too little is flatly wrong. My first extended time with him was in Little Rock in late 1991, working with him on a campaign speech on national security. As we talked through each paragraph, he did not react as other candidates I have seen in similar situations. He did not ask how the listeners might react to what he would say, although that, of course, was an unspoken criterion. Quite unconsciously, I thought, at the end of almost every section he had approved, he said, "Yes. I *believe* that."

Indeed, I think that his tendency has always been to believe too much, not too little. And, immensely talented, throughout his life he was able to have it all, to avoid making truly hard choices. But I saw, over the four years I worked with him, how he moved ever more confidently in making such choices, beginning with the attack on Baghdad in the spring of 1993.

Some critics of the President's decision alleged that he acted out of political calculation. In fact, that couldn't be farther from the truth. The next day, I happened on the President and two of his senior White House aides as they sat in a little garden off the West Wing. His two advisors were questioning the attack on the grounds that the inevitable pictures on CNN of civilian casualties would create a negative public backlash in the United States. I argued, with some heat, that the President could not now go back on the decision that he had made. Yes, we would see casualties on CNN. But while we would never know how many people would be saved by deterring further Iraqi terrorism nor ever see their faces, their lives were real as well. And they hung in the balance. The President dismissed these last-minute hesitations.

The attack took place as scheduled at 4:22 EDT on June 26. Since it was the middle of the night in Baghdad, we would have no photographic evidence of the results for some hours. We had hoped that there would be immediate CNN coverage of the results, but their correspondents had gone from Iraq to Amman, Jordan. The President, Vice President, and a few others gathered in the little dining room off the Oval Office some minutes before the President was due to go to his desk to televise an address to the nation. We heard that CNN had received confirmation that the headquarters had, indeed, been hit — the report coming to a CNN employee from a relative living in Baghdad. The President asked if we could be sure of this report. I told him that we could have only "relative" certainty. He seemed only moderately amused.

The intelligence headquarters was, in fact, badly damaged. There were civilian casualties in the immediate vicinity. Years later, the President was to remember the name of one of those who died, with concern for the loss of life but not, I believe, with regret for having ordered the attack. For it probably has helped deter further Iraqi terrorism. This suggests that deterrence of such state-sponsored terrorism remains possible. It is also a positive fact that the number of terrorist attacks was lower in the late 1990s than it was a decade earlier. Total terrorist attacks in 1987 numbered 666; in 1998, there were 273.[3]

So much for the good news. There is bad news, too. While the number of terrorist incidents has decreased, they have become more destructive, with many claiming more victims.[4] The casualty rates of recent attacks against Americans form a tragic litany of loss: the World Trade Center bombing (six dead, more than a thousand injured); Oklahoma City (168 dead, more than 500 injured); Khobar Towers (19 dead, some 500 wounded); U.S. embassies in Kenya and Tanzania (more than 250 dead and upwards of 5,000 wounded).

Moreover, the profile of the terrorists is changing in ways that make them harder to deter. And access to weapons of mass destruction is easier in a world of globalization.

These factors do not conclusively mean that America will suffer a WMD terrorist attack on our soil within the next five years. But given the consequences and the increasing probability, our society needs to act, not out of hysteria, which is neither warranted by the facts nor useful as a spur to effective action, but out of prudence. If such an attack occurs, we must be able to say, looking back on this period, that we did everything we could to prevent it and to deal with its devastating consequences.

The hard truth is that we are not doing so.

2.

The Changing Face of Terror

According to a 1998 government study commissioned by Attorney General Reno, "the single most significant deficiency in the nation's ability to combat terrorism is a lack of information, particularly regarding domestic terrorism." The report expressed major concerns over "increased activity by small cells of terrorists or individuals who are inspired by, but not affiliated with, terrorist groups, thus making them harder to identify and stop."[5]

This is true as well, though perhaps to a lesser extent, with international terrorists. They more often act in organized groups, but the ties of such groups to each other — and to foreign governments — are increasingly murky. As *New York Times* reporter Tim Weiner observed in the wake of the 1998 U.S. Embassy bombings in Africa,

> The networks are by nature almost impossible to unravel. The chain of command in a sophisticated group connects the intellectual author of the terror to the attackers who carry out his will. But that chain has many links, and no one person in the chain may know the identity of the next. The man who builds the bomb may know nothing of the man who pays him, or the man who drives the bomb to its target. So locating a bomber or his car may lead nowhere.[6]

Most important, the aim of both domestic and foreign terrorists seems to be changing. While political terror remains a reality, as in the case of Hamas, more and more, the postmodern terrorist is motivated simply by *hate*. Hatred of the West. Hatred of the United States Government as the destroyer of liberties at home and of traditional values abroad. Hatred of modern technology and a modern, godless, global society. Hatred of "them": other men, women, and children who, because different in belief or ethnic heritage, are seen as less worthy, less good, less human. Hatred inspired by religious feeling, in contradiction to the tenets of all major religions. Hatred, and, thus, revenge. As Unabomber Ted Kaczynski, who killed three people and injured almost thirty before his capture in 1995, wrote in his diary in April 1971, "I act merely from my desire for revenge . . . I believe in nothing."[7] (Kaczynski was in the class behind me at college. I do not recall him. I'm grateful he did not recall me.)

For such people, the murder and maiming of innocents is an existential act that is driven by the very worst angels of their nature. Acting alone or in shadowy groupings like those of Usama bin Ladin, these terrorists are harder to identify before they strike and to apprehend after they do. Acting without clear ties to foreign governments, they cannot be stopped by threats or retaliation against those governments. Acting without clear political goals, they are not self-deterred by concerns about popular reaction to their acts. Religious fanatics, whose only constituent is God, believe they answer to a higher authority. Brian Jenkins writes, "Whether that god speaks through the mouth of some angry sheik, extremist rabbi, fundamentalist preacher, or mad guru in Tokyo, if he says that it is permissible to kill indiscriminately, then the constraints of conventional morality fall away."[8] As "Meggie," a member of the antisemitic and racist

Christian Identity movement, explains in an essay on the World Wide Web,

> The Bible is chock full of things we are to hate. I think Solomon, known as the wisest man, said it best. *If anyone respects and fears God, he will hate evil. For wisdom hates pride, arrogance, corruption, and deceit of every kind* (Proverbs 8:13, TLB). This includes people who hate God . . .
>
> Is there a thinking person in this country that would say we have justice anymore? Can they really not say this country is going to hell in a hand basket at breakneck speed? Can they say that Yah reigns supreme here? I don't think so. Could our problems stem from our refusing to hate? What does Yahweh say? **HATE EVIL . . .** (Amos 5:15, TLB).[9]

Such messages contribute to an atmosphere of intolerance and divisiveness that, at the extreme, could be used to justify violence.

Acting against the symbols of the global technological, economic, and cultural forces the new terrorists like McVeigh hate — whether federal buildings, corporate headquarters, military bases, abortion clinics, or U.S. embassies — they put at increasing risk the nation, citizens, and businesses seen as at the heart of those global forces: America and Americans.

It follows that while these criminals are drawn to traditional means of destruction — guns and explosives — they will turn also to weapons of mass destruction. The bullet and bomb were seen as "heroic" by traditional, politically motivated terrorists. The new terrorists are haters, not self-anointed heroes. Their aim is to lash out, to kill. And how better to kill than using weapons of mass destruction?

3.

Global World, Global Weapons

Gaining access to weapons of mass destruction is not a simple task.

While biological agents are relatively easy to grow or obtain, transforming them into substances that can be spread effectively is a far more complex procedure. And once a terrorist has a weaponized agent, he still faces the challenge of delivery. Poisoning a water supply is much harder than it sounds, as sunlight and chlorine kill waterborne organisms. To launch aerosolized pathogens successfully indoors, a terrorist would need knowledge "on the rate at which the air is exchanged in a building being attacked, the number of cubic feet of space serviced by the air handling system, and the dosage required to inflict a human casualty with the agent being used" in order for mass casualties to result.[10] Outdoor dispersal depends heavily on the weather; ultraviolet rays destroy most pathogens, and wind can blow a bioweapon far from its intended target. Moreover, production of bioweapons is risky. According to Karl Lowe:

> Even the best vaccines can be overpowered by large doses of agent, a problem that makes most laboratories so concerned with safety. Because a biological agent's producers and deliverers are likely to come into contact with very high doses, they would be at extraordinary risk unless wearing a properly fitted mask whenever they are exposed (making it hard to remain unobtrusive when attempting to disseminate the agent). This is particularly true if the terrorist group wants to produce a dry agent since an electrostatic charge is imparted to particles during drying and humans attract them quite readily.[11]

Similarly, the manufacture of chemical weapons can be unpredictable and dangerous. Making sarin, for example, involves high temperatures and the use of a highly corrosive chemical that is difficult to handle. Moreover, if the terrorists aim to stockpile the sarin, they must distill excess hydrochloric acid from the product, which is an extremely hazardous procedure. Because handling and storing the virulent chemicals is so dangerous, terrorists might be attracted to binary chemical weapons, in which two relatively safe precursors are mixed together at short notice to produce the toxic agent. But manual mixing would be enormously perilous. On the other hand, obtaining or developing an automated mixer would require significant resources and expertise.[12]

A lump of plutonium the size of an apple is big enough to build a nuclear bomb. There are, however, numerous obstacles involved in manufacturing even a small amount of weapons-grade material. Stealing or diverting such material, while possible, would likely demand extensive resources. Even assuming a nation or terrorist group could acquire sufficient enriched fissile material, additional high-explosive components would need to be developed and tested in order to make the material into a weapon. Handling the plutonium or highly enriched uranium would pose serious safety hazards. And the weapons would need a delivery system — itself a complex undertaking.

But the end of the Cold War and the rising tide of globalization are eroding these technical barriers. Terrorists are exploiting global forces to gain access to the keys of mass destruction.

The Internet has enabled societal fringe groups, religious cults, and extremist political organizations, traditionally geographically confined, to build large organizational networks, exchange information, and combine resources. For example, Ramzi Ahmed Yousef, the mastermind of the World Trade Center bombing, used the Internet to send encrypted messages.[13] Subcomandante Marcos, the leader of a rebel movement in the Chiapas region of Mexico, used his organization's Web site to spread propaganda for its cause.

The Internet also is an easily accessible resource of manuals for mayhem and murder. Uncle Fester's Silent Death includes recipes for botulism, shellfish toxin, and ricin. *The Jolly Roger Cookbook* covers topics like making fertilizer bombs and buying explosives and propellants. *The Terrorist Handbook* and *Anarchist's Cookbook* offer similar "how-to's" for destruction. It takes a matter of minutes to track down such texts using popular Internet search engines.

The globalization of the chemical industry has led to a rise in international flows of precursor chemicals — and makes such flows increasingly hard to monitor. Many chemicals that could be used to make chemical weapons have legitimate commercial and even medical uses. For example, some of the ingredients used to make sarin are consumed by commercial industry in millions of tons per year. Even more specialized sarin precursors are legitimately employed to make products like pesticides and fire retardants.[14] And because trade flows are so extensive, would-be terrorists have a greater ability to order weapons components in a piecemeal fashion, thus mitigating suspicion.

The collapse of the USSR, combined with the wholesale transformation of Russia's society and market, has exposed the nuclear security system of the former Soviet Union to unprecedented risks. In November 1998, William C. Potter, director of the Center for Nonproliferation Studies at the Monterey Institute of International Studies in California, who had visited ten Russian nuclear-materials sites that year, reported that, "many of the storage buildings which contain approximately 70,000 nuclear weapons equivalents of highly enriched uranium and plutonium . . . have no perimeter fences, armed guards, vehicle barriers, operational surveillance cameras and metal and radiation detectors at entrances."[15] In September 1998 one building at an institute in Moscow had been found completely unguarded although it contained 100 kilograms of highly enriched uranium. The institute could not afford a $200-per-month guard.[16]

Along with the problem of Russian "loose nukes" are what might be termed "loose geeks" and "loose spooks" — former Soviet scientists and KGB operatives with WMD expertise. These individuals, once privileged members of the elite, now may find themselves unemployed or struggling to provide for their families. Economic vulnerability could lead such persons to sell their savvy on the WMD black market.

Globalization has dramatically multiplied the flows of goods across borders, making it effectively impossible to check what comes in and goes out of our country. Referring to the drug trade, one U.S. official noted, "A lot is hidden in plain sight." In 1996, 75 million cars, 3.5 million trucks and railroad cars, and 254 million people crossed from Mexico into America. At some of the thirty-eight official border crossings, fewer than 5 percent of the vehicles were searched.[17]

And as modern societies become more dependent on integrated, highly technical infrastructures — the systems that run our banks, our airways, our telecommunications, our utilities — we become more vulnerable to new forms of attack, especially cyberterror.

This is not futurology or science fiction or nail-biting fiction. It is not scare-mongering or hysteria. It is not deductions from the present time, extended to the future. This is the present. It is now. It is here. We have crossed the threshold to the era of high-tech terror, including the use of weapons of mass destruction.

At 8:05 A.M. on March 20, 1995, members of the Aum Shinrikyo (Supreme Truth) launched a WMD terrorist attack on the crowded Tokyo subway. Five two-person teams disguised as businessmen placed eleven sarin-filled plastic bags on trains headed for a central hub station. As the trains neared the station, one member of each team punctured the bag with the tip of an umbrella while the other cult member kept watch. The clear puddles of sarin evaporated slowly, giving all but one of the terrorists sufficient time to escape. As the poisonous fumes spread throughout the packed cars and onto the rush-hour platforms, hundreds of commuters were overcome — staggering and collapsing in sixteen stations along the three subway lines. The final toll was twelve people dead and more than five thousand injured. Had the Aum used better-quality sarin and a more sophisticated method of dispersal, the incident could have been even worse — with casualties in the tens of thousands.[18]

This attack could just as well have taken place in the United States, or against American citizens. Indeed, in April 1990, the Aum — which was also experimenting with biological agents — sent a convoy of trucks armed with botulism microbes on a mission to attack U.S. bases. The trucks sprayed clouds of invisible mist at American Navy installations at Yokohama and Yokosuka. Fortunately, no one got sick as a result; the strain may have been weak, or Aum's delivery methods flawed. But the Aum continued trying to cultivate bacteria — including anthrax, Ebola, and Q fever — testing their weapons, always unsuccessfully, from rooftops and trucks throughout Tokyo.[19]

It may have been because making germ weapons proved so hard that the Aum resorted to sarin in their March 1995 assault. In fact, the cult had originally planned to release the nerve gas in the United States in June 1994. For reasons that remain unclear, they attacked the Japanese city of Matsumoto instead; 7 people died as a result and more than 150 were injured.

The Aum is not the only group to have pursued WMD capabilities.

- In 1984, members of an Oregon cult led by Bhagwan Shree Rajneesh contaminated restaurant salad bars with home-grown salmonella bacteria in an effort to affect the outcome of a local election. As a result 750 people became ill and 45 were hospitalized.[20]
- In 1993, the terrorists who bombed the World Trade Center allegedly laced their weapon with cyanide. U.S. District Court sentencing judge Kevin Duffy said, "Thank God the sodium cyanide burned instead of vaporizing [or] everybody in the north tower would have been killed."[21]
- In August 1994, reportedly as part of a sting operation, German officials seized 363 grams of plutonium from a Lufthansa flight arriving in Munich from Moscow.[22]
- In December 1994, Czech police arrested a Czech, a Russian, and a Byelorussian with ties to the nuclear industry and seized 2.72 kilograms of weapons-grade highly enriched uranium.[23]
- In March 1995, Douglas Baker and Leroy Wheeler of the right-wing Minnesota Patriots Council were convicted of unlawful possession of biological weapons — specifically ricin — with the apparent intent to poison Internal Revenue Service agents and a deputy U.S. marshal.[24]
- In May 1995, Larry Wayne Harris, who had ties to the white supremacist group Aryan Nation, was arrested for misrepresenting himself in ordering three vials of freeze-dried bubonic plague bacteria from American Type Culture Collection in Maryland.[25]
- In 1993, Thomas Lewis Lavy, an American with ties to survivalist groups, was stopped by Canadian border officials

while he was attempting to smuggle 130 grams of ricin from Alaska into Canada.[26]

In addition, the reported actions of governments demonstrate the dangers:

- In 1941, the British government conducted experiments at Gruinard Island off the coast of Scotland to see whether anthrax could be successfully delivered by bombs. The result: Yes, it could. And Gruinard was uninhabitable for decades since anthrax spores survived in the soil.
- In 1968, the United States conducted an extensive strategic test of a bioweapon powder. Enough ships to have made the world's fifth-largest independent navy were positioned around the Johnston Atoll, 1,000 miles southwest of Hawaii. At sunset, a Marine jet flew a "line-source laydown," releasing small amounts of weaponized particles with every mile of flight. The particles traveled over the ocean, where barges loaded with hundreds of rhesus monkeys were stationed. The monkeys were taken back to Johnston Atoll. Within days, half the monkeys had died. Military analysts concluded that a similar laydown over an American city would likely kill more people than a 10-megaton hydrogen bomb.[27]
- On April 2, 1979, a plume of anthrax leaked from a secret Soviet research facility on the outskirts of Sverdlovsk (now called Yekaterinaburg), 850 miles east of Moscow. This facility, known as Compound 19, was a bioweapons factory. As the poisonous cloud made its way downwind, unsuspecting villagers and livestock breathed its lethal fumes. Within days, a serious outbreak had begun. Doctors were baffled; first they thought it was pneumonia, then the severity of patients' chest pain led them to diagnose heart attacks. Eventually, specialists

from Moscow arrived and confirmed the disease was anthrax. Antibiotics were largely ineffective. Some people died outside the hospital, at home, or even in the streets. While the incident continues to be shrouded in secrecy, an estimated ninety-six people lost their lives.[28]

■ Since 1992, more fissile material is known to have been stolen from the former Soviet Union than the United States was able to produce in the first three years of the Manhattan Project.[29] This is especially alarming when you keep in mind that producing or acquiring fissile material presents the hardest and most time-consuming aspect of developing a nuclear bomb — not constructing the device itself. I recall that the usual estimate of our government experts was generally ten years or so for another nation to build the bomb. Most of that period was required for production of weapons-grade fissile material. If it could be stolen or bought, the estimate of a decade would be radically shortened.

■ As of 1998, twenty-seven nations were known to have nuclear, biological, or chemical weapons. Russia alone has a declared arsenal of forty thousand tons of chemical weapons that it promised by treaty to destroy but now cannot afford to do.[30] These weapons states pose a double danger: not only of using their arsenals themselves, but of increasing — intentionally or otherwise — the weapons' availability to terrorists.

■ Iraq has declared that it possessed the following in the 1990s: 2,245 gallons of anthrax, enough to kill billions; 5,125 gallons of botulinum toxin, enough to wipe out the population of the Earth several times; and 4 metric tons of VX, a nerve agent so deadly that a single drop can kill.[31] After Saddam Hussein turned away United Nations weapons inspectors in December 1998, these substances remained unaccounted for, along with dozens of other WMD components, including at least

157 aerial bombs filled with germ agents, at least 25 missile warheads containing germ agents, more than 30,000 munitions filled with chemical weapons, 4,000 tons of precursor chemicals, and design drawings and materials for building nuclear weapons and ballistic materials.[32]

Which weapon of mass destruction are we most likely to see in a terrorist assault in the United States or against our citizens and interests abroad?

Chemical weapons are certainly the easiest to use and the cheapest to develop. Nuclear weapons are the most dramatic, but they are expensive and difficult to acquire and deploy. Many experts lean toward biological weapons, which are easier to make than nuclear devices and far more lethal than their chemical cousins. This gruesome combination of availability and killing capacity could render bioweapons irresistible. "It is really a matter of time," microbiologist Raymond Zilinskas of the University of Maryland Biotechnology Institute has concluded. "I don't understand why it hasn't happened already."[33]

Whatever the likelihood of such an attack, the consequences could be so catastrophic that we must do what we can to forestall one. At the same time, on top of all you have just read about the dangers of weapons of mass destruction in the hands of terrorists, there is another instrument that could wreak widespread havoc. One that is still more likely to be used against us — and soon. Thus, the nightmare in the next chapter.

CHAPTER TWO

eTERROR, eCRIME

Allenwood, PA
January 19, 2002

Felice Trout
Attorney at Law
3307 M Street, NW
Washington, DC 20007

Dear Ms. Trout:

Maybe you're really busy, but you *are* my lawyer and I want an answer *now* to my last letter. Prison is bad enough, especially when I shouldn't be here. As I said, I don't like television, don't much like any of the other people here, and I DON'T SEE WHY I CAN'T HAVE A COMPUTER FOR E-MAILS. Have you talked yet to the judge, or warden, or whoever?

Please,
Casey Gates

■ ■ ■

January 24

Dear Casey:

I did talk to the prison authorities, again, as I did last month. They still refuse and they are getting impatient with your demands. One even said to me, "We don't give murderers pistols in prison. Why should we give a hacker a computer?" The fact is, they seldom do.

Casey, I know you feel wronged. But maybe if you'd been more forthcoming at your trial on what you did and why, the judge wouldn't have been so hard and I could have mounted a better defense. Protecting your friend might have seemed like the right thing, but remember: He's free and out of the country and you're not. Think about it.

At some point, you will come up for parole. If you don't show some contrition, or awareness of the consequences of your action, you won't convince them you deserve any consideration. I took this case as a friend of your father. But I, like him, am losing patience. Here is what your hacking produced: hundreds of millions of dollars for the Russian Mafia, some of it likely to a terrorist organization in return for cooperation in a drug-producing area; the collapse of EBUY, one of the largest U.S. Internet companies; a consequent dive in the NASDAQ that wiped out many people's savings; hundreds of lawsuits against EBUY and the major credit-card companies; and God knows what else. Your "neat idea" may have been a game for you, but it wasn't for your friend, and you are left holding the bag. How can you complain, given the results of what you did? Please do tell me what happened. If you expect me to help you in the future, I must know. Or I can't go on representing you. I should have insisted on this before.

Sincerely,
Felice Trout

■　■　■

February 23

Dear Ms. Trout:

O.K. I'm sorry for what happened, but it wasn't my fault.
I'll tell you some of what I did, to see if it persuades you. And to
tell you the truth, I'm still kind of proud I was able to do it.

It was my friend Denis's idea. I didn't know him that well, but
we used to hang together. Hacking. We were good at it. (Good
enough that we didn't bother with the fancy monikers that the
less serious, uncool, show-offs use. Believe me, the really serious
folks don't need to get off by showing off. You and your friends
know what you did, and that's enough.) So we wanted to try
something that would have been really wild. We downloaded
free tools from the Internet and got into the Commerce
Department system. From there we tried to get into a French
telecommunications company to read some of its files. Easily
traced. The French would have blamed the U.S., and maybe
there would have been a fight between the two governments.
Nothing serious, but fun to read about. But we couldn't figure
out a way to hack into the French company's systems.

In any case, we wanted to try something bigger. Denis
suggested we try to get into EBUY's database systems where
they keep the credit-card numbers of their customers. I agreed.
Not to steal them, really, but to see whether we could do it.
So we tried. And came close. So I really got interested in the
challenge. And after a while, we got in.

No problem, really, getting into the public Web server, the
company's public face. Then came the firewall in front of their
databases. They had a commercially available version that wasn't
bad. But typically, human error defeated them. Denis said he had
a cousin who had recently worked there and still had a few valid
passwords. Now I know his Russian friends probably stole them or
bought them from a current employee. By the way, I think he

probably met them at last year's Def Con convention of hackers in
Las Vegas. Most of the people who go there are "good" hackers
like me — yes, I know you don't think I am — but it also attracts
the bad guys. I guess they offered Denis a lot of money. Oh yes,
to answer your question: I didn't talk at my trial — and still don't
know if I'll tell anyone all this except for my lawyer — because
Denis called me just before he left and told me what his
Russian friends would do to me if I *did* talk. I was scared.

Anyway, the company didn't change its passwords often
enough, simple human mistake, and we used them to get
through. Once we got past the firewall, we could exploit the
"trust relationship" between the various servers and their
private data banks to find the credit cards, many thousands of
them. But it wasn't easy. I'm not going to tell you exactly how
we did it. I guess I'd call this my own "proprietary information."
But it took some time and we had to work around the company's
intrusion detection monitors. I *can* tell you how we did that.

We used a DDoS attack — that's Distributed Denial of
Service — to set up our direct operation against the data bank.
We used a DDoS attack called Trinoo. You hack into a software
company and get the list of its customers to which it is sending a
warning about a vulnerability in the system it sold them. Many of
the customers won't act on it, or won't act soon. So you use the
list and exploit the vulnerability to get into their systems, and
plant "Zombies," or instructions that will be activated later. You
then make them all send repeated, bogus network requests to a
single Web site of your choosing at a time of your choosing. So we
launched our Zombies, many thousands of them, at EBUY, and for
a whole day and most of the night their router couldn't handle
the flood and shut down. Too many Zombies. A real Night of the
Living Dead. Their network staff are, after all, human beings, and
they were probably so tired the next day, so tense, and so on the

lookout for new Zombies that they let down their guard against us as we worked inside on their database. And stole the credit-card numbers. By the time they noticed anything, we were long gone.

I did not, I repeat *not*, know that Denis was going to give them to the Russians, or that they would use them all at once to make all that money, or how they would use the money. I'm sorry about what happened to EBUY and the credit-card companies and the NASDAQ and all the lawsuits (although I'll bet you lawyers aren't). But as you can see, it wasn't my fault.

Is there some way you can use this information to get me paroled, without the Russians knowing?

If you talk to my father, without revealing this info can you try to make him understand this just seemed like a cool idea? Maybe he won't. Maybe it's just generational. But I hope *you* do.

And can you try one more time to get me a computer? Seriously. *It's all I think about.*

Please,
Casey

■ ■ ■

The Internet has changed almost everything in our lives. It would be folly not to recognize that it has also changed the lives of terrorists and international criminals. It greatly enhances their ability not only to act, but also to act *together*. This helps to create a new nexus of danger. Add to the threats described in the previous chapter new cyberthreats and the widening reach of international criminal gangs. This requires that we organize ourselves to attack the problem whole rather than piecemeal. Hence the proposal made at this chapter's end.

1.

Cyberterror: The Next Front Line?

My students at Georgetown University cannot conceal their smiles when we spend a class on the threat of cyberterror and cybercrime. Many live in cyberspace, and they don't fully accept the fact that the personal computer, for all its benefits, can also be a powerful instrument of terror. It is cheaper, more easily deployed, and safer to use than almost any other weapon a terrorist or criminal can obtain. An ordinary laptop with Internet access is all that's needed to cause considerable harm from anywhere in the world. A Justice Department official who prosecutes such crimes met with my students recently, and he told us that my hypothetical story of Casey Gates, including the consequences of his escapade, is entirely possible.

Indeed, in January 2000 a hacker broke into the files of CD Universe, an online music seller, stole a large number of credit-card numbers and tried to blackmail the company by threatening to publish the numbers unless the company paid him off. The company refused; he began to publish the numbers on the Internet; and credit-card companies had to replace the thousands of cards held by CD Universe shoppers. (A few months later, the FBI assisted in the arrest by British and Canadian authorities of two British youths for a similar operation.) Experts believe that these were no miracles of hacking; small Internet companies, lacking sophisticated defenses, are quite vulnerable to such attacks. And in February 2000, some of our largest Internet merchants were shut down for extended periods of time by a series of DDoS attacks.

The problem is compounded not only by the difficulties in tracing such attacks back through the multiple (often foreign) sites to their original source, which could be a cybercafé open to public use, but also by the fact that judges are loath to impose harsh penalties on most hackers when they are caught and prosecuted. As the Justice Department official told us, the hackers are usually bright young people with their whole lives before them. Why ruin them? (Especially, he might have added, since they are mostly middle-class kids who probably remind the judges of their own.) The result: Only a handful of miscreants have actually been convicted and sentenced to serve time.

The judges are wrong. Whether as terrorism or crime, malevolent hacking represents a serious threat. A part of the danger is that the pool of potential cyberterrorists is much larger than the number of those who might be able to develop and use, say, anthrax. My students laugh when I reverse the warning of the 1960s and tell them that I don't trust anyone *under* thirty — because they have been raised with the knowledge, and probably access to all the tools, that a cyberterrorist needs. But the crime is no laughing matter.

According to the President's Commission on Critical Infrastructure Protection (PCCIP), the global population with the skills for a cyberattack has grown from some thousands in the early 1980s to seventeen million in 1996, and will reach nineteen million by 2001. The menu of malevolent options for cyberterror has multiplied as well. The number of computer viruses has ballooned from a handful in the early 1980s to thousands in 1996 and potentially tens of thousands by 2001. In addition to viruses (such as PAPA, Mad Cow, I Love You, and Armageddon), wrongdoers can also turn to computer worms, or independent programs that copy themselves from one computer to another across a network; Trojan horses, or code fragments that hide themselves inside programs and perform disguised functions, such as stealing passwords; logic bombs, or computer programs that self-execute when the user performs a triggering action; trap doors, which allow developers to sneak back into programs that they built; chipping, the process of putting malicious functions into hardware chips as opposed to software; and, a new concern in early 2000, Trinoo and other large-scale denial-of-service attacks.

Armed with these and other destructive digital tools, millions of computer-savvy individuals could wreak havoc against the United States, other governments, businesses, and critical infrastructures. Why would they want to? Some just for kicks, or for prestige, or because of the challenge. Some targets, like the Defense Department, are to be attacked because, like Mount Everest, "it is there." As hacker Kevin Poulson, alias Dark Dante, explained, "To be physically inside an office [Poulson sometimes broke into his targets literally as well as electronically], finding the flaws in the system and what works, was intellectually challenging. It proved irresistible. It wasn't for ego or money. It was for curiosity. A need for adventure. An intellectual challenge and an adrenaline rush. It was fun. And at the time it seemed pretty harmless." (Poulson was caught after breaking into a Pacific Bell telephone system switching center and manipulating calls during radio call-in competitions in order to win all the prizes — an act of greed that seems to weaken his claim that money was no motivation.)[1]

And while most terrorists up to now have preferred traditional means of attack, or may have been tempted by weapons of mass destruction, cyberterror may also attract them for a variety of reasons. Carrying out a cyberattack presents no immediate physical danger to the perpetrator. A strike can be launched from a remote location, offering greater anonymity. The relative simplicity of the equipment and skills involved means an individual can more easily act alone, without recourse to a larger group or government. And he can disguise his attack by working through sites in a number of countries. If national borders are becoming increasingly porous through globalization, cyberborders are almost nonexistent. It would not be terribly difficult or expensive for a group of a few dozen malevolent computer experts, operating from different sites around the world, to conduct simultaneous and highly damaging attacks on our infrastructure: power grids, financial institutions, 911 systems, and the like. Pause for a moment and consider the chaos that would result. No explosions, as in a bombing attack by foreign aircraft. But some of the same effects.

Even those who lack the skill to devise their own computer viruses can find information on the Internet to help them learn to break into networked systems. Tools intended to enhance computer security, such as SATAN (Security Administrating Tool for Analyzing Networks), can be downloaded by would-be hackers to launch broad-based, automated scans of other networks to identify their weak points. Netcat, a similar system administration tool, can be downloaded and used for "IP spoofing" (appropriating another computer's electronic address or identity), "packet sniffing" (eavesdropping on data like passwords or log-ins as they pass through the network), or "SYN bombing" (overwhelming a network with bogus requests for information).[2] And the targets of a cyberattack may never know they were hit, which could appeal to the terrorist who seeks not only anonymity but the private, perverse pleasure of possessing secret knowledge that he or she has manipulated other people's lives (or deaths).

Cyberterror also offers a vast array of targets, as the world becomes ever more wired in the midst of an information explosion.[3] The number of Internet devices accessing the World Wide Web is skyrocketing from thirty-two million in 1996 to hundreds of millions in 2001. And as information networks continue to merge (for example, the public telecommunications network with the Internet), their vulnerabilities, and the difficulty of tracing cyberattacks, will multiply as well. Remember, also, what a stake our economy has in information technologies, which may be fueling a third of our economic growth.

For the terrorist with exceptional sensitivity, a cyberattack may not seem so severe — likening it to a reverse neutron bomb, destroying things but not people. Some digital strikes could be bloodless but highly expensive, such as a Wednesday night attack on New York City's electric power supply and telecommunications. Gridlock and pandemonium would naturally ensue. Worse, inflicting such a blackout before the Treasury Department had settled on securities coming due on Thursday could also have dramatic repercussions on our nation's economic stability, because of the billions of dollars of transactions at stake.

Yet to assume that all cyberattacks would be bloodless is to dangerously deceive ourselves. A malicious cyberterrorist could easily wreak terrible damage on human lives. In the spring of 1998, I had lunch with Dick Clarke, the President's newly appointed counterterrorism coordinator. The food became less appetizing as we concocted the deadliest cyberschemes we could imagine, from assaults on emergency 911 services to airports, hospitals, and nuclear power plants.

I won't describe the scenarios we came up with because, unlike building a nuclear device, you *could* try this at home. But consider some of the plots James Adams describes in his book *The Next World War:*

> A CyberTerrorist will remotely access the processing control systems of a cereal manufacturer, change the levels of iron supplement, and sicken and kill the children of a nation enjoying their food . . .

A CyberTerrorist will attack the next generation of air-traffic control systems, and collide two large civilian aircraft . . .

A CyberTerrorist will remotely alter the formulas of medication at pharmaceutical manufacturers.[4]

Moreover, as the President's Commission has noted, "For an adversary willing to take greater risks, cyberattacks could be combined with physical attacks, against facilities or against human targets, in an effort to paralyze or panic large segments of society, damage our capability to respond to incidents (by disabling the 911 system of emergency communications, for example), hamper our ability to deploy conventional military forces, and otherwise limit the freedom of action of our national leadership."[5]

Would that the threat were merely theoretical. But as with weapons of mass destruction, the genie is well outside the bottle. According to the Defense Information Systems Agency, there were 250,000 attempted penetrations of Department of Defense computer systems in 1995 alone. By the decade's end, the number of attacks was believed to approach 500,000 a year.[6]

In 1994, two hackers reportedly invaded the computers at Rome Air Force Base in New York for more than two weeks. And in the winter of 1997, the e-mail system at Langley Air Force Base in Virginia was swamped by some thirty thousand messages that virtually shut down the system for several hours. Investigators later determined that the messages had originated in Australia and Estonia, before traveling through several intermediate points, including the White House computer system. Those responsible were never discovered.[7] Also that year, a young hacker in Sweden jammed the 911 lines in Miami, disrupted service, harassed the operators, and diverted emergency calls. He also broke into a telephone system and generated sixty thousand unauthorized calls.[8]

A June 1997 exercise called Eligible Receiver dramatically illustrated how vulnerable our military and political establishments are to digital assault. A group of specialists from the National Security Agency, armed only with basic computers and techniques that any hacker could download from the Internet, simulated power blackouts and 911 overloads in Washington and various other cities. Then, teams in diverse locations (including one on board a ship in the Pacific) tried to break into unclassified systems at four regional military commands and the National Military Command Center in Washington. They succeeded in gaining supervisory-level access to three dozen networks, from which point it was possible to change key data and disrupt e-mail and phones. Meanwhile, officials who tried to respond were stymied by hacker-fed disinformation. As one official ruefully concluded, "Coordination within the executive branch was fraught with confusion. We found that within the Defense Department, we lacked the ability to integrate the picture well, and the rest of the government was not prepared at all to handle this. It was a fairly wrenching experience for all of us."[9]

In February 1998, just as America was preparing for possible deployment to the Persian Gulf, two high school students in northern California, assisted by another teenager in Israel, broke into eleven networks at defense installations around the country. While the systems were unclassified, they included sensitive information on numerous administrative, logistic, and personnel matters. And though Deputy Defense Secretary John Hamre later called it "the most organized and systematic attack the Pentagon has seen to date," it took a whole week before officials were even sure a coordinated attack was under way.[10]

A March 1998 survey prepared by the Computer Security Institute, in conjunction with the FBI, indicated that attacks on

U.S. computer systems had risen 22 percent since 1996. Sixty-four percent of computer security specialists at U.S. businesses, government agencies, universities, and private organizations reported security intrusions within the past twelve months, and the number of companies that had been attacked via the Internet more than tripled between 1996 and 1997.[11]

In April 1998, a group of hackers called the Masters of Downloading/2016216 broke into a military computer system at the heart of the Defense Department's communications network. Pentagon officials, acknowledging the incident, said the invaded program was unclassified, but one of the hackers allegedly claimed, "I think international terrorist groups would be interested in the data we could gain access to. Governments would buy it for intelligence purposes."[12]

And what I believe was the first-known electronic attack by a terrorist group on a target country's computer system has also already occurred: In 1997, ethnic Tamil Tiger guerrillas tried to crash the computer systems of Sri Lankan embassies by flooding them with e-mail messages.

Our intelligence agencies are dangerously underequipped to deal with cyberthreats. They lack sufficient personnel: Computer experts can earn much higher salaries working for private firms. And there reportedly is friction between the FBI's National Infrastructure Protection Center (which is supposed to "fuse" the work of local, state, and federal authorities) and the other agencies of the government involved in defending against cyberattacks. The FBI hesitates to share information on incidents that may involve criminality, since it could thus taint the evidence it would use in a prosecution. The other agencies naturally resent being kept in the dark. A satisfactory solution to the dilemma has not yet been found.

CYBERCRIME: CASH BY COMPUTER

The world may be entering the age of cyberterrorism — and it could age us fast. But we are already well into the era of cyber-crime, and it is taking an expensive toll.

Digital crime poses a huge, and growing, tax on doing inter-national business. This tax, in turn, is passed on to consumers — which means the cyberthieves are stealing from you. Estimates on private-sector financial losses from cybercrime range from a few hundred million to billions of dollars. One report has sug-gested that losses could by now be between $20 billion and $40 billion worldwide.[13]

The hard and dangerous fact is that no one knows the full extent of the damage. Businesses are reluctant to reveal that elec-tronic security has been breached, for fear of undermining crucial investor and consumer confidence. According to an FBI survey, fewer than one-fifth of all cyberattacks are reported to law enforcement.[14]

To its credit, Citibank did report and pursue Vladimir Levin, a twenty-four-year-old mathematics graduate from St. Petersburg University "accused of being the mastermind of the biggest bank heist in the brief history of cyberspace."[15] In 1994, Levin led a group of hackers in breaking into Citibank's digital vaults and moving a total of $10 million to accounts in San Francisco, Amsterdam, Germany, Finland, and Israel. In the end, Levin was caught not through slip-ups during the burglary but because of his sloppy money laundering. Citibank since has strengthened its networks to prevent such heists in the future.[16]

2.

A Silent Crisis — Transnational Crime

Sir Arthur Conan Doyle observed in 1891, "The more featureless and commonplace a crime is, the more difficult it is to bring it home." More than a century later, daily acts of crime, orchestrated by organized transnational forces, are exposing our people to violence and fear and tearing at the fabric of our society. Yet since the impact of transnational crime rarely makes splashy national headlines because its effects are widespread and continuous instead of a one-time assault, many Americans remain unaware of the extent to which it affects their lives.

Transnational crime is a tremendous problem, both for the American government and for each of us as citizens. It undermines and erodes democracies worldwide. Fledgling democratic institutions in countries such as Russia can all too easily be corrupted. Voters may be tempted by a return to authoritarianism in order to break free from the suffocating tentacles of criminal gangs. More mature democracies are even in danger, as drug traffickers' penetration of Colombia's political and economic institutions has shown. And it can weaken stability in critical regions of the world, whether it be Russia, or China, or the Latin American and Caribbean countries on our doorstep. It also puts a terrible burden on judicial and law-enforcement systems, claiming the lives of dedicated officials from Italy to Mexico. Worst of all, it hurts people — including but not limited to our own.

I remember the moment when the reach of the criminals first became vivid to me. It was during a 1993 cabinet meeting on an unrelated issue. A senior cabinet colleague, a combat veteran known for his calm toughness, told me that his counterpart in the friendly government of a nation very important to us, a senior minister in a position that had little to do with security issues, was being threatened by criminals and feared for his life. The reach of the criminals was so strong that his foreign friend did not know to whom he could talk in his own government. As he told me this, the American cabinet officer seemed shaken. In the following weeks, as I recall, we did what we could to be helpful. I know his foreign counterpart survived whatever threat there was. But I, too, was impressed that such a thing could happen within the government of a large, sophisticated nation.

My memory of this incident is clear. But, in retrospect, it was also unusual. While I have vivid memories of every terrorist incident, every military intervention, every financial shock, I have very few recollections of dealing with specific cases of transnational crime, even though such crime probably was doing greater daily damage to American citizens than all the other threats we faced, combined. And still is. Transnational crime has become a silent crisis — largely hidden from public consciousness, yet looming larger each day. The UN's 1999 Human Development Report estimates that the annual gross profits of these criminal syndicates is greater than the GDP of the United Kingdom! Like the giant iceberg that sank the *Titanic,* international crime is capable of inflicting enormous losses. If we don't change our course and attack this problem with the urgency it deserves, we as a society may simply come to accept such crime as a fact of modern life. That would mean that the drug traffickers, gun runners, extortionists, contract killers, counterfeiters, and cyberthieves had won.

Consider some of the costs of this "crime tax" on American citizens and society:

■ The international drug trade reportedly costs us about $200 billion every year in health care, lost productivity, and revenues — not to mention the incalculable human losses of families and lives destroyed. During the four-year period of 1988–91, the number of Americans needing emergency-room treatment because of drug use was more than twice the number of our wounded during World War II.[17]

- Every year, some $1 billion worth of stolen vehicles is removed from the United States and sent to other countries. The price tag for this cross-border carjacking shows up in your insurance.

- Unknown billions of dollars are lost each year to American businesses because of cybercrime, as discussed above.

In an era of globalization, these threats and dangers will only grow worse. Increasingly porous borders are enabling people to move more easily. Modern communications and advanced encryption technology are making it easier for transnational criminals to hatch their plans and hide their tracks. And the extraordinary volume of international capital flows facilitates money laundering.

The allure of profits, the aid of global communications, and the commonality of risks have fostered new links among transnational crime organizations. Cooperation between Colombian and Mexican drug cartels has given Colombians greater access to U.S. borders and Mexicans a share in the cocaine and heroin trade. Colombians have also worked with the Sicilian Mafia to exploit the European market, while Mexican smugglers have assisted Chinese criminal organizations in trafficking illegal immigrants into the United States.[18] Criminal opportunities are even overcoming politics: In El Salvador, paramilitaries of the right and the left are joining together in carjacking and theft, as are Palestinian and Israeli car thieves.

3.

A Deadly Nexus

Even more dangerous are the growing ties between these multinational masters of the underworld and terrorist organizations, especially in a world where weapons of mass destruction are proliferating. In interagency meetings on the subject, I used to refer to these connections as the nexus. From the start, President Clinton has pushed for more attention to the ways in which terrorists, criminals, and technology can combine to threaten us. In his State of the Union address on January 27, 2000, he warned that "the same technological advances that have shrunk cell phones to fit in the palms of our hands can also make weapons of terror easier to conceal and easier to use. . . . I predict to you, when most of us are long gone, but some time in the next ten to twenty years, the major security threat this country will face will come from . . . the narco-traffickers and the terrorists and the organized criminals, who will be organized together, working together, with increasing access to ever more sophisticated chemical and biological weapons."

In fact, they are already "working together." Hizbollah sells black-market cigarettes on the border of Brazil, Argentina, and Paraguay. Usama bin Ladin's people traffick heroin in Afghanistan. Russian criminals cooperate with drug cartels in the Caribbean. The Aum Shinrikyo in Japan was reportedly cooperating with former Soviet Mafia groups in smuggling nuclear materials and conventional munitions out of Russia.[19] And over the past decade in Colombia, a country of direct strategic importance to our own, the alliance between drug cartels and the guerrilla-terrorist movement has almost torn our neighbor apart. Even in 1985–90, before the crisis reached its current proportions, more than one thousand police officers, seventy journalists, sixty judges, and four presidential candidates were murdered by criminal cartels.[20]

Why have the Colombian drug syndicates reached beyond their borders to establish links to the terrorist organization Sendero Luminoso (Shining Path) in Peru? Because the drug cartels get armed protection. And the terrorists get big bucks. The result? Innocent citizens throughout our hemisphere see their communities corroded by drugs and violence.[21]

Drug traffickers aren't the only criminals forging ties to terrorists. In the 1990s, U.S. authorities became aware of a sophisticated counterfeiting operation that was spreading high-quality fake $100 bills to terrorists in Lebanon, the Irish Republican Army, the Japanese Red Army, and others. Repeatedly, the United States altered the real bill. The counterfeiters rapidly matched it. No one is sure who was behind the operation. Some believe it was Hizbollah, using Iranian Revolutionary Guard materials and training. Others suggest the forgers were North Korean, because at least one North Korean diplomat was arrested with stacks of the "supernotes" on hand.

In March 1996, the United States attempted to break the vicious cycle with the ugliest greenback ever produced: an enlarged, off-center Ben Franklin gazing out at the bearer with what looks like a sneer of reproach — perhaps conveying his low opinion of anyone who would carry so much money. Unfortunately, counterfeiters (allegedly the North Koreans) already have copied what they call the Big Head bill. And as the U.S. Treasury did not withdraw the old currency from circulation, the supernote survives.[22]

If a foreign government did to the American people what transnational crime is *already* doing, and what terrorists using weapons of mass destruction or cyberattacks *could* do, we would certainly go to war. Yet a forceful response to these modern threats is extremely difficult to devise. As Claire Sterling concludes, "Modern criminal power has surpassed the ability of governments to contain it. . . . If the (governments) go down to dismal defeat in the war against crime, it will be largely because they are hampered by all the baggage of statehood — patriotism, politics, accountable governments, human rights, legal strictures, international conventions, bureaucracy, diplomacy — whereas the big criminal syndicates have no national allegiances, no laws but their own, no frontiers."[23]

More broadly, the forces of globalization are fueling the terrorists, drug traffickers, criminal gangs, and cyberthieves who disregard national borders. Thomas Friedman has pointed out, "Globalization gives them both the added incentive to hate America and the added power to do something about it."[24] At a meeting I attended at Georgetown University, Mexican Ministry of Interior official Jorge Tello Peón used Alvin Toffler's Third Wave theory of revolutionary transformation in the information age to illustrate how the tides of globalization can overwhelm traditional crime-fighting strategies. Tello used the example of the struggle against drugs. Traditional antidrug strategies require consumption controls, yet the wave of the future is rising consumption. Traditional antidrug strategies demand tough controls on borders and financial flows, yet the wave of the future is freer trade, the free flow of capital, and deregulated markets. Traditional antidrug strategies call for communications controls, yet the wave of the future is people's growing ability to share and access knowledge. These waves cannot be reversed any more than King Canute could stay dry. But we *can* give our efforts to deter, defeat, and when necessary deal with the consequences of terrorism and international crime a greater urgency and focus.

We have made a start. The Counterterrorism Center, effectively built by Director of Central Intelligence John Deutch and his successor, George Tenet (both first-rate public servants), has helped in the disruption of several dozen terrorist cells, as well as in foiling some major attacks. Unlike the rest of the CIA, where analysts and operations officers inhabit different worlds, at the Counterterrorism Center they work shoulder-to-shoulder, pooling resources and expertise. And, recognizing that terrorism no longer has any regard for boundaries, they also work extremely closely with the FBI and its new Domestic Counterterrorism Center. Indeed, the Counterterrorism Center is staffed by both CIA and FBI personnel. This may seem a logical and obvious way of doing business. But the animosity between the two organizations would have made this almost impossible only a few years ago.

For a while, the animosity was exacerbated by the establishment of a few dozen FBI offices around the world. They are needed to help their host governments in the fight against transnational crime and terrorism and to help collect evidence when crimes are committed against American citizens. CIA stations have a different role — intelligence collection and, very occasionally, covert actions. But at first the CIA objected to the FBI's expansion abroad, on its "turf." I invited the senior leader of each agency to lunch to encourage them to work together. It was hard going. The CIA official even said, "Russia is ours." But he relented, as he had to. The fact is that criminal influence is raising questions about the degree to which Russia belongs even to the *Russians*. In more recent years, the CIA and the FBI have worked much more closely on their common turf abroad. And the FBI and their Russian counterparts are working together, in extraordinary ways, against Russian criminals on both Russian and American soil.

In the spring of 1998, President Clinton approved a long-term, comprehensive national strategy to fight international crime and reduce its impact on American citizens. Through the Nunn-Lugar Cooperative Threat Reduction program launched in 1992, we've worked to stanch the spread of Russian nuclear materials at the source. The Department of Defense has added $1 billion for chemical and biological defense to its Five-Year Defense Plan and expanded its anthrax vaccination program. Representatives from key federal government agencies are working with local emergency professionals in cities across the country, providing WMD response training and equipment to America's 120 largest urban centers.

But we still have a long way to go. I will always remember the Saturday morning in January 1995 when we were informed by authorities in Manila of a raid on the apartment of Ramzi Ahmed Yousef, a young Kuwati-born Arab of Palestinian and Pakistani parents. Fortuitously, a fire had forced its occupants to flee, leaving behind them incriminating papers, computer files, and bomb-making materials. The police had rounded up and interrogated two Yousef associates who revealed a plot to destroy a number of American jets over the Pacific.

The mechanics of the plan had been tested successfully on a Philippines Airlines flight, creating an explosion that killed a Japanese passenger. You could call it a BYOB assault: Build Your Own Bomb on board. The terrorist would fly like a normal traveler. When the plane reached altitude, he would go to the lavatory and construct a small explosive device. The key component was nitroglycerin, which he hid in a bottle of contact lens solution. When the bomb was complete, the terrorist would stash it above the ceiling tile in the bathroom. He would leave the plane at its first scheduled stop. The plane would blow up before the next.

The Philippine authorities had found only one bomb, but Yousef's plan called for six. I called the President to inform him of the serious situation. The President decided to ground all U.S.-bound Pacific flights under American flag. We reached the FAA, which issued the necessary orders. But to my frustration, which led to incredulity, we were unable to locate the secretary of transportation. His department was closed that day, and there was no answer even on its central telephone number. It was only hours later that we reached him to get his formal approval of the FAA's action.

We have much more progress to make in protecting our cities and citizens here at home. Exercises held in 1998 in Washington, San Jose, and Boston revealed a need for intensive training and support for first responders. In the Washington drill, a simulated nerve gas attack, rescuers found that downdrafts from emergency helicopters would have spread the gas. In San Jose, a simulated gas attack on city council offices found firefighters and police units stuck outside for three hours trying to put on protective suits. In Boston, shortages of proper gear meant some emergency personnel had to rely on garden hoses and a child's wading pool to wash down mock victims.[25]

We also need to do a better job of intelligence collection on emerging threats. Critics expressed amazement at the CIA's failure to predict India's test of a nuclear bomb in 1998. Yet I believe a far more egregious lapse was the fact that no one was paying attention to Aum Shinrikyo at the time of the Tokyo attack — despite the fact that they had about fifty thousand members, including membership in Russia three times as large as their Japanese constituency, more than $1 billion worth of assets, and offices in Bonn, New York, Moscow, and Sri Lanka; openly preached an anti-American and anti-Western message; and ran a deadly brewery of chemical and biological agents.

There is no silver bullet, no one piece of legislation, no funding appropriation, no single conference or report that can make this nexus of emerging threats disappear. What is needed, therefore, is a greater sense of urgency, more political will, and a new way of thinking as we pursue the attack.

It is time for the government to organize itself to address the nexus in a serious way. In writing this, I mean no criticism of Richard A. Clarke, the newly appointed "czar" who oversees these programs. He is not widely known outside Washington but should be. I first met Dick Clarke in 1992, when he briefed Sandy Berger and me on Somalia. I was impressed with the breadth of his knowledge and his unusual degree of willingness to take responsibility for his opinions. He became one of the most valued members of our National Security Council (NSC) staff.

Dick has the look, if not the demeanor, of the career civil servant he is, with reddish-gray, receding hair, a fair complexion that betrays its rare exposure to the sun, and an intense manner relieved by a genuine if dark sense of humor. He is a bulldog of a bureaucrat, notorious among his colleagues for utter devotion to those he works for, fierce loyalty and support toward those who work for him, and a bluntness toward those at his level that has not earned him universal affection. President Clinton's highest praise for someone is to say that he or she wakes up in the morning wanting to do something. Dick is such a man — and he does not mind banging heads together, or wounding egos, in the process. He is one of the smartest, most effective public servants I have known.

It was Dick who pushed through Presidential Decision Directive 42 in October 1995, which orders executive-branch agencies to increase the priority and resources they devote to international crime. And Dick has spearheaded other government-wide blueprints for action that have since been created in the areas of combating terrorism and protecting our nation's critical infrastructure. In May 1998, he assumed a newly created position — National Coordinator for Security, Infrastructure Protection and Counter-Terrorism.

These efforts are an important start in disciplining the government's response to new threats. But they are not nearly enough. In retrospect, I wish I had expended more capital trying to reform the bureaucracy to deal with the problem.

There is a tendency within government to try to compartmentalize the problem and fit it into boxes. There are issue boxes: Proliferation. Traditional terrorism. Modern terrorism. Crime. Critical infrastructure security. There are jurisdictional boxes: International. National. State. Local. Government. Business. There are response boxes: Law enforcement. Diplomacy. Intelligence. Emergency management. Each involves a separate organization, ethos, and approach. As Pentagon spokesman Kenneth Bacon replied when asked about the response to the terrorist bombing of Khobar Towers, "This is the FBI's job. We don't ask the FBI to fly F-16s over Iraq and they don't ask us to take over their investigations."[26]

These boxes are distinct, discrete, and disunited — but the threats they aim to address are just the opposite. As the world evolves, and with it the face of modern terror and crime, our definitions of the problem must be revised as well. For example, as Deputy Secretary of Defense John Hamre observes, "We have a nineteenth-century view of national security. If a problem develops outside of the borders of the United States, it is a national security problem. If it is inside of U.S. borders, it is law enforcement. But there are no borders in cyberspace."[27]

Similarly, when is terrorism crime, and when is crime really terrorism? The National Liberation Front in Vietnam, the Palestine Liberation Organization, and other similar groups argued that their political purposes made their attacks on innocent civilians acts of war, and neither terror nor crime. (Tell that to the victims.) Now, when revenge and hate motivate the existential killers like McVeigh and the Unabomber, can their actions be termed political terror, or are they simply crimes — which is to say, blatant murder? Secretary of State Madeleine Albright illustrated this shift in perspective when she declared before the staff of the bombed embassy in Nairobi, "Terror is not a form of political expression and certainly not a manifestation of religious faith. It is murder, plain and simple. . . ."[28]

The fact is, acts of terror and crime are not so different. And in an era of globalization, the line between national and international action has blurred — certainly in the eyes of terrorists and criminals. Nor should we make too much of the distinctions between the means they employ. It is wrong to argue, as some have done, that because terrorists currently use car bombs and conventional explosives, we shouldn't waste more time or resources on the threat of WMD terrorism. A strong response to one problem need not result in neglect for the other. Both traditional and twenty-first-century terror are real dangers. America must focus on both.

Until we see the problem of emerging threats whole, our efforts to deter and deal with it will be run in a piecemeal, and at worst counterproductive, fashion. Consider, for example, the problem we faced when the first news of the disastrous explosions at the World Trade Center and on flight TWA 800 reached the White House. Were the incidents terrorism? Crime? Freakish accidents? Were they national or international affairs? Each potential answer implied a separate box. There was no single office we could turn to that would see and deal with the problem whole — and no one we could put on the ground with the clear authority and institutional neutrality to mediate and balance competing interests.

In 1997, I attended an exercise held by federal, state, and local authorities on how to respond to a hypothetical chemical attack on the MCI Center in Washington (which became the inspiration for my own nightmare scenario). The officials were divided into teams. At one table, representatives from the FBI and the Federal Emergency Management Agency, or FEMA, were discussing how they would react, based on Presidential Decision Directive 39 — a directive I'd endorsed and the President had signed. I was struck by how the FEMA representative consistently deferred to his FBI colleague, as the directive said he should. But it is not clear that the FBI's desire to collect evidence for a criminal investigation should necessarily trump FEMA's efforts to bring swift aid to the victims, or that the FBI can be impartial in deciding between the two priorities.

In a newspaper profile of Dick Clarke, he remarks, "The national coordinator will have a great deal of access to senior levels of government — access but not authority. . . . The national coordinator's only weapon . . . will be persuasion."[29] If this doesn't sound like the Dick I know, it *is* an accurate reflection of his job. But mere coordination may not be enough to meet today's modern threats. Because as long as bureaucratic politics and human nature remain unchanged, no agency will ever voluntarily cede its power to another.

It is time to adopt a radical solution to this problem, going far beyond identifying a lead agency for each box. One step in the right direction was recommended in July 1999 by the congressionally mandated commission on how to organize government activities against the spread of weapons of mass destruction. The commission argued that the government's failure to organize effectively to combat proliferation demands the creation of a new position: the National Director for Combating Proliferation.

Similarly, in dealing with the related problem of terrorism, we need to provide for a central *command* structure that can coordinate policy decisions, resolve operational disputes among the agencies, and, through an operational staff like that of FEMA, actually take charge of possible terrorist incidents on the ground. That central authority needs to tie together all the elements of the threats I have described. Only an Assistant to the President for such issues, in the White House, would have the power and institutional perspective to force cooperation from a wide span of agencies, both in Washington and on the site of any incidents. Some argue that this function should be placed in the National Security Council. I disagree. The NSC should not be involved in domestic operations (it has no mandate to do so) and, with due respect to Oliver North, it should not directly run operations. But the new Assistant to the President should coordinate very closely with the NSC as well as with senior domestic-policy advisors.

To ensure such cooperation, this new Assistant to the President could share staff members with the National Security Council, based on a model we developed in 1993 in which the National Economic Council and NSC share staff members on international economic issues. Unless they are schizoid, the staff members must work to bring their two bosses together since each must approve their work. The system worked well. It also could work well in helping a new Assistant to the President coordinate our national fight against international crime, terrorism, and the proliferation of weapons of mass destruction.

Any suggestion to create a new "czar" in the White House raises bureaucratic hackles in the agencies — and in the current offices of the White House. When discussing this idea recently, I was asked whether I would have supported it while still the national security advisor. Since it would have reduced my authority, I instantly replied, "Of course not." I would have been wrong. Sooner or later, I believe such a command structure will, of necessity, be formed. Why not now, before the need becomes still more apparent in some badly managed disaster somewhere in the United States?

A reorganized government must also be bolder in tackling new threats at their source. For example, when I was in government, there was a raging argument about whether to go beyond freezing the financial assets of terrorist organizations to attacking them, and perhaps siphoning them off, through covert means. While respect for the integrity of the international banking system is indeed important, the stakes are too high to sideline this weapon in our antiterror arsenal. The many millions of dollars that finance terror, from renting safe houses to doctoring passports to buying powerful explosives, are both a crucial asset and a significant vulnerability. Our intelligence community should be tasked with new urgency to show us the money, and then to attack it, with the proper safeguards that govern all our covert actions.

Our executive branch is unlikely to move rapidly on the issue if we do not progress in shielding ourselves against nexus threats within our society as a whole. But for any effort to be successful, we need to move beyond partisan wrangling. It took more than a year, and the Oklahoma City bombing, before Congress passed President Clinton's antiterrorism legislation in 1996. Even then, some key law-enforcement tools were excised from the bill: roving wiretap authority, so a suspect could be monitored whether he used the phone in his living room or a pay phone down the street; and chemical markers for the most common explosives, including black and smokeless powder, so that we could more easily trace and track down anyone who builds a bomb. There are many other serious proposals for ways we could toughen our laws, from tightening the loophole that permits cultivation of lethal bacteria from natural sources to criminalizing possession of potential WMD materials. Each deserves an honest debate. The burden of proof should be on those who would take away our freedoms in order to meet a potential threat. But we owe it to ourselves to put politics aside as we review the merits, case by case, of every constructive proposal.

It is tempting to censor the preachers of hate and destruction who roam the Internet. Certainly, posting recipes for ricin and fertilizer bombs can serve little good for society. But censorship of this new, powerful information vehicle should be treated with as much suspicion as censorship of our newspapers. Moreover, any ban would be hard to enforce on the Net's vast and fluid terrain. And inevitably, driving such speech underground would only increase its cachet. Instead, we should better utilize the Internet to learn more about potentially dangerous groups and individuals, to keep tabs on what they are up to, and to bring to justice those who violate our laws.

We also need to intensify our prevention and preparedness efforts for dealing with WMD attacks on our soil. Thanks to the Nunn-Lugar-Domenici program, 120 major metropolitan areas are slated to receive training and equipment and take part in exercises by 2001. But as of early 1999, only forty-six cities had received classroom training and fewer than a dozen had participated in a full-scale drill. Critics complain that the program offers too much lecturing, not enough hands-on training, and virtually no opportunity for refresher courses. And many urban officials are still unsure which federal agency to turn to in an emergency.

In January 1999, President Clinton made an important speech calling for increased attention and funding to meet the twenty-first-century terrorism threat, including some $2.8 billion to defend against chemical, biological, and cyberattacks by developing new vaccines, stockpiling antibiotics, setting up emergency medical teams in major cities, and establishing a "Cyber Corps" of skilled computer experts to deal swiftly with digital strikes. The President's speech was a welcome step forward, but most of the funds were for preexisting programs — enhancing but not expanding our preparedness. More would be needed, as President Clinton recognized in calling in January 2000 for another $2 billion to be spent on the cyberattack front.

Another area for greater cooperation is between government and private industry. Businesses pay a significant price for international organized crime and electronic thievery. Yet a lack of trust between business and government is hindering both from effective action.

Only the private sector has the knowledge, expertise, and access to identify and address its vulnerabilities to cybercrime and cyberterrorism. Only the federal government has the legal authority, law enforcement tools, and defense and intelligence means to detect and deter the most serious cyberthreats. Unless both groups find common ground, businesses will be picked off individually and the nation as a whole will suffer.

Of course, our government needs to maintain a clear-eyed view of the problem. It must find a way to mobilize public support without prompting unwarranted panic. And it must have the strength to never, ever yield to terrorist provocation.

To build public support for tough action against new threats, we must draw the connection between these dangers and our people's daily lives. Terrorism is receiving a great deal of public attention, but the problem of international crime is not. Yet cocaine from the Andean jungles and heroin produced in Southeast Asia's Golden Triangle wind up in our cities, on our streets, in our schools. Fraud schemes and other crimes run by international gangs cost Americans tens of billions every year. By publicizing the scope, severity, and significance of these threats, we can take the silence out of the "silent crisis" — preventing our people from ever accepting that transnational crime need become simply another part of the global landscape. At the same time, every sector of society has a real responsibility not to glamorize these crimes or romanticize their perpetrators. Lastly, all of us need to understand that terrorists measure their victory not only in fatalities but in fear. The purest way to defeat them, therefore, is never to be cowed.

I know from experience that this is not an easy task. In the fall of 1995, the United States Secret Service informed me they had credible, if not conclusive, evidence of a very specific foreign death threat against me. At their recommendation, I spent several months in the protection of Blair House, the official guest house across Pennsylvania Avenue from the White House, and a safe house not far from there. I rode in a bullet-proof limo and spent many evenings shooting pool (badly) with my highly trained and extraordinarily competent detail of Secret Service agents.

One day, I insisted that I take a walk. As I strolled up Connecticut Avenue, preoccupied and not paying attention, I stepped off the curb and was nearly struck — by the Secret Service car trailing behind. "You almost got killed!" my lead agent exclaimed with a look of mock horror. I argued that the car was moving too slowly to do me any real damage, but he was unpersuaded. "You almost got killed," my agent replied, "because I'd have had to strangle you myself to keep you from saying what happened and ruining our reputation!"

The threat — real or unsubstantiated — certainly altered my life for a while. But such moments helped me keep the threat from altering my outlook.

By refusing to let terrorists terrify, we take away their power. In President Clinton's words,

Make no mistake about it: The bombs that kill and maim innocent people are not really aimed at them, but at the spirit of our whole country and the spirit of freedom. Therefore, the struggle against terrorism involves more than the new security measures I have ordered and the others I am seeking. Ultimately, it requires the confident will of the American people to retain our convictions for freedom and peace and to remain the indispensable force in creating a better world at the dawn of a new century.[30]

CHAPTER THREE

Ambiguous Warfare

MEMORANDUM
FOR THE PRESIDENT

From Chief of Staff
August 5, 2004

You asked how we got ourselves into the current predicament, in which you are under assault by your political enemies during a tough reelection campaign for failing to react to the murder of almost one hundred American citizens (almost certainly by the government of I***), as well as for the temporary blockage of the Panama Canal and a severe blow to our tourist industry. I have pulled from the files the summary minutes of the most important NSC meetings for your review:

SUMMARY MINUTES AND CONCLUSIONS
OF MEETING OF NATIONAL SECURITY COUNCIL

April 19, 2004

Meeting began at 10:03 A.M.

Participants

The President
The Vice President
The Secretary of State
The Secretary of Defense
The Secretary of the Treasury
The Attorney General
The White House Chief of Staff
The National Security Advisor
The Chairman, Joint Chiefs of Staff
The Director of Central Intelligence
The Ambassador to the United Nations
The Deputy National Security Advisor

The President asked the National Security Advisor to review the events of the past week, since last they had met.

The National Security Advisor reported that the incident the previous evening in the Strait of Hormuz raised the most serious issues. As they all recalled, he said, the American strike with Tomahawk cruise missiles against I*** a few weeks ago on April 2 had been entirely successful. Even opinion in most of the Arab world, not to mention the reaction of the Russian and French governments, had been that the American response was justified and proportionate given the heavy losses suffered at the MCI Center last year.

The President praised the work of the CIA and FBI in uncovering the nebulous but real ties of the MCI terrorists to the I*** government.

The Attorney General noted that a fair measure of luck was involved, as well, and that we should not count on finding such indirect links in the future. And we still hadn't caught the three who carried out the attack. But we would, sooner or later.

The National Security Advisor returned to the previous evening's incident. The attack on our ship by I*** was not unexpected although we had reinforced our naval presence before our April 2 strike and had warned I*** against any response. The issue now, in his view, was not whether we responded, but when and how.

The President asked the Secretary of Defense to report on the I*** attack.

The Secretary of Defense replied that our frigate, on routine patrol 1 kilometer outside I***'s territorial waters, had suffered minor damage in the attack by three swift boats. One American sailor was dead; three injured. Damage to the attackers was unknown. The Secretary voiced his strong belief that an immediate American response was necessary.

The Vice President concurred.

The President asked for options for a retaliatory response. He added that any response must be accompanied by a further buildup of American forces in the region, to send an unequivocal message that further attacks on American forces would be punished severely. We must not get into a series of tit-for-tat exchanges. Could such a scenario lead even to a ground war in the region?

The Director of Central Intelligence said that the I*** attack of the previous evening was probably a face saver. I*** still had many options, including direct or indirect assaults on her Gulf neighbors, in order to drive a wedge between them and the U.S.

The Chairman of the Joint Chiefs of Staff stated that there was no question the U.S. could achieve escalation dominance in any escalation scenario. He recommended not only an enhanced naval presence, but also that elements of the 4th Infantry Division (Mechanized) be deployed from Fort Hood to Kuwait. With their advanced precision-guided munitions, in the event of any conventional conflict these units should hold their own until reinforced. On the basis of our far better intelligence and air power, we should be able to defeat a larger force. Should it appear necessary, we could also deploy heavier forces.

The Secretary of State asked whether American forces were actually that much more capable.

The Secretary of Defense remarked that this was more a question of military than diplomatic judgment and that, in fact, U.S. forces were far more capable than the Secretary of State might be aware. Recent improvements in our information links meant that our theater commanders could not only use smart, precision-guided weapons but could act smarter themselves. They could use the new technologies to see any battlefield and issue orders far faster than any opponent. He invited the Secretary of State to the Pentagon to get updated, should he so wish, in order to understand better these military calculations and to learn about the effectiveness of weapons like the Apache Longbow, which, working with immediate intelligence supplied by unmanned aerial vehicles, could devastate enemy armored vehicles.

The Secretary of State noted that neither diplomatic nor military matters were the exclusive concern of any department, including Defense. While reserving on his final recommendation, he expressed his and his experts' concern that a further attack on I*** would increase nationalistic sentiment there and decrease the chances of any change in the nature of the regime or its policies.

The Secretary of Defense recalled hearing the same hopes before and wondered when those changes in I***'s regime or policies might actually occur. How long, he asked, would we continue to hear this argument?

The Secretary of State answered that we would hear it as long as it was true.

The President suggested that the argument about internal I*** politics had been sufficiently covered at this and previous meetings and asked whether a major buildup in the Gulf would degrade our ability to deter an attack on the Korean peninsula.

The Chairman of the JCS stated that there was no doubt we could prevail if there were a conflict there, but that a buildup in the Gulf would degrade the rapidity with which we could reinforce in Korea. As it was, the buildup in the Gulf would mean delaying a rotation of units for our peacekeepers in Bosnia, Kosovo, and Colombia.

The National Security Advisor argued that while a Persian Gulf contingency could erode our military deterrent position in Korea, a failure to respond strongly to the previous night's attack would erode deterrence in Korea and elsewhere still more through its psychological and political effect.

The Chief of Staff stated that the American public's reaction to the Tomahawk attack on April 2 had been very positive. Any failure to respond now, especially after taking casualties last night, would be unthinkable.

The President stated that if we proceed further down this road, and it looked as though we must, the public must be prepared for further casualties. This was not an arcade game, although it might appear so on television. Otherwise, the public could turn on the whole enterprise in revulsion against not only U.S. casualties but footage of civilian deaths in I***.

The Vice President said that the problem wasn't only casualties. Further military action must have a clear, achievable purpose that can be presented to the public. Without it, the reaction to casualties would be still worse.

The President asked the Secretary of Defense and Chairman of the JCS to report to him that evening with the options they had prepared for a further retaliatory strike against I***. He asked that the same group meet with him in the Residence that evening at 8 P.M.

Meeting ended at 11:37 A.M.

Conclusions

Defense/JCS to prepare to present options for retaliatory strikes by close of business today.

Defense/JCS to brief on measures to reinforce U.S. military position in Gulf, for President's approval.

State and NSC to prepare diplomatic plan to accompany further strikes, including recommendations regarding Presidential calls to leaders in the region and key allies, as necessary.

State/US Mission to the UN to prepare any necessary actions at the Security Council.

NSC to prepare press guidance for today's briefings and draft Presidential statement to announce new strikes.

NSC to prepare talking points for Presidential calls to Congressional leaders.

■　■　■

SUMMARY MINUTES AND CONCLUSIONS
OF MEETING OF NATIONAL SECURITY COUNCIL

June 25, 2004

Meeting began at 3:02 P.M.

*Participants: Same as at meetings of April 19, April 25, 26, 28,
May 4, May 24, and June 10.*

The President began by stating that he assumed, but could only assume, that, unhappily, we knew why there had been no military response from I*** to our air attacks of April 27. He again congratulated the Defense Department on the efficiency with which the buildup and attacks had been conducted. There could be little doubt that our overwhelming military power had deterred further military action by I***. But he also had little, or no, doubt about the real nature of their response — that I*** was behind the recent terrorist outrage in the Panama Canal.

He asked the National Security Advisor to bring the group up to date.

The National Security Advisor said that he would defer to the Attorney General and Director of Central Intelligence on the status of the investigation into the explosion and sinking in the canal. There still had been no claims of responsibility for the attack. The Panamanian government was doing what it could, with our help, but held out little hope of catching those responsible now that two weeks had passed. The question before us: Could we retaliate against I*** based only on the belief that they were responsible? If not, what were the chances now of gaining some degree of proof? What would be the effect of failing to act?

The Director of Central Intelligence stated that she saw little chance of finding a link between the terrorists, even if identified, and I***. We were lucky last time. They probably would not make the same mistakes this time. And the American cruise ship had been an easy target — you could check your bags into your cabin without their being screened; the screening procedures for the ship's personnel were lax.

The Attorney General said that despite the press statements by unnamed FBI officials, there seemed little likelihood of making a case against I***.

The Secretary of State said that it was conceivable — not likely, but conceivable — that the attack had been carried out by an enemy of I*** in order to stimulate an American attack against I***. Or it could have been carried out by guerrillas in Colombia unhappy with the peace deal . . . or narco criminals . . . or anyone with an interest in shutting the canal.

The Secretary of Defense agreed that any of these were *possible*. Maybe. But should that possibility deter us from exacting a cost for the murder of eighty-eight Americans, including twelve servicemen on leave and nine children, as well as thirty-three foreign tourists? Everyone in the Persian Gulf, and around the world, thought that I*** was behind it. A failure to act would make us look impotent — and that look would not be deceiving.

The Chairman of the JCS spoke strongly of the families of those who had died and the need to act in their behalf. And if we did not, this incident would encourage other enemies of the U.S. to act in similar fashion rather than taking on the United States directly. This could have profound implications for our military position in the future.

The President agreed. We had to do something or our position would be weakened. And the American public would never accept a failure to do anything in response to such a loss. In any case, he had promised the day of the attack that we would track the terrorists down and see justice done, no matter what. He could not and would not eat those words.

The Vice President recalled his own record as a hard-liner on issues of terrorism, but said he had no choice but to raise a warning flag. Attacking I*** with no evidence might be popular for a few days. But there would then be a very strong reaction on editorial pages and probably in the public about our going off half-cocked without any factual basis for our action. He recalled a statement by President Kennedy about Vietnam — that the public cheered a war against a visible enemy but with no visible foe your choices are very hard.

The Chief of Staff said that he reluctantly agreed.

The Secretary of State noted that if we acted without evidence of I***'s guilt, reaction on "the street" in the Arab world would be very harsh, undercutting not only our position in the Gulf but that of friendly governments. We could expect the condemnation of most governments around the world, including even most of our allies. We would probably have to veto a resolution attacking us at the UN Security Council.

The Secretary of Defense pointed out that a failure to act would make us a laughing stock with the same Arab opinion and the same governments around the world.

The National Security Advisor said that, in short, we were damned if we do and damned if we don't.

The President thanked him for his insight.

Meeting ended at 4:12 P.M.

1.

Military Change

How will future Presidents deal with this nightmare: the difficulty of confronting an enemy who answers our growing military might not only through unconventional means but anonymously as well?

Let us start with the good news: the current modernization of our armed forces — the so-called Revolution in Military Affairs (RMA). This, like previous periods of innovation, is a revolution that will both increase our military strength and test our wisdom in how to use it. Then let us imagine the difficult new terrain on which future opponents may respond to our growing military power — the terrain of ambiguity, on which we must learn to fight more effectively as well.

■ ■ ■

The communications revolution is allowing and promoting change in our military forces just as it is enhancing the productivity of American businesses. We have entered into a period of rapid innovation in our nation's military organization and operational doctrines that will give our armed forces an extraordinary new capacity to fight and win this new century's wars. How well we guide, adapt to, and exploit this wave of change will shape our nation's military security well into the future.

There have been a number of such revolutions in the past. All were driven by changes in technology. At the Battle of Agincourt, British soldiers used new technology and tactics to crush a well-financed French army at least four times their size. After luring the enemy into a head-on attack, British longbow archers found easy targets in the armored French knights. When the weakened, weary French finally reached the English lines, they were finished off with axes and swords. The railroad, the telegraph, and the mass-produced rifle transformed the nature of nineteenth-century war, accelerating mobilization of forces, enabling commanders to transport armies more quickly, facilitating coordination of troop movements, and intensifying the lethality of combat.

In World War II, the German Blitzkrieg combined the best of tanks, communications, and precision strikes to spread across the continent. The aircraft carrier transformed war at sea from the barrages of the big guns to long-distance exchanges of air strikes. And nuclear weapons, with their potential for mass destruction, fundamentally changed strategic doctrine by making deterrence through the threat of destruction, rather than destruction itself, the primary purpose of our most lethal military weapons.

Now, the same information revolution that is having such profound effects on our civilian lives is also transforming our military. We saw a new stage in the Revolution in Military Affairs in Desert Storm, where unmanned aircraft beamed reconnaissance images to commanders, high-tech satellite systems let aircraft and troops know their location at all times, and smart weapons enabled precision strikes with greatly reduced risks to Americans. Indeed, according to General John J. Sheehan, "one F-117 sortie with laser-guided bombs was able to destroy the same types of targets that required 1,500 B-17 sorties in 1943 and 176 F-4 sorties in 1970."[1] We see it in Bosnia, where a broad intelligence umbrella has helped to keep the pressure on the parties to the Dayton Accords. Apache helicopters flying overhead can transmit detailed pictures from the ground to a satellite, record them on video, or send them straight to headquarters. Electronic communications down to walkie-talkies and field telephones can be overheard. Even in darkness, airborne infrared sensors can pick up the heat emissions that secret movements of troops would generate.[2] Such digital documentation has been essential in discouraging a return to fighting.

But these examples, impressive though they are, are just the leading edge of the RMA. Less than 10 percent of the munitions used against Iraqi forces during the Gulf War were precision guided. That percentage will grow on future battlefields. And perhaps even more important than the accuracy of our ordnance is the growing ability of U.S. forces to dominate information flows on and around a battlefield, and thus to dominate the battlefield itself.

The implications of information dominance are huge. As Eliot Cohen writes in his excellent article "A Revolution in Warfare":

> Such a transformation . . . might lead, for example, to a drastic shrinking of the military, a casting aside of old forms of organization and creation of new ones, a slashing of current force structure, and the investment of unusually large sums in research and development.
>
> Such a revolution would touch virtually all aspects of the military establishment. Cruise missiles and unmanned aerial vehicles would replace fighter planes and tanks as chess pieces in the game of military power. Today's military organizations — divisions, fleets and air wings — could disappear or give way to

successors that would look very different. And if the forces themselves changed, so too would the people, as new career possibilities, educational requirements, and promotion paths became
essential. New elites would gain in importance: "information warriors," for example, might supplant tanks and fighter pilots as
groups from which the military establishment draws the bulk of its
leaders.[3]

Our military understands very well that this is a time of
change. "Force XXI Operations," an army guide written in 1994,
begins with the recognition that "We live in a dynamic world, an
era of contradictory trends shaped by two great forces, one strategic, the other technical — the advent of the Information Age. The
scale and pace of recent change have made traditional means of
defining future military operations inadequate." But as with previous revolutions in military affairs, we are only just beginning to
explore its meaning. The dawn of the Information Age is not the
end of mystery.

The RMA poses an important question of priorities: How much
of our military resources should we use to finance this revolution, even at the expense of our existing more traditional forces?
And if we place our bets heavily on the current technology, will
we then miss the following wave as we build what is called the
military after the next?

The current balance has been struck through what some of our
planners call wing walking. Imagine our nation as a barnstorm-
ing daredevil, balanced on the wing of an airplane flying into the
winds of an uncertain future. Their point is that if we don't hold
on to both struts — the strut of continuity and the strut of
change — we risk getting swept away.

Secretary of Defense William Cohen and Chairman of the Joint
Chiefs General John Shalikashvili adopted this approach in the
1997 Quadrennial Defense Review (QDR), rejecting a strategy

that would have placed both hands on the strut of change. As they explained,

> While [such a strategy] might appear "bold" to some, it is not best for America. The approach we chose balances the needs, and risks, of today with those of the future, paying for steady increases in modernization to fully realize the Revolution in Military Affairs by making reductions in support structures and, to a modest extent, force structure. This is clearly the most prudent way to defend our interests now and into the next century.[4]

Numerous critics attacked them for an overly cautious approach. It will be years before it is clear who was right.

Led by former Deputy Chairman of the Joint Chiefs of Staff Admiral William Owens, former Army Chief of Staff Gordon Sullivan, and others, the military has put considerable thought into what the Revolution in Military Affairs will look like and its organizational and strategic implications.

In ten years, or considerably sooner, American forces will be able to dominate a battlefield with weapons and technology that might now seem drawn from the pages of science fiction. Some are designed to enhance surveillance and reconnaissance. Global-positioning satellite systems already enable our troops — from the sailor on the open sea to the soldier in the tangled jungle — to pinpoint their precise locations. Converted Boeing 707s known as J-STARS (Joint Surveillance Target Attack Radar Systems) use radar to scan a battlefield from the sky and send maps back to troops on the ground. Unmanned aerial vehicles (UAVs) equipped with cameras can lurk unnoticed above an enemy encampment and beam the images back to our "shooters." Micro-UAVs are also in development; these tiny flying spies just inches long are part of a next generation of UAVs already being tested and built, including the Global Hawk and Dark Star. The latter can spy on enemies far above their reach at an altitude of 45,000 feet.

Other technologies are being developed to reduce the risk of casualties to both American soldiers and foreign civilians. Planned for 2004: combat systems called the Land Warrior (with video imaging, Global Positioning System, or GPS, and even e-mail for the individual soldier) and the Objective Individual Combat Weapon, a replacement for the M-16, with a device on its barrel to measure the distance to a target and smart bullets that can detonate in the vicinity of an enemy, showering him with deadly shrapnel. Other projects just in their infancy include a vortex launcher that produces a cannonball of air, a radio-frequency weapon that disables electronic equipment, and a sound-wave weapon that can penetrate the human body and vibrate internal organs.

Perhaps more important, other technology will allow us to process our intelligence with unprecedented speed through computers, bringing comprehensive, immediate knowledge to commanders and combatants alike. Individual soldiers with portable computers will be able to pull down the data they need, tailored to their specifications. With a common view of the battlespace and a common sense of what needs to be done, decision making will be sped, the accuracy of strikes will be improved, and, one can hope, conflicts will be minimized and brought to a swifter conclusion.

Proponents of the RMA believe it can help to reconcile several competing tensions: the need for American leadership in a global era, the tightening of defense budgets, and the lowered tolerance of the U.S. public for casualties in war. In the words of the director of the Defense Advanced Research Projects Agency, "These systems will use the most advanced technologies to let machines perform today's most hazardous missions, thus minimizing casualties to the military's most important resource, its people."[5]

The ultimate expression of this new war-fighting wizardry is the proposal for Rapid Dominance capabilities. This ambitious strategic concept is being developed by Harlan Ullman and James Wade with a group of former senior Defense officials and military leaders. The goal of Rapid Dominance is to paralyze an enemy's will to fight by inflicting an overwhelming level of "shock and awe" — or, as the authors explain, the nonnuclear equivalent of dropping the atomic bombs on Japan. Unlike the doctrine of Decisive Force that characterized Desert Storm, Rapid Dominance goes beyond the direct use of military might:

> It will mean the ability to control the environment and to master all levels of an opponent's activities to affect will, perception and understanding. This could include means of communication, transportation, food production, water supply and other aspects of infrastructure as well as the denial of military responses. Deception, misinformation, and disinformation are key components in this assault on the will and understanding of the opponent.
>
> . . . Rapid Dominance will strive to achieve a dominance that is so complete and victory that is so swift that an adversary's losses in both manpower and material could be relatively light, and yet the message is so unmistakable that resistance would be seen as futile.[6]

All this would be underpinned by futuristic technologies, from 3-D virtual environments that commanders could use for planning to robots that could provide a force presence in areas too dangerous for our troops. And, in the longer term, space-based systems — from high-resolution sensors to antimissile lasers — can improve both our intelligence and weapons accuracy.*

America's advantage lies not only in the development of these systems. Indeed, much of this technology is now available on the open market. (My highly accurate, handheld Global Positioning System will guide me to within a few feet of navigation markers during my weekend sails on the Chesapeake Bay.) What is unique is America's ability to fuse these technologies into a "system of systems" that will give our military complete information dominance within a 200-by-200 mile battlespace. In the words of Secretary of Defense Cohen,

> This system of systems will integrate the laptop, the microchip, the microwave, the videocam, the satellite and the sensor. It will connect the cockpit, the quarterdeck, the control panel and the command post and link the shooter to the commander to the supplier. It will aim to collect and distribute a steady flow of information to U.S. forces throughout the battlespace, while denying the enemy the ability to do the same.[7]

This advantage would be what many have described as that of a chess player who can see all the pieces while the opponent can see only some. That is true. But it is also more than that: Imagine such a battlefield to be a game of chess in which each move must be made within thirty seconds or forfeited. Using not only advanced, real-time intelligence, but also computer-aided

---

*My impression, based on participation in preparations for a military strategic-scenario exercise conducted after I left the White House, is that military planners are also thinking more carefully about space-based systems and their potential applications than the policy officials and legal experts who need to look at the arms-control implications are.

command-and-control systems, the U.S. commander can repeatedly act before the enemy has had a chance to react to the previous move.

When you add to this highly accurate precision-guided missiles that can strike, without warning, from many miles away, the psychological effects of information superiority are almost as potent as the physical. Imagine you were a Bosnian Serb in 1995, as U.S. troops used electronic warfare to find and cripple your radar and anti-aircraft missiles, and then hit you with accurate long-range strikes against which you had no effective response. No wonder you'd have concluded you stood a better chance of survival at the negotiating table than on the battlefield.

This combination of extraordinary situational awareness, nearly *simultaneous* rather than sequential operations, and massive, accurate firepower will lead to a very different battlefield. Massed formations of ground troops, as we saw in Desert Storm, will become a thing of the past. Instead of attrition warfare, where we try to grind an opponent down, information superiority and advanced precision weapons will allow us to make decisions faster and better than the enemy, besieging all his weak points at once across the entire battlespace. In sum, they will make our soldiers more deadly while helping them stay alive.

As the army's "Force XXI Operations" pamphlet explains,

> Looking at conventional and high-intensity warfare, recent military-technical developments point toward an increase in the depth, breadth and height of the battlefield. This extension of the battle-space with fewer soldiers in it is an evolutionary trend in the conduct of war. The continuing ability to target the enemy, combined with rapid information processing and distribution, smart systems, and smart munitions, will accelerate this phenomenon. As armies seek to survive, formations will be more dispersed, contributing to the empty battlefield. Commanders will seek to avoid

linear actions, close-in combat, stable fronts, and long operational pauses. Recent U.S. operations show that deep battle has advanced beyond the concept of attacking the enemy's follow-on forces in a sequenced approach to shape the close battle to one of simultaneous attack to stun, then rapidly defeat the enemy.[8]

2.

Back to the Future: From Chancellorsville to Fort Hood, Texas

A former Army Chief of Staff, General Gordon Sullivan is a soldier's soldier. More than once, I had the unhappy experience, but also the honor, of joining him when he consoled the families of our soldiers who had lost their lives, or talked with the wounded as they lay in their beds, thinking about how their lives had been changed by a bullet or shell fragment. An emotional, plainspoken man who loves the army and its people, is steeped in its history, and is devoted especially to those who have seen combat, as he did, in Vietnam, you might expect him to be a conservative planner, instinctively resistant to change. You would be wrong.

In early May 1997, I toured the battlefield of Chancellorsville with General Sullivan and Hal Nelson, the retired army historian. We had been to Gettysburg a few years before. It is fascinating to observe the ground from the point of view of professional soldiers. As they describe what they see, their eyes become the eyes of Burnside and Hooker, Jackson and Lee. They speak of what must have been going through their predecessors' minds as they not only made their tactical decisions, but worried about logistics, communications, their relations with civilian authorities — and their own reputations.

That day, General Sullivan reflected on the difficulties of reform, on how earlier generals had tried to apply the lessons of the recent past to their immediate problems, with huge stakes in lives and fortunes. Immediate reform does not always mean immediate success. For example, a few months before the battle at Chancellorsville, Hooker had seen Burnside's mistakes in attacking Lee's entrenched positions at Fredericksburg, at a terrible cost in lives and defeat. So at Chancellorsville, having replaced Burnside as the Union commander, Hooker hunkered down when an attack would have carried the day. He had learned the right lesson about the advantages of entrenchment but applied it at the wrong time and in the wrong way. Hooker also reformed his command structure, but his new command methods apparently failed him. The Union suffered another severe setback.

Hooker did not fail simply because he tried unsuccessfully to adapt. He also lost his nerve at key moments. But as we drove around the battlefield, we were sobered by how harsh the judgment of history can be when a military (or any) commander moves either too rapidly or too slowly in adopting reforms.

As we drove through the Wilderness on the same dirt road that Jackson and his troops followed as they broke off from the main Confederate forces to circle and surprise the unsuspecting Union's right flank, General Sullivan turned to the importance of the Revolution in Military Affairs, with its emphasis on accurate intelligence and rapid maneuver. To make his point, he punched the radio button in his car. Soon, he said, each of our battlefield vehicle commanders would be able, with just one touch of a button, to inform headquarters of his or her exact location. Just as we can put into the cockpits of our planes almost instantaneous intelligence about ground-missile threats, so in the not-too-distant future, he said, we could give our tactical ground commanders near-instant imagery of what lies beyond the next hill.

As Army Chief of Staff in the early 1990s, it was Gordon Sullivan who pushed the army toward change. I could see his pride in the progress at Fort Hood, in central Texas, when I accompanied him there in June 1998.

Fort Hood is not only hot. It is huge — 340 square miles of motor depots with rows of tanks, armored personnel carriers, and Humvees; facilities to house and care for forty-one thousand soldiers and ninety thousand family members; test ranges; and the headquarters buildings of the III Armored Corps. It is the nation's largest armor installation, home to two army divisions. One of them, the 4th Infantry Division (Mechanized), is in the process of becoming the first "digitized" division in the U.S. Army. While maintaining its readiness for conventional deployment abroad, it also is intensively incorporating the new technologies and command structures of the RMA. At a cost of some $2.4 billion, its metamorphosis should be complete, subject to further refinements, early in this century. A second Fort Hood division, the 1st Cavalry, should be similarly transformed by 2003. In 2004, the III Armored Corps is scheduled to become the army's first Digital Corps.

The 4th Infantry Division is already equipped with many of tomorrow's technologies, which bring unprecedented information to every level of command and radically reduce the time required to make battlefield decisions. I saw them use All Source Analysis Systems (ASAS) — desktop computers that integrate and fuse the streams of intelligence being transmitted to commanders by J-STARS, UAVs, U-2 spy planes, satellites, and more. Capable of processing hundreds of reports per hour, the ASAS can be housed in mobile trailers and kept as close or as far from the battlefield as needed. With the click of a mouse, battlefield commanders from corps through brigade will be able to obtain a comprehensive picture of enemy deployments, capabilities, and courses of action — and plot their targets accordingly.

Other networks are bringing better situational awareness to the lowest tactical level: the individual soldier. Computers attached to the dashboards of Humvees, tanks, trucks, and Bradley Fighting Vehicles can display a common picture of the battlefield, integrate data from multiple intelligence sources, and link the troops together through a digital communications system.[9] This means that all soldiers can see where they are, where their teammates are, and where the enemy is hiding. It reveals to the quartermasters who is running short of what, so they can better plan refueling and resupply. It reduces the likelihood of friendly fire, while enhancing the accuracy of strikes. And it strengthens the lethality, survivability, and speed of our troops in the field.

Computers also are aiding operations off the battlefield. Previously, military planners and commanders plotted maneuvers with acetate overlays, using overhead projectors, grease pencils, and maps to manually chart a battle's progression. These time-consuming, static displays are being replaced by computer monitors that offer a real-time, dynamic picture of how enemy and friendly forces are moving. With a light pen, a commander can plot out potential movements on his or her screen and through the computer analyze their tactical implications and anticipate future logistics needs, all with unprecedented speed. Moreover, these electronic staff-planning meetings can be shared up and down the line — providing common command awareness of why a decision is made.

One Fort Hood commander described to me how the digital corps would dominate the battlefield of the future. He called it Find-Kill-Finish. First, they would locate the enemy through sophisticated sensors. Then they would take away the enemy's flexibility with "shaping fires" against his mobile reserves and artillery, constraining his room for maneuver. Finally, they would engage in a firefight on the ground, one whose parameters were closely limited by the earlier shaping strikes. Whereas previous battles were linear and sequential, these would be continuous. Whereas previous battles required time to plan, prepare, and execute each operation, now situational awareness would enable immediate, simultaneous actions.

The army is not the only service experimenting with new technology. At training exercises at Camp Pendleton in California, young Marines with computers strapped to their chests and antennas rising up from their shoulders are learning how electronic networks can enhance their war-fighting capacity. Marine Corps Commandant General Charles Krulak describes "the strategic corporal" of the future, who will have tremendous power at his fingertips. At the other end of the spectrum, tomorrow's Marine Corps generals are looking forward to what one officer calls a "God's-eye view of the battlespace" — informed by situation reports from every man and woman in the field.[10]

All of this is real, if embryonic. It is not the wish list of Beltway technoconsultants or the fantasy of Rand Corporation theoreticians. It is being built at places like Fort Hood. The 4th Infantry Division was the first on Utah Beach in June 1944. It could be the first to prevail on tomorrow's digital terrain.

THE QUANDARY OF COMMAND

As is so often the case, technological change will have important organizational as well as strategic implications. For American military commanders, the "fog of war" is being lifted — swept away by a flood of information from a sea of intelligence sources. The challenge our leaders face today is how to organize and act on this knowledge. Colonel James Blaker is the former senior advisor to the vice chairman of the Joint Chiefs of Staff who worked closely with Admiral Owens on developing the Joint Chiefs' approach to the RMA. Right now, he says, our armed forces can process only some 10 percent of this information. The info-flood will only swell as technology improves. As General Sheehan, the retired commander of our Atlantic forces and a brilliant leader in our operations in Haiti, points out,

> By 2010, our C4ISR systems will be capable of transmitting and processing 1.5 trillion bits of information a minute.* This represents an exponential increase over time from the days of the World War I telegraph, when our rate was 30 words per minute; through the World War II, Korea and Vietnam-era teletype, with a 66 words per minute rate; to the pre-Pentium computers used in Desert Storm with a rate of 192,000 bits of information a minute.[11]

There is no point in having and processing all this information if our commanders cannot use it quickly enough to stay one or more steps ahead of an enemy. That means a different kind of command structure.

First, the different branches of our armed forces, working with our intelligence community, must move from an evolving capacity to act together in joint operations to the ability to act in a truly integrated fashion. As American forces moved into Haiti in the fall of 1994, considerable satisfaction was taken at the fact that *for the first time* army helicopters operated from navy aircraft carriers. This did indeed reflect a highly successful planning operation

---

*C4ISR refers to technologies and systems that provide command, control, communications, computer processing, and intelligence in the service of surveillance and reconnaissance.

directed by the Joint Chiefs. But in the future, such integration of operations must be normal, not cause for congratulation. Moreover, it must be as instantaneous as it is instinctive. As with our approach to terrorism, crime, and proliferation, we have to break down the boxes in our military structures as well.

Battlefield command — indeed, the nature of military leadership — will have to adapt to technological change as well. Combat operations are conducted through hierarchical structures. This is inherent in the meaning of the word *command*. Yet the information flows of the twenty-first-century force will increasingly be "Internetted" and nonhierarchical — diffusing authority and enabling different combat elements to directly coordinate their actions. How to make the hierarchical and horizontal fit together is one of the challenges being grappled with at Fort Hood.

Consider this change through the eyes of commanders at three levels: the platoon leader in the field; the division or corps commander of the battlefield; and the Commander in Chief and his senior military advisors. For the platoon leader, more information *could* mean far less battlefield discipline. How do you persuade your soldiers to charge when they can see what awaits them on the other side of the hill? If a pawn could see a knight that was hovering around the corner, would it still carry out its move? Thus far, the army has put its most sophisticated radars in only the lead Apaches and tanks "so the quarterback can make the decisions." But the less of a monopoly on intelligence there is at the top, the more essential strong leadership will become.

This becomes increasingly important at the division or corps commander level. While electronic communications will permit battalion leaders to take part in common planning, once a commander's order has been issued, it must be obeyed absolutely. But without the inherent power that comes from possessing more information, tomorrow's commanders will need to draw their authority all the more from other sources — whether force of personality, military tradition, or inspiring a sense of loyalty. As one Fort Hood general remarked to me, "You cannot digitize leadership." If tomorrow's foot soldiers will have more battlefield knowledge than yesterday's four-star generals, tomorrow's generals will have to convince as well as command, inspire as well as instruct.

The issue of *hierarchical* discipline around the battlefield becomes an issue of *self*-discipline in Washington. When Washington can watch a battle unfolding in real time, how do you keep the Joint Chiefs of Staff, and even the President, from weighing in? This has been a potential problem since the days of the Civil War, when the telegraph made it possible for political leaders to communicate with generals in the field. As Eliot Cohen has observed, the Union's military telegraph system was placed under civilian control, enabling Secretary of War Edwin M. Stanton to monitor — and meddle in — the affairs of his military leaders. Similarly, President Johnson's insistence on choosing specific bombing targets in Vietnam had a demoralizing effect on our military and made him needlessly vulnerable to charges of ill-advised micromanagement.

President Clinton wisely stayed out of tactical decisions, though he always reviewed general military plans. In any case, it always took too long to get information on an ongoing operation for the President to have interfered. In part, it was because the Pentagon resisted sharing details that still were in doubt. Most military officers know that "the first report from the battlefield is always wrong." Even when the Pentagon is relatively confident of the facts, it is best to treat carefully all reports of the first few hours of an operation.

During the June 1995 rescue of Captain Scott O'Grady, a downed American pilot in Bosnia, I began receiving half-hourly updates beginning in the early evening. It wasn't long, however, before reports started reaching me faster from our intelligence services than from the Pentagon itself. This should and will change — but such change will allow dangerous, amateur meddling from Washington in unfolding military operations.

Self-discipline will be a challenge not only for the White House and the Department of Defense, but also for members of Congress and the press — neither famous for restraint. Not only will battle information be available in real time, but it will be chronicled on tape as well. How long before posturing politicians insist on holding near-immediate congressional investigations that dissect every decision of a division commander? How long before CNN reviews the battle with a Monday morning analyst crowing into the camera, "Let's go to the videotape!"?

Interference from Washington as operations are under way could lead to confusion and delay. And instant replays by Congress and the press could lead to a climate of instant recrimination, fueling risk aversion among battle commanders who fear being made the next "tapegoat." Technologies designed to strengthen our hand could tie our hands instead. Whether the sergeant in the Humvee, the division commander at headquarters, or the President in the Oval Office, the challenge is the same: how to maximize the benefits of instant information while maintaining command structures that work.

It will be very hard, but who is better at handling this tension between discipline and individual initiative than America's men and women in uniform? Prior to his 1994 trip to Europe for the fiftieth anniversary of D day, President Clinton hosted a group of World War II veterans and historians at the White House. All of us there were particularly impressed by the emphasis they laid on the way that battle was a struggle not just between two armies but between two opposing ideas, and the qualities those ideas engendered in their respective fighting forces. As Stephen Ambrose reminded the President, and as his books brilliantly illustrate, only American forces could have acted as they did. When the American forces first landed at Omaha Beach, everything seemed to go wrong. Landing craft were destroyed. Tanks were lost in the ocean. Men chest-deep in cold water were easy prey for enemy guns. But when the troops made their way to the unfamiliar shores, having lost their officers, surrounded by strangers from other units, they did not radio back, "What now? We need to have orders to move." Instead, they began to form groups of their own and to improvise their own assaults. As President Clinton said later, "They were . . . driven by the voice of free will and responsibility, nurtured in Sunday schools, town halls, and sandlot ball games. The voice that told them to stand up and move forward, saying, 'You can do it. And if you don't, no one else will.' "[12] Not only in that tactical sense, but in a broader sense as well, our democratic culture promotes a spirit of individual responsibility that accommodates to the demands of a common cause.

REVOLUTIONARY REPERCUSSIONS

The Revolution in Military Affairs will reinforce and perhaps accelerate trends on two other fronts as well: public opinion at home and the attitudes of our allies and friends abroad.

As the potential power of the RMA becomes clear, the contradictory trends in public opinion that we have seen since Desert Storm will intensify. The tolerance for casualties could shrink as precision-guided munitions work their apparent magic. At the same time, for the same reason, the demand for using military force may grow. And with the heightened perception of military omnipotence, so may come a sense of ex post facto omniresponsibility. Years after the devastating genocide in Rwanda, scholars and reporters maintain that simply because the United States possessed such power, we had — and reneged on — a moral obligation to intervene to stop the slaughter. Our power does indeed require that we consider carefully its use in such circumstances — and there is no doubt that the United States shares the blame for a failure by the international community in Rwanda. But the possession of such power does not bring with it an automatic responsibility to use it.

The same mentality of American omniresponsibility is evident abroad. The perception of unparalleled American strength has led us to be viewed as an "Atlas that shrugged" in indifference whenever we've chosen not to use it. The pernicious corollary has been a reduced willingness and capacity of our partners to share the burdens of leadership. We see this in our partners' growing reluctance to let us use their soil for our operations. If they are convinced that we can project long-distance power, why should they assume the political risk of cooperation? At the same time, they depend on us more than ever for intelligence, logistics support, and leadership.

Our partners must have the muscle and means to pull their own weight in joint missions, including peacekeeping operations. But is it in our interest to push them to develop information-dominance systems? Was it in our interest to support, albeit reluctantly, the development of nuclear weapons by our allies? Joseph Nye and Admiral William Owens have argued for what they term an information umbrella, in which America would provide situational awareness to other nations. Access to real-time, accurate knowledge of an unfolding crisis or military conflict is a key to effective coalitions. By clarifying the issues at hand, it helps resolve differences among disparate partners — in short, helps coalitions coalesce.[13]

CHANGE ISN'T CHEAP

Some believe the Revolution in Military Affairs will save tax-payer dollars, as technological advances permit reductions in personnel. Others say these supposed savings are exaggerated or will be offset by the need to pay computer-savvy soldiers competitive wages. But these budget debates miss the real bottom line: The RMA is a subset of, not a substitute for, a strong, conventional American defense. We will still need troops to seize and occupy enemy territory and take part in operations other than war.

A *visible* American presence abroad, from our aircraft carriers to our army and air force units stationed in theaters around the world, has profound political and psychological importance. When China conducted provocative missile tests in the Taiwan Straits in the spring of 1996, the aircraft carriers we sent to the region helped defuse a dangerous confrontation. And the thirty-seven thousand American servicemen and women in South Korea, standing watch over the last fault line of the Cold War, are a crucial guarantor against aggression in a region of profound importance to our nation.

The broader question is how much we should be spending on our capacity to fight and win conventional wars — a capacity the RMA unquestionably will enhance.

The end of the Cold War has not reduced the importance of power. We are still confronted with the necessity of deterring — and if necessary defeating — the multiple regional threats produced by the regimes of men like Saddam Hussein and Kim Chong-Il. Consequently, it is entirely premature to abandon our strategy of preserving (and, as necessary, strengthening) the forces necessary to fight two large regional conflicts nearly simultaneously, as developed in the 1993 Bottom-Up Review (the Pentagon blueprint for defense planning in Clinton's first term) and reaffirmed by the Quadrennial Defense Review (QDR). In fact, the crisis in Kosovo in 1999 stretched our forces very thin. For a period of time we had no aircraft carrier in the Pacific.

Why was this so dangerous? Why must we be able to fight one conflict while successfully deterring another? If there were a long delay before we could fight on a second front, a potential enemy could be tempted to attack while we were still hunkered down on the first. Such a prospect could inhibit a President from responding to an attack in the Persian Gulf — or even prevent the Joint Chiefs of Staff from recommending such a response in the first place.

I saw the merit of the two-theater strategy myself in the summer of 1994, easily the most perilous period during my time at the NSC. We were reaching the endgame of negotiations with North Korea on freezing their dangerous nuclear program. To put strength behind our diplomatic efforts, we threatened North Korea with sanctions if they didn't agree to freeze and reverse their nuclear program. North Korea countered with a threat of force against the South if sanctions were imposed. We thus went through intensive planning on what a Korean conflict would entail — concluding that it would be very bloody, with heavy civilian as well as military casualties, but we would win. To deter the North Koreans, whose moderation in times of crisis is unproven, we quietly deployed more forces both to the Korean Peninsula and off its shores. Within months, when Saddam made another threatening move against Kuwait, we reinforced in the Persian Gulf as well.

Knowing that we had the means and mobility to manage both deployments was crucial to President Clinton's ability to go to the brink and hold firm. The result? North Korea signed on. Saddam backed down. Two major crises were averted. We must not lose the capacity (which is eroding) to avert them in the future.

Achievements like these rely heavily on our superior hardware and readiness. But at Fort Hood I was reminded especially of the human factor — the caliber of our military men and women. The fanciest weapons systems in the world are worthless without the people trained to use them.

During my tenure as national security advisor, I was consistently impressed by the emphasis General Shalikashvili and Secretary of Defense William Perry placed on our soldiers' quality of life. They firmly believed that just as our troops cared for us, we had a sacred duty to care for them. This includes a predictable lifestyle, a good workday, and a supportive living environment. At Fort Hood, I saw the pride the soldiers took in their base; one young soldier referred to part of the newly refurbished gym as "my weight room." Base funding is crucial for families, too; the army, for example, is the largest certified child-care provider in the nation.

But tighter defense budgets have been taking their toll. Fort Hood saw its funding drop from $741 million in fiscal year 1996 to $590 million in fiscal year 1999. Training resources have been maintained, but base operations have suffered. Even more alarming is the financial pressure our troops and their families are feeling. All the technical and master sergeants I met at Fort Hood said they would be leaving once their tours were up because they could not afford to stay. I heard about soldiers working at McDonald's to supplement their income — putting their lives on the line by day, flipping burgers at night. Others had volunteered for service in Bosnia not only out of loyalty to our country but also because the hazard pay was too lucrative to ignore. And yet, the extra money in their wallets was offset by the high toll on their spouses and children in loneliness, uncertainty, and stress.

The pressures will only get greater as the Revolution in Military Affairs moves ahead. As digital technology becomes more and more prevalent, every unit will need to be manned by computer-literate soldiers, information warriors at least as comfortable with computers as they are with their M-16s. But when corporations pay computer-skilled workers as much as two and a half times our soldiers' current wages, and the private sector pays some 13.5 percent more than the military across the board,[14] a 3, 4, or even 5 percent annual military pay raise isn't nearly enough to compete. As General Sullivan once said to me, today's army isn't hollow — but it is fragile. A survey of military personnel presented by the Center for Strategic and International Studies in early 2000 showed that our soldiers believe strongly in their mission but are increasingly stressed by the quality of their lives in the military.[15]

The costs of the Revolution in Military Affairs can be met, in part, by expanding defense budgets and by greater efficiencies — for example, in deciding we cannot afford the multiplicity of next-generation fighter aircraft that seem designed as much to meet the demands of each branch of the military as to meet the needs of the next century's battlefields. Overcoming congressional opposition to closing more redundant bases and to cutting the pork out of the Defense budget would also help. In December 1999, Senator John McCain called it a disgrace that the Congress voted for $6 billion worth of programs even though it was unrequested by the military. But at some point, even if there are short-term costs, the hand on the strut of continuity will also have to be loosened as we adapt to the change inherent in the Revolution in Military Affairs. And reasonable experts inside and beyond the Pentagon believe that, while RMA programs are very expensive, in the long run it will neither cost nor save great quantities of the taxpayers' treasure. As one senior Pentagon official puts it, "It will do what technology always does — raise the unit cost. But it will also raise unit productivity."

3.

Ambiguous Warfare

It will be a few years more before Defense planners, the President, and the Congress will have to make final decisions on how to refashion our force structure and military doctrines as the Revolution in Military Affairs becomes a more complete reality. As the capability of our military forces increases, at no small cost, it will be appropriate and necessary to make adjustments. The size and shape of a subsequent streamlining must be made in the context of a threat analysis and revision of military doctrines *at that time*. In a few years, for example, the actuarial tables for the remaining years of the North Korean regime, if any, should be more clear. Until that is the case it would be premature to degrade our ability to act forcefully in two different regions at more or less the same time.

If the specifics of those decisions about the coming shape of our forces are not yet clear, one point is almost beyond argument: For the foreseeable future, the military power of the United States will be overwhelming when matched against any enemy. But before we breathe a sigh of complacent relief, we must recognize that such enemies will not necessarily meet us on the battlefield, as our unfortunate, hypothetical President discovered at the beginning of this chapter. Our nation's unparalleled — indeed, unapproachable — power has sparked a new concern among our military planners: what they call asymmetrical warfare.

Asymmetrical warfare, also known as the David Effect, pits a relatively puny future foe against the giant of our military might. Such an enemy, whether a foreign government, state-sponsored actor, or criminal group with a grudge, could choose to match the prospect of our twenty-first-century weapons with harrowing, unorthodox responses, such as terrorist attacks, ambushes of peacekeepers, or the taking of American hostages. This use of low cunning against our high technology may not produce battlefield wins, but it *will* raise the cost of America's role in conflicts. And as we saw in Somalia, such gruesome affairs can increase the public and congressional pressures for the withdrawal of American troops and the end of an operation.

How to respond to a slingshot attack will test our resolve and restraint. But something worse has concerned me since a series of meetings in the Situation Room a few years ago. We were engaged in contingency planning to map our military response in case we discovered that a foreign state was responsible for a terrorist attack on American servicemen. As we worked it through, I became convinced that we face a more difficult challenge than the threat of asymmetrical warfare. It is the growing likelihood of what I would call ambiguous warfare, in which no one takes responsibility for a strike at our interests, and proof of our suspicions is hard to come by. As suggested at the beginning of this chapter, this is more than a threat. It could be a nightmare. What do we do when a future enemy not only uses asymmetrical means against us but successfully denies responsibility? After our Baghdad strike in 1993, some critics argued that we hadn't sufficiently proven Iraqi complicity in the plot against President Bush. Future attacks could be much less clear. What if we were certain we knew who was responsible but couldn't compile the evidence? And even if we felt we were certain, wouldn't it always be possible that another hostile government or group was exploiting the opportunity to poke us in the eye? Would a missile strike — and attendant casualties — be worth the risk?

The fact is, conventional military means may not always be the best, and must not be the only, way to exact a sufficient price when we are attacked by terrorist groups and/or their state sponsors. Our Tomahawks may be sharply accurate, but in fighting terrorism they are a blunt instrument. Shortly after America's missile strikes against Usama bin Ladin, former CIA employee Raymond Close argued in the *Washington Post* that "we can't defeat terrorism with bombs and bombast." He warned that our strikes against bin Ladin had sent a dangerous message to our enemies worldwide: "Accelerate your efforts to acquire new and deadly high-technology weapons — and manufacture and store those weapons in hard shelters in the midst of your civilian population."[16]

But should we simply do nothing? No. That would be unacceptable. It would send a dangerous signal of weakness to terrorists and, indeed, to friends around the world.

When confronted by governments with murky ties to terrorists, or by those terrorist organizations themselves, we need to secure more options for action between launching missiles, especially without a clear basis, or meekly accepting our fate. As Maxwell Taylor wrote in 1960 in calling for a policy of flexible deterrence to meet the Cold War threat, "it will permit our national leaders a wide range of choice when at some critical moment of history they must determine the appropriate military reaction required by our national interest."[17]

Sanctions may work, but they require patience — and lack not only the "punch" of more forceful measures but also the precision. Seeing innocent civilians suffer and the perpetrators left unscathed does not make for satisfactory retaliation. In addition, the most successful sanctions require multilateral support.

In a case of terrorism of ambiguous origin it is highly unlikely to be forthcoming.

In short, faced with the likelihood of ambiguous warfare, America needs to ready itself to fight on ambiguous terrain. This will require means of action that are controversial: a greater capacity for covert action not only by the CIA but also by the Department of Defense, including cyberattacks, or "information operations," against terrorist organizations and the states that sponsor them.

As Bruce Berkowitz and Allan Goodman have pointed out, American officials often used covert action during the Cold War as a "middle option" against a superpower rival. Secrecy seemed to add both flexibility and efficiency by eliminating the onus of public scrutiny and debate. But covert action has costs that must be carefully weighed as well — primarily, anger (or at least an erosion of trust) from allies and the public as the facts of an operation emerge; and the absence of "reality checks" to keep a covert mission running sensibly.[18] Indeed, there may sometimes have been recourse to covert action simply because of its convenience as a way to "do something."

Berkowitz and Goodman suggest two scenarios in which covert action is valid. The first is when awareness of U.S. involvement would undermine an operation; for example, if our backing of a foreign political party would corrode the party's credibility. The second is to avoid sparking a cycle of escalation by putting an adversary in the position of having to retaliate against us. This was true, I believe, in the case of our assistance to the Afghan resistance against the forces of the Soviet Union. No one with any intelligence (in either sense of the word) could fail to see our hand in the operation. But if we had supplied the aid formally, we would have forced the Soviet Union to respond in ways that would have been dangerous for us both.

Similarly, deniability is useful when we need to strike back at a government or group we are quite certain has attacked us, but we can't publicly amass the proof. It may be that our response will be truly covert; a damaging event might take place that would appear spontaneous, raising only suspicions that an external agency was involved. Or it might be that others could have a pretty good idea that we were behind such an event but could not prove it. In either case, the ambiguity of our response might well send a better message of deterrence than "bombs and bombast."

A menu of antiterrorist covert actions should include a range of measures that are far less lethal than the use of missiles — as well as some that are. To the degree that there is uncertainty about the responsibility for a terrorist attack on us, the retaliatory action could be reduced in its force. In any event, our strictures against assassination should not, I believe, be relaxed. Yes, the death of a Hitler or Pol Pot would have made the world a better place and saved many lives. But until a clear red line can be drawn between such as they and more run-of-the-mill despots, and a system devised to ensure that the distinction is maintained in a responsible fashion, the return to political killing as an instrument of American policy would be more dangerous than useful.

Are there covert means short of assassination that are potentially available to us in the ambiguous warfare of the future? Yes. But our means to conduct such covert action are limited by both capacity and policy. The CIA's clandestine service has been shrinking since the end of the Cold War, with experienced personnel moving on and not enough new recruits coming in to replace them in number or ability. Current salaries are too low to attract people with the talents and the willingness to assume the risks that a successful clandestine career demands. The CIA is addressing these problems, and recent increases in the budget should help, but there is a long way to go.

On the policy side, there is understandable resistance to covertly attacking the financial resources of terrorists. But as argued in the previous chapter, the lives of potential victims are more important than the risk to depositor confidence that such covert action might create.

Our focus should be on two areas in which we could be better equipped than we are to conduct ambiguous operations.

When we do resort to military force, we should consider enhancing or creating new forms of covert action. First, we could deploy more Delta Forces — small units that could conduct quiet or covert operations deep within offending states. And second, it is feasible to produce bombs and missiles that disintegrate on impact, leaving no "calling card" behind. Such sophisticated weapons wouldn't fool anyone as to their source, but they would provide the most forceful ambiguous response to terrorist attacks in which responsibility is obvious but unclaimed. Of course, their use would raise very difficult questions of congressional authorization and public accountability.

There is another form of covert action that offers a wider, more effective range of possibilities than human campaigns: information operations. This is not a new concept. During the Civil War, Union operatives tapped into Confederate telegraph lines, not only gaining intelligence but sending false messages to sow confusion. Today, more than ever, computers provide the tools for attack. Their potential use raises the same concerns about accountability. But that is reason to resolve the problems rather than dismiss the possible use of this weapon.

Information operations could include gaining control over an enemy's decision-making process and cycle, and exploiting his data or communications systems without his knowledge. They also require protecting one's own computer and communications systems from intrusion, disruption, and destruction. The United

States already has begun to explore this terrain through new units like the army's Land Information Warfare Activity, or LIWA. As a focal point for information-warfare expertise, LIWA provides small field-support teams — including specialists in information security, computer security, military deception, psychological operations, and command-and-control targeting — to bolster a battlefield commander's primary staff in planning operations.

But so far, the Pentagon tends to view information operations as an *adjunct of* the battlefield, instead of an *alternative to* it. We need to consider information warfare more broadly defined, not merely supporting military operations but substituting for them — thus giving future Presidents options that could make the difference between passivity and the use of blunt instruments.

What could this mean? *Washington Post* writer Bradley Graham reports that:

> The government has explored ways of planting computer viruses or "logic bombs" in foreign networks to sow confusion and disruption. It has considered manipulating cyberspace to disable an enemy air defense network without firing a shot, shut off power and phone service in major cities, feed false information about troop locations into an adversary's computers and morph video images onto foreign television stations.[19]

Ultimately, the warning shot of information weapons could help dissuade an enemy from engaging in conventional warfare — all with minimal casualties and, if desired, the cloak of deniability.

Of course, using offensive information operations poses problems as well. There is the problem of acquiring sufficiently detailed knowledge of any system we were attacking; for example, we would want to leave hospitals untouched, even as we shut down a power grid. There is the problem of collecting evidence of hostile intent before acting against an enemy; we would want to be armed with as strong a case as possible. There is the problem of conducting acts of war behind the public's back, and the corrosive effect that has on the compact between the government and the governed. And there is the problem of paranoia — because as soon as it is known that the United States is in the business of shutting down power grids, any time a country's lights go out, they may assume that Uncle Sam is to blame. This could provoke aggressive retaliation.

Finally, some have argued that offensive use of information operations would break an existing taboo, prompting others to target our more vulnerable information infrastructure. Surely, this gives too much moral credit to terrorists and their state sponsors, who are highly unlikely to be bound by taboos and would pursue their capacities regardless, as might other governments. Indeed, there are reports that the Serbs sought to use cyber-attacks against NATO during the Kosovo crisis. And in November 1999 the *Liberation Army Daily*, an official Chinese military journal, called for the development of their cyberwarfare capacities, an "all-conquering offensive technology . . . electronic bombs which saturate the enemy's cyberspace."[20]

In a June 1998 Senate hearing, when asked if America was developing offensive information-operations capabilities, Director of Central Intelligence George Tenet said the nation can be confident "we're not asleep at the switch in this regard." But further details are intensely guarded. As one Senate staffer remarked, "Whenever you get into the offensive stuff, you very quickly run into a security brick wall. The Defense Department has next to nothing to say about this in an unclassified form."[21] It is not possible, in this book, to go much farther.

As of 2000, there reportedly has been no presidential directive on the development of U.S. offensive capabilities for cyber-weapons, and virtually zero public debate on guidelines for their use, where to place military command authority, when peacetime intelligence gathering crosses the line into an act of war, what the likelihood and likely form of foreign retaliation would be, and whether we have the legal and institutional framework in place to oversee covert cyberoperations.

While we need to keep secret the specifics of our capabilities, we cannot afford to delay debate and discussion of the concept any longer. There are complex organizational issues to be resolved. For example, where will decision making be centralized? How will we get real-time information to policy makers in the White House so they can authorize attacks against unconventional targets like banks and telephone networks? And how will we meet the need for congressional notification, when part of the strength of information operations is the speed with which they move?

One solution to the organizational problems would be to fold information operations into the portfolio of the new Assistant to the President proposed in chapter 2. While the Department of Defense and CIA would be responsible for developing our cyberstrike capacity, the White House would coordinate its actual use. Information warfare moves too fast to enable congressional oversight of every action, but congressional approval should be required for any overall attack.

It is time to get serious and bring our planning for information warfare into line with its enormous potential. Covert computer operations can be among our greatest weapons in the twenty-first-century world. Will we use them to seize the high ground on ambiguous terrain? Or will we only watch as they are used against us?

CHAPTER FOUR

Peacekeeping As Permanent Band-Aid

Our military does more than deter and fight wars. Increasingly, it is being asked to make or keep the peace in messy foreign domestic disputes. This, too, has its dangers and dilemmas:

From the journal of Lt. Col. Lanny Jones, U.S. Army:

March 22, 2003

San Vicente del Caguan, Colombia

I don't like it. Not just the town. The situation. It's very, very tense. And I don't really know why we're here. Yes, to help keep a kind of peace. But for how long? What are we trying to get done? How will we know when we've done it? And how many of us or them will get hurt in the meantime?

To be honest, I wish I had more of a combat command. That's why I'm a soldier. Yes, peacekeeping is important. But I did my tour in Bosnia. It's wrong to say it, but it may be easier to kill people in combat than to convince people to like a peace. This is hard.

But here I am, with my battalion. And I miss Laura. But they say it's only until early next year. So they say. But they said we'd be out of Bosnia in a year and we've still got people there. And in Kosovo, where things don't get better enough for us to leave or worse enough to make us do something different.

I'd feel better about it if I knew where the talks in Rio were going to come out. At least the government and guerrillas — I mean FARC (got to be respectful) — reached enough agreement to get a kind of peace and to hold "elections." They better do more than that before the elections next year. But not my job to worry about that. Mine's tough enough: we in UNOMCO — sounds more like a gas station than the "UN observer mission in Colombia" — are supposed to "observe and verify" the disarmament, demobilization, and even reintegration of the two sides and to give the UN cops in CIVPOL our muscle as they train the local police and help local security restore "law and order." And we've got to help get the Colombians in this area ready for the elections next January.

Not easy. But my guys seem ready. And this will be a hell of a lot more interesting than duty at the Pentagon. (Although then I'd be with Laura and the kids.)

I'm glad Dick's here as my Exec. He did a good job with me in Bosnia. Smart guy. Already reading novels by Latin authors. Wish I had the time. Or enough interest. Maybe I will. But I wish Dick wasn't wound so tight. Maybe it's who he is. Maybe it's trouble at home.

I'll need him to be on the top of his game when the rules of the game are so unclear — including even our rules of engagement. "Chinese Chapter VII" they're called, though no one can tell me why. We can protect ourselves but no offensive acts. And we've got to get the guerrillas down from the hills and into the cantonment areas. Well, we'll be more "persuasive" if we make it clear nobody screws with us. Nobody. But we can't push the folks around or this will be a hostile environment, and in a hurry. I wonder if the people want us here. They must. God knows they've suffered from the war. I'm glad we have Venezuelan troops with us in the same sector. The FARC must like them a whole lot better than us. Now that I think of it, I don't guess the people who've been making money on their coca fields up outside town will be pleased to see us, either. And the death squads — I mean paramilitary? They're probably not so glad we're here, even if they've been going after FARC sympathizers.

We'll see. It'll all depend on how the FARC acts. 20,000 of them or so in the country. How many up in our hills? Intelligence says maybe a few thousand. But they're not sure. "The guerrillas in the mist." We can't force them to come to the cantonments and give up their weapons. I know they're tired of the fighting. Our aid to the government helped convince them. But the guerrillas still control almost half the country and are doing well from the drug deals. I wonder if they will play ball. Might have been better to let them keep their half and divide the country? No. It would be the world's first narco-state. But mine not to wonder why. We've got an agreement and we'll see how it all turns out. *We'll see.*

One year and back to Laura and the kids. She's strong. She can manage alone. I like that. But I don't like it, too. None of us like thinking that maybe, after a while, they don't notice so much that we're not there at home.

Speaking of worrying about not being missed at home: Dick is here. Got to go. I should ask him about why he seems uptight. And I *will* write in this journal every day. Wish I had in Bosnia.

November 11, 2003

This is one hell of a Veterans Day. I haven't been good about keeping this journal. But maybe writing in it tonight will help me think about what to do.

I can't blame Dick personally, though he probably overreacted. Do I stand by him, defend him when the investigation begins, as it will? Or do I say I think he acted too quickly? Even if I don't really blame him? Did he react the way I would have? Or did he order the shooting because he was mad about the "Dear John"? Three busted marriages in the unit since March. And his was the worst.

I have no doubt they'll all try to blame him. The C. government . . . the UN . . . our embassy in Bogota, maybe even the Pentagon. Killing a "Robin Hood" is what he did, kind of, and it's made our job harder. The people here were never real happy with us. They liked our helping bring "peace." They didn't like it that we didn't bring law and order, or jobs, right away. And they don't like our killing this guy who is now becoming a local hero. Never mind that he killed people and was a narco. And shot at us. I think.

It's a shame, because we've been making some progress, not bad in a place they call "Locombia," the Mad Country. A thousand of the FARC demobed, *almost* as many weapons given up. But many more guns weren't. Not surprising: A gun is not a bad tool for making money. In fact, I wouldn't be surprised if some of the bandits are guys we'd demobilized and who can't find work now. More robberies, more murders, more incidents on the roads outside town and the poor guys in CIVPOL, good cops and good trainers, are overwhelmed. One told me they are way undermanned not just here but around the world. They don't get the same chance at advance planning for peacekeeping operations like this. Their headquarters in NY isn't even in the main UN building. Military can deploy so much faster than the police advisors. That's what the military does — deploy abroad. But there's no international or even national police force trained and ready to do this.

So day before yesterday it's Dick who ends up making a police decision. At least he didn't act like the U.S. soldier in Haiti (before we got tougher) who stood by while thugs beat up a civilian. In our training they said that our soldier in Haiti had a "nine millimeter pistol and a 1,000 mile stare." That sure wasn't what Dick did.

His "local hero" holes up in a room above a store in a village outside town. Local police are after him for a minor bust because they can't get him for the coca they know he's been moving. CIVPOL helped them get the goods on the guy and were advising them on the arrest. The guy has an automatic rifle. CIVPOL calls for help. We send a platoon. Further standoff. I send Dick (should I have gone myself?). (Maybe I'd better destroy this entry after I write it.)

The guy over the store must have panicked. Shoots off a few rounds. No one hit. Our platoon leader looks at Dick. Dick orders return fire. Platoon takes out the shooter in spectacular fashion.

Turns out the guy had numerous relatives. And had made a few donations to help out the village school, etc. A Robin Hood, except he wasn't robbing from the rich, he was screwing over our druggies back home. But that doesn't mean much to the villagers here who have real problems of their own. So last night we see anti-American slogans go up on the walls. I've asked the Venezuelans to help out with patrolling in the area. And Dick is still working on his report. At least CNN wasn't around. So maybe it didn't really happen, as far as the World cares.

Poor Dick. He showed me the first page of the book he just started reading, *The General in His Labyrinth* by, I think, Márquez. He gave me a piece of paper with the words the general says to his servant: "Let's go as fast as we can. No one loves us here."

We'll see. Doesn't look to me like it will be very "fast."

1.

Things Fall Apart

The destruction within Colombia — its near dismemberment — is part of a sad pattern.

At the beginning of the twenty-first-century, the number of armed conflicts worldwide hovers around some twenty-five each year. Millions of people lose their lives in the fighting, which frequently targets civilians; according to the United Nations, wars in the 1990s alone killed two million children, seriously injured or disabled six million, rendered twelve million homeless, and severely traumatized ten million more. In 1998, these conflicts contributed to the flight of around thirteen million people seeking foreign refuge, and prompted an estimated eighteen million more to join the desperate ranks of the internally displaced. Big numbers. Pause for a moment and think of them as human beings, not statistics — as prisoners left to starve in labor camps, as pregnant women hacked to death by machetes, or simply as families uprooted and perhaps torn apart.

Virtually all of these violent conflicts were not between states but within them; not the result of foreign invasion but of neighbor turned on neighbor. Today, fractured states, civil wars, and ethnic conflicts kill more people and present far greater challenges to our diplomats and soldiers than more traditional threats. Dangerous as they are, we know how to deal with threats that reach across borders. But the fact is that we are still groping to find our way in dealing with internal conflicts.

The worst of the nightmare is for the millions of people suffering directly from violence and disorder. But I believe that unless we learn to act with greater efficiency in conducting peacekeeping operations — and with much greater clarity about the long-term purposes of such efforts — these conflicts will become something of a nightmare for us, as well.

Why the number and scope of these conflicts?

Before 1989, they were exacerbated by Cold War tensions and rivalries. Pursuit of geostrategic gain led the United States and Soviet Union to interfere in internal conflicts from Central America to Angola to Cambodia. Today, with superpower confrontation passed, such proxy wars are no longer likely. But the collapse of the Soviet Union and its empire has lifted the lid on a seething cauldron of suppressed hostilities. We have seen the murderous effects — in Bosnia, in Kosovo, in Nagorno-Karabakh — when ancient hatreds are combined with modern weaponry. And the fate of states such as Angola, Sudan, Somalia, Liberia, Burundi, Rwanda, and Sierra Leone has shown how internal conflicts can set back the fortunes of an entire continent. Northern Ireland, Colombia, and Indonesia show that such cases are by no means limited to Africa and the former Soviet Union.

While wars between states are generally fought over territory, the causes of internal conflict are varied. In some cases, such as Colombia and Peru, ideology motivates, or is used to justify, divisive clashes for political power. In others, such as Kosovo or East Timor, one side is seeking some form of independence or autonomy. The growing number of current crises reflects increasing ethnic or religious tensions, fueled by social stress and economic dislocation in an era of whirlwind change. Scarce resources, overpopulation, environmental degradation, and poverty are keeping the world's poorest nations on the outskirts of the global economy. Modern communications have made the gaps between the haves and have-nots more apparent, while enabling scapegoaters and preachers of hate to amplify their message. And the same communications allow separatist groups to reach out more easily for support from their ethnic kin abroad. People uprooted and buffeted by change are seeking refuge within their own ethnicity, especially as foreign (largely American) culture threatens their own through the communication networks of the global village. Weapons are abundant, available, and cheap, while hope too often is in short supply. When these factors are combined with weak, dysfunctional governments that cannot meet the basic needs of their people, the erosion or even collapse of authority may result — the phenomenon of the "failed state."

Often, these crises occur in regions least equipped to handle their consequences, whether they be unchecked violence, refugee flows, starvation, or disease. Given these complex, unsavory conditions and their seeming intractability, it may be tempting to turn our backs on civil conflicts, especially when they occur in nations far from America's shores. But the fact is that even a distant war in a tiny, impoverished nation can affect American interests both at home and around the world.

The effects of an internal conflict can spill over into neighboring countries, including regions of strategic importance or even the United States. The military coup in Haiti and ensuing internal repression prompted thousands of Haitians to risk their lives on the high seas, seeking sanctuary on American soil. Conflict in Africa can affect our supplies of oil. The breakdown of law and order in Colombia has benefited narco-traffickers, who export drugs and violence to American streets and schools. The war in Bosnia could have sparked a wider conflagration in Europe, affecting some of America's NATO allies and many of the continent's new democracies. And even though a spread of Bosnia's fighting was prevented, nearby nations felt the shock waves of war in economic dislocation and streams of refugees.

Nor will a nation preoccupied or paralyzed by conflict make a strong, reliable partner for the United States. While the conflict in Chechnya was consuming the time and energy of Russian officials, issues such as fighting nuclear proliferation suffered. As long as Africa is racked by civil war and ethnic strife, it will be able to neither devote its full attention to catching up in the international economy nor pull its weight in the global fight against drugs, disease, and crime. And while an isolated conflict might not impinge on U.S. interests, the cumulative effect of dozens of conflicts on the increasingly integrated world stage inevitably will hinder our ability to shape a more secure, prosperous future. As our own economic health continues to grow more dependent on that of others, internal conflict "over there" will have even greater effects on our own interests here in the United States.

In addition, there is a moral imperative that is all the deeper with our superpower status. How can America sit on the sidelines when innocent civilians are being slaughtered, or starved, or made to suffer before our eyes? We lose credibility on other issues if we turn our backs on humanitarian tragedies. More important, it is wrong to do so. With our great power comes great responsibility and leadership in human as well as geopolitical terms. Not acting, when you can, is as much a decision as becoming involved. This does not mean we *must* always act. But there are consequences when we do not.

This becomes all the more true in the era of CNN, because when cameras cover civil conflicts as they unfold and satellites beam them into our living rooms, pressures to act are accelerated and recriminations for inaction are amplified. But television coverage is itself selective and subject to human biases. By 1999, the deaths in the conflict in Southern Sudan had become more than *one hundred times* those in the terrible crisis in Kosovo. Yet Kosovo was front and center on the nightly news, whereas Sudan — at war for more than fifteen years — has gone virtually unnoticed.

Yes, our attention should focus mostly where our interests are greatest. And yes, our interests in Kosovo probably are greater than in Sudan. But shouldn't a human cost one hundred times greater in Sudan at least make equal its claim to international attention?

Whether because of the claims on our interests or the appeals to our collective conscience, dealing with such conflicts has become a central issue on our national security agenda. We and the rest of the international community have found some success and probably more setbacks in our approaches to the problem. Certainly, through early warning systems and efforts to address fundamental causes, we should do all we can to prevent conflicts, when they occur, but we all should take a hard look not only at *whether* to get involved — the question in most of our contemporary debates on the issue — but *how*. This means focusing on three questions:

- How best do we pursue diplomatic solutions to internal conflicts?
- How best do we conduct peacekeeping operations to reinforce diplomatic agreements?
- And perhaps most important, while least examined: What are the proper *purposes* of our diplomatic and peacekeeping efforts?

2.

The Tools of Diplomacy: Honest Brokering and Coercion

The first response to internal conflicts has been to seek their resolution through diplomatic means. Sometimes we act as an *honest broker* — as in the conflicts between Israel and the Palestinians or between the Catholics and Protestants in Northern Ireland. In other cases, our diplomacy and power are more directly linked in an effort to *coerce* one or more parties into agreement — as was the case in Haiti and Bosnia. To illustrate the point, let us briefly delve into recent history.

BROKERING PEACE

Acting as an honest broker can be the more difficult response for a diplomat. The United States certainly has real influence that it can bring to bear. But this kind of diplomacy primarily requires reason, patience, and often enough cajolery, because it relies less on power.

I was continuously impressed by the patient skill that Secretary of State Warren Christopher brought to his mission to bring peace between the Israelis and the Palestinians, as well as the Syrians and other neighbors. Together with the immensely talented and experienced Special Middle East Coordinator Dennis Ross, he threw himself into repeated efforts to bridge the gap. And from the start, the President took a particular interest in this cause, in no small part because of his close personal relationship with the late Prime Minister Yitzhak Rabin.*

The repeated trips our secretary of state took to the region had a price. He was criticized for spending so much time on this issue at the expense of others. But the strength of our interests in that region and the depth of our ties to Israel made his judgment the right one. If not for the death of Rabin, the efforts of the President and Secretary Christopher would have borne more fruit. As

---

*Perhaps the hardest thing I had to do was tell the President that his friend was dead, when our initial reports had been that he might survive the assassin's bullets. The President was unable to concentrate behind his desk while waiting for news and had walked to the putting green on the south lawn, standing there as much as trying to swing his putter, perhaps recalling the dramatic signing ceremony there, a ceremony Rabin had made possible. When I walked toward him with the final report, he saw my face and visibly sagged. When I gave him the news, it was as if someone had punched him.

it was, the progress that was made laid the foundation for the future progress that has and will come. It is a legacy of which Warren Christopher should be proud.

Through coincidence and a developing personal interest, I became more involved in the effort to end "the Troubles" in Northern Ireland. In early November 1993, suffering from a cold and uncertain of what to say, I was meeting at the Capitol with the Congressional Ad Hoc Committee on Irish Affairs. It included those members of the House of Representatives who were most assertive in their belief that the United States should reverse its long-standing refusal to take an active role on Northern Ireland — an issue that the British government considered an internal affair and thus of no diplomatic interest to us. Included in the dozen or so around the table were such strong supporters of Irish nationalism as Representatives Peter King, Richard Neal (a friend of mine from western Massachusetts), Benjamin Gilman, and Tom Manton.

I had agreed to the meeting at the recommendation of Nancy Soderberg, then the staff director of the NSC and previously the foreign-policy coordinator in Little Rock of the 1992 Clinton campaign. Her work as the chief foreign-policy staff member for Senator Ted Kennedy had given her a strong background and interest in Irish affairs, as well as a wide range of contacts both in the North and in the Irish Republic. So she recognized that in the fall of 1993 we faced both a problem and an opportunity.

The previous year, not coincidentally on the eve of the New York primary, then-Governor Clinton had pledged to appoint a special peace envoy to Northern Ireland and to give a visa for entry into the United States to Gerry Adams, the president of Sinn Fein. Sinn Fein's close ties to the Irish Republican Army, and Adams's own past involvement in the IRA and thus with its ter- rorist activities, had barred him from such a visa in the past. In any case, either action would be a sharp departure from U.S. policy and an affront to our British allies. The candidate had made his pledge without the prior knowledge of his foreign-policy advisors. When Soderberg later joined the campaign, she worried about how to reconcile his words with the realities of our relations with the British. In April 1993, Adams applied for a visa. Without much debate within the Administration it was denied. IRA bombings in September and October did nothing to make us think we were wrong.

In late October, however, the situation was changing. Mayor David Dinkins, running for reelection in New York City, wrote the President asking him to reconsider and give Adams a visa. We were on autopilot when we sent the President a reply for his signature. Drafted by mid-level officials wedded to the language of the British position, it included phrases that were code for an absolute adherence to London's view of the matter. The President's reply quickly became public, of course, and produced an unpleasant backlash. It was clear to me that I didn't sufficiently understand either the issue or the views of those calling for a change in our policy. I did not want to get involved in a domestic political dispute (an attitude for which I was occasionally criticized by some of the President's political advisors), but I would be meeting with both Democrats and Republicans at the meeting.

At the start of the meeting, I made no commitments to change our policy but said that I wanted to hear their views. King, Neal, and others laid out their case for American involvement. When they were done, I pledged to look into the question with a fresh mind and to take the time to do so seriously, despite the pressures of the current crises in Somalia, Bosnia, Haiti, and Russia. Representative Joe Kennedy, who had arrived late, immediately challenged me. They had heard such statements before from other Administrations, he said with obvious disdain, and they never meant anything. I asked if he was saying I had just lied. Perhaps surprised that an Administration official would object to such badgering by a member of Congress, he said that he was not, and repeated this in a subsequent generous note. I left the meeting intrigued by the issue (all the more so when recalling the occasional arguments between my English father and my mother, whose origins were largely Irish). And the exchange with Kennedy on the issue solidified my commitment to engaging on it.

In the ensuing weeks, Soderberg, who was the driving force behind our policies, became convinced that changes could be taking place within Sinn Fein and the IRA that would offer us an opportunity — even an obligation — to become engaged productively. A group of Irish Americans led by Bruce Morrison (recently a member of Congress) and Niall O'Dowd, publisher of the *Irish Voice*, had helped secure a weeklong cease-fire in September. In December John Hume, a Catholic moderate and leader in the civil-rights movement in Northern Ireland (and later Nobel laureate), urged us to grant Adams a visa — reversing the position he had taken six months earlier. Senator Ted Kennedy, a longtime foe of the IRA, also recommended doing so.

If Soderberg thought there was some chance of change, British intelligence and our FBI did not. Throughout the coming months and years, they did all they could to convince us that Sinn Fein and the IRA were both one and the same — and irrevocably committed to terrorism. At one later meeting with a senior British intelligence official I pressed, as tactfully as I could, for evidence of their absolute view. Little was forthcoming. I noted their ambassador, in a rare unguarded moment, looking acutely embarrassed. We had no independent intelligence sources in Northern Ireland (we don't spy within the United Kingdom) and thus had less reliable information from our intelligence community on this issue than on any confronting us during the first Clinton term, save North Korea.

To their great credit, however, the British and Irish governments issued a joint declaration on December 15, 1993, that gave further sign of change. For the first time, the Irish government agreed that the consent of the majority in Northern Ireland (at least for now the Protestants) is a condition for the reunification of the island, while the British agreed that reunification is an option if the majority so desired.

While not yet convinced that a visa should be issued to Adams, we at the NSC came increasingly to the view that it would make sense to test the IRA through Sinn Fein. Would American efforts to encourage Adams and his party into the fold lead to a diminution of violence — even a cease-fire? Soderberg argued that this was a win-win proposition. If such an approach worked, predictable British irritation with our policy would diminish and the benefits could be very large. If it did not, then a policy of supporting the isolation of Sinn Fein and the IRA would have a strong basis of fact. To dangle the visa for Adams without committing ourselves, the President on December 21 issued a statement saying that, "We will keep the issue under review as the developing situation warrants, especially in light of events flowing from the 15 December Joint Declaration . . ."

The issue soon came to a head. The mainstream National Committee on Foreign Policy in New York City invited Adams to a February 1 conference on peace. On January 28 and 29 Adams issued statements that did not renounce violence as clearly as we urged but represented a step in the right direction. Soderberg and I recommended giving him a one-day visa to attend the conference, in part because Adams could then hear from Irish Americans that they wanted peace. Despite the objections of the State and Justice Departments, the President issued the order and

Adams went to New York, together with a number of other Northern Irish leaders. The President had taken a step into territory no American President had entered before. Even Woodrow Wilson had refused to take a position on Irish independence in 1919, for fear of offending the British.

Not surprisingly, there was a furious backlash in London. Her Majesty's Government was very unhappy. Privately, the ambassador and others were very clear in their negative view. But British officials tried not to make things worse in their public statements. Prime Minister John Major, with whom the President had a much better relationship than portrayed by the press, quietly signaled his strong disappointment. I saw little spillover, however, to our very close work with the British on other issues. The British press, on the other hand, was apoplectic — as was our own ambassador to London. His successor, Admiral William Crowe, was also to be a skeptic about our approach, but always in a constructive and useful way.

The reaction in London made it all the more important that we use our involvement not only to urge Sinn Fein toward peace but also to make sure that we were working just as closely with the Protestant Unionists — and were seen to be balanced in our approach and contacts. As I was to make clear repeatedly to both sides, it was also imperative that we not have our own substantive plan for peace, which would draw immediate fire, but that we act as a channel of communication while urging both sides onward.

Over the following few years, I often met with, and more often spoke on the telephone with, the leaders of the parties on each side and officials in the British and Irish governments. At my first such meeting, with Jim Molyneaux, the outgoing leader of the Ulster Unionist Party, I could see that even at the most difficult moments these conversations would always be enjoyable and often amusing. Ian Paisley, the radical, anti-Catholic leader of the

Democratic Unionist Party, had recently called Molyneaux a Neville Chamberlain for his moderate behavior. I asked Molyneaux how it felt to be so branded. He laughed and said he was rather pleased. He was making progress. After all, he said, only a few weeks earlier Paisley had called him Judas Iscariot.

Even Paisley could be rather engaging at his most outrageous moments. When I once called him to invite him, with all the other leaders, to a White House event, he not only refused but treated me to a diatribe on the sins of the American government that was so inventive that I found myself not wanting to cut him off, for the sheer pleasure of listening to our common language used in such colorful fashion. When I finally did so, by suggesting that I took it we should put him in the "decline" column, I asked if he might wish to send his son, who we thought was in the United States. Another voice unexpectedly broke in, from an extension on the line, and the son told us, in less colorful but no less direct terms, what he thought of our invitation.

The more pragmatic Protestant leaders, however, like David Trimble (Molyneaux's successor) gradually came to accept the American role. I had a particular admiration for two Loyalist leaders, Gary McMichael and David Ervine, who had had paramilitary ties and now stood courageously for an end to the violence. They had seen firsthand the effects of the bombs and bullets and were all the more attached to the vision of peace. Their role in restraining the Protestant militia has never been given its due.

By August 1994, six months after the Adams visa, we had little to show for our involvement. But once again, the issue was forced on us by new applications for visas. Joe Cahill, a man with ties to the IRA, together with his associate Pat Treanor, applied for entry to the United States. Our ambassador to Ireland, Jean Kennedy Smith, strongly supported the request. Again, State and Justice strongly opposed it. And once again, the President rolled the dice, although not blindly. We had some reason to believe, from their statements, that approval could lead to an IRA cease-fire. The visas were issued on August 30, for a shorter period than requested. The next day, the IRA declared a cease-fire. A month and a half later, the Loyalists followed suit.

Over the next fifteen months we held constant meetings with all the parties, including Gerry Adams. My first meeting with him was in private, at his room in a Washington hotel. After a time, he was welcomed at the White House. Engaging, with a nice sense of humor, Adams would never reveal the exact nature of his dealings with the IRA (in which he clearly still had great influence), but he was remarkably open in his moods — either hopeful or discouraged about further flexibility in their position as we worked to encourage all sides to enter into negotiations. I could never be sure whether he was having us on and was simply the human face of the IRA, as some British analysts contended, or whether he was trying to bring the IRA along to a peaceful future in which Sinn Fein and Adams himself could be at the political center of things. I inclined to our remaining open to the latter view, with our hands on our wallets, in part because of my sense of Adams and in part because it was the only possibility that could lead to the IRA's abandoning violence — and thus was worth testing.

Although by the early fall of 1995 there was not yet agreement on how to hold talks among the parties, the President decided to visit Northern Ireland and Dublin in November. Partly because of our using his approaching visit to encourage London and Dublin to make it a success, on the eve of his arrival the two governments announced the formation of a commission to oversee the decommissioning of weapons (the most contentious issue) and the establishment of a target date (late February) for the beginning of talks. The President was buoyed by this announcement, and his visit was perhaps the emotional high point of his first term. He bathed in the warmth of huge crowds in the north and in Dublin. Even the reporters accompanying him were swept away. Nancy Soderberg, Kathy Stephens (our consul in Belfast), and Mary Ann Peters (the NSC staff member responsible for Ireland) had spent many hours ensuring that the Catholics and Protestants received equal time and attention on the President's schedule. It was particularly heartening to see that his reception was equally warm in the two communities.

I was overwhelmed by the occasion. As I sat watching the ceremony of the lighting of the Christmas tree in Belfast, with the orange decorations adorning a green tree, I thought of my parents and their differences on the issue. Even as I wanted to give much of the credit to the President and his decisions, I also thought of how hard it had been for the Irish government and, even more, the British to move forward as far as they had — not to mention the parties and people of Northern Ireland who knew that the benefits of peace were accompanied by the risk of a backlash by its enemies. When the President had offered me a bottle of champagne on the flight over, a few days earlier, I had reminded him that we still had a long way to go.

At a similar moment, as American troops peacefully entered Haiti in September 1994, I told a group of reporters that we should never be too high at such times, just as we should never let ourselves get too low at the hard moments. After a minute or two of this, Helen Thomas, the UPI legend, yelled at me, "Tony, aren't you even a *little* bit happy?" I certainly was more than a little bit happy in Belfast.

But in two months, as we had feared, the carnage of an IRA bomb at Canary Wharf ended the cease-fire. It was finally reestablished in 1997. Talks led by former Senator George Mitchell, certainly one of the most skilled public servants of this generation, finally led to the Good Friday Agreement among the parties in 1998 and its reassertion in late 1999. Its combination of interim power-sharing arrangements and framework for talks about the final status of Northern Ireland was a great step forward — but not an irreversible one. However the history of the next few years evolves, the progress of the recent past shows what can be done when leadership is shown — shown by men and women like John Hume, David Trimble, George Mitchell (who surely deserved a piece of the Nobel peace prize), Gerry Adams, David Ervine, and Gary McMichael (all of whom literally took risks for peace), and the British and Irish officials who pushed it all along, together with President Clinton.

In the end, it is the people of Northern Ireland who deserve most of the credit for the progress and who will finally decide whether they will claim their peace for good. I am sure that despite predictable setbacks, they will do so. I saw it in the faces in the crowds of November 1995. I heard it in the voices of those with whom I spoke during that visit, the men and women who told me about the everyday things that peace allowed — like visiting the shops or pubs they wanted to, without fear. They were speaking of something the President once stated as our goal in the Middle East: "the quiet miracle of a normal life."

What gave the United States the leverage we used in making our contribution to the progress toward this miracle? We could talk to all the parties at a time when they had great difficulty speaking to each other. More than once, we were assured by two historic antagonists that they would follow a constructive script at a forthcoming meeting, only to see the encounter fall apart in mutual hostility. British and Sinn Fein representatives, especially, grated on each other in ways they themselves did not recognize. At one point, in nearly simultaneous telephone conversations, an official of each expressed to me his bewilderment at the inability of the Bosnians to talk to each other — just as he was, once again, reviewing for me the indelible sins of his British or Irish interlocutors.

Our ability to deal with all sides depended in large part on our repairing the damage with the British. Prime Minister Major deserves much more appreciation than he has received for his going as far as he did, on the thinnest of majorities, on the issue. His grace in dealing with us, despite his initial anger at our decision to become involved, was reflected in a letter he wrote me as I left the White House in 1997. "I have valued enormously the close contact and co-operation between you and No. 10," he concluded, "— even on those occasions when you have somehow overcome your natural reticence about offering advice to other governments in sensitive areas!"

The prospect of increasing American aid and investment in Northern Ireland also was important. It was at our Trade and Investment conference in May 1995 that senior British officials and Gerry Adams first met. The International Fund for Ireland (at which we were very ably represented by Jim Lyons) supported projects benefiting both Catholics and Protestants. The role of Irish America was crucial. It had a particular weight when American friends like Peter King or Bruce Morrison or Ted Kennedy or Jean Kennedy Smith or Chris Dodd urged flexibility on Sinn Fein. As in Israel, the popularity of President Clinton was a factor that any politician in Northern Ireland had to take into account. I never saw any, save Paisley, turn down a photo opportunity with him. Such opportunities could be used by us to encourage progress.

In addition, we could carefully and without endorsement or disapproval give each side a sense of where the others stood, to help encourage them in the belief that flexibility might be met in kind. At the same time, of course, each side tried to use us as a means of influencing the other. This gave us a chance to engage them. But as in the Middle East, each had a tendency to believe we had more influence than we did, despite our disavowals, and then to blame us when we failed to "deliver." Gerry Adams would ask for "guarantees" of British concessions in return for his considering new moves — something only the British themselves could provide. It is always essential that an "honest broker" be clear about what that role can provide — and what it cannot.

All these forms of leverage helped us make what contribution we did. But there were times when I would joke with my colleagues about how much simpler it is when we have at our disposal the leverage provided by the threat of American force.

USING POWER FOR PEACE

Any negotiator is always looking for leverage: a carrot, a stick, an appeal to reason, an explanation of why it is in the interest of the other side to do what you want him to do, an effort to make the other think doing something you want was his idea rather than yours. Negotiating for the United States certainly has its frustrations (including the necessity of convincing a skeptical Congress of the wisdom of making any concession on any issue, no matter what benefit it might bring). But there is no nation that can confer greater benefits or potentially do greater harm than ours. This power is worth more than the skills of the wiliest of diplomats — if we put it properly at the service of our diplomacy. On those occasions when we move beyond bargaining to coercion, including the use of military power, it is vital to bear two points in mind.

It does no good to be prepared to use force, or other instruments of power, if others do not believe you have the political will to actually use it in a sufficiently coercive manner. And a corollary: Never threaten the use of force unless you have already made a decision to use it. Once you have made the decision, use that fact, if you can, to try to resolve an issue before striking.

The story of our efforts to deal with the problems of Haiti and Bosnia in 1994 and 1995 demonstrates our initial failure to follow the first precept and our success, finally, in following the second.

If the trip to Ireland was to be the high point of the four years, Black October 1993, was the low. On October 3, the American casualties in a firefight in Mogadishu, Somalia, came on the same day as the dramatic confrontation between President Yeltsin and his enemies in the streets of Moscow. After some heated debate among his advisors, the President held firm against congressional pressures to beat an immediate retreat from Somalia. After a compromise with congressional leaders on the timetable, we built up our forces and then drew them down over the next six months in an orderly fashion. To do otherwise would have made it open season on Americans around the world. The potential message: Kill and humiliate our people and the United States will immediately retreat.

In fact, in tactical terms U.S. Army Rangers had fought very bravely and inflicted even more damage than they suffered. I went to Fort Campbell with some other officials to greet their unit when it returned. I found a number of the relatives of those who had been killed and was incredibly impressed by their bravery. (Others of the families were understandably unable to overcome their bitterness.) At a later meeting the President held with some of the veterans of the fight, one of the Rangers told me that he was ready to serve anywhere, anytime he was ordered to do so. He said it in a very matter-of-fact way. He took his duty for granted. We should not take such men and women for granted.

Mogadishu was a strategic setback, not only in perceptions of the United States abroad, but in our confidence at home. We had tried to do more than we could in setting our goals in early 1993. Congressional and public anger was reflected within the Administration by a flurry of implicit finger pointing and then the requested resignation of Secretary of Defense Les Aspin. This was especially painful to me, as Les was a good friend who had a fine record of public service over many years. After he died in May 1995, his funeral service in Wisconsin was an outpouring of love for our rumpled, respected friend.

However much we may have denied it to others and ourselves, this loss of confidence in the wake of the October 3 confrontation in Somalia played a role, I believe, in our reaction to another setback, a week later, in the harbor at Port-au-Prince, Haiti. The previous July, we had helped broker an agreement with the de facto rulers of Haiti for President Jean-Bertrand Aristide to return. Aristide was the legally elected president who had been overthrown in a bloody coup in September 1991. He was and remains a controversial figure: the object of deep suspicion among the elites in Haiti and conservatives in the United States and of near adoration by the poor in Haiti. I have spent many hours with him. He is an extraordinarily intelligent and complex man: He is at one and the same time deeply, even mystically attached to "the people" and their welfare; a coldly calculating politician; a charming and warm interlocutor; and a democrat, but one who plays by the winner-takes-all rules of Haiti's political culture, in part because he is determined never again to be in the position of weakness that allowed his enemies to almost kill him in 1991.

President Bush had committed the United States to helping restore democracy to Haiti, which meant Aristide's restoration. There was no doubt in our minds that until this was accomplished, the brutal repression used by General Raoul Cedras and his fellow rulers to hold on to power would not only be a blot on the region but would also generate pressures for an exodus of the Haitian people to our shores. This exodus had forced Clinton to reverse his criticism of the Bush Administration for its policy of preventing their coming here. He now adopted a similar stance himself. This was painful to the President not only as a political embarrassment but even more, I was sure, on its merits.

Under the terms of the July 1993, Governor's Island Agreement, signed by both Cedras and Aristide, about six hundred military engineers and trainers would enter Haiti to begin the work of reconstruction, including retraining the army, before Aristide's return. With the permission of the Cedras regime, the landing ship USS *Harlan County* arrived at Port-au-Prince on October 11 to provide two hundred of these troops, Americans and Canadians, who had no real combat capacity. In a clear effort to overturn the Governor's Island Agreement, Cedras dispatched hundreds of thugs to the port, where they prevented the ship's docking and unloading.

It was a stand-off. The ship's soldiers couldn't fight their way ashore. Even if they gained land, what would they do in the wake of the collapse of the agreement? In Washington, there was little — in retrospect, too little — debate in our meetings about whether to use force to compel Cedras's compliance. Instead, we ordered the ship's withdrawal, announced new sanctions against the regime, and ordered a number of American warships to patrol off Haiti's shores.

It was a terrible humiliation. On top of Somalia and the continuing, bloody shelling of Sarajevo, we seemed unable or unwilling to bring American power to bear in effective ways.

We all did some soul searching during that time. My model for a national security advisor was that of the behind-the-scenes consensus builder who helped present the communal views of senior advisors to the President. But as Colin Powell urged me to do in a conversation just before he completed his duties that September, I decided to change my approach. I would stay behind the scenes (probably a mistake, as discussed in chapter 6). And I would do my best always to try to achieve consensus and to make sure that my colleagues' views always had a fair hearing with the President. But I would be less hesitant in voicing my own views when they differed from those of my colleagues, even if it prevented consensus or put me more at odds with them — whether on NATO enlargement, Bosnia, Haiti, or other issues. (On almost every issue, our ambassador at the United Nations, Madeleine Albright, and I were to share the same view even if our approaches occasionally differed.)

In the fall of 1993 there was little dispute among us on the importance of working to gain the agreement of our allies to issuing an ultimatum to the Serbs that they withdraw their forces from around Sarajevo and stop its shelling, or face bombing attacks on those forces. At a NATO summit at the turn of the year, the President's personal diplomacy helped gain the ultimatum. It worked, and while Bosnia remained a cancer on our foreign policy and topic A on our agenda, the situation there eased somewhat until the autumn of 1994.

Haiti, however, was a different matter. After the *Harlan County* incident, we persisted in pursuing a solution on a number of fronts, pushing for stronger sanctions at the UN, pressing Cedras to return to the terms of the previous agreement, urging Aristide to be flexible in naming a prime minister who could act with some legitimacy in an interim period. But by March, I was convinced that our strategy would not work. Larry Rossin, a skilled and gutsy Foreign Service officer who handled Haiti on the NSC staff, knew the country very well. He was convinced that without the real threat of force, or its use, Cedras would never give in. It was also clear that Aristide would not agree to any formula that might marginalize him, which an effective prime minister acting in Port-au-Prince might do. Based on our experience the previous October, I saw no reason to doubt Rossin's analysis of the regime, and I had watched Aristide bob and weave in a number of meetings with the President. We needed a new approach.

There was no point in further pressing Aristide to agree to any kind of "internal solution," with a new prime minister, since the idea only was driving him and his supporters to greater mistrust of us. If they completely lost patience, the situation could explode. Strobe Talbott, the deputy secretary of state, and I began a series of meetings with Aristide at his hotel room in Washington. At Strobe's suggestion, I began by asking Aristide for *his* views on the situation, since it was entirely possible that he knew more about Haiti than a foreigner like me did. This helped us begin a dialogue of somewhat greater trust, since he had been treated earlier only to constant lectures from the American side. We developed standing pleasantries — for example, taking turns serving coffee to the others attending our meetings.

In early April, on a flight with the President to Cleveland for the opening-day game that would inaugurate the new Jacobs Field (a kind of Camden Yards without the charm), I spoke at some length with George Stephanopoulos, a good friend who could judge well the President's views. I told him that I believed that only force, or a credible threat, would remove Cedras and restore Aristide. On the return flight, I told the President that I wanted to pursue this line of thought. He did not commit himself, but he did not discourage me.

The Pentagon had been developing possible plans for military action against Haiti, on a contingency basis. At a meeting with the President on April 15 in the Cabinet Room, General Shalikashvili laid out their plans, very fairly and well. He clearly had serious doubts. I then made the case to the President, as I had with my colleagues before, for moving to a force-based strategy. The State Department reiterated its opposition, calling for more sanctions. I argued, unsuccessfully, that the sanctions would add still more refugees without moving Cedras. We had to act. There had always been a powerful economic push for migration. The repression of the Cedras era added a new class of migrants who were politically at risk. This made it untenable over time for us to stanch the flow of economic migrants without placing the political refugees at risk. As the Vice President said at one meeting, in moral terms we could not sustain a policy of returning the Haitian migrants like "throwing crabs back into a barrel." But we also could not indefinitely place them in holding camps in a third country or allow the whole tide into the United States.

Despite such arguments, the President decided to stay on the sanctions course. In frustration, I asked that the President consider deciding that force would be used, if necessary, down the road and that the State Department submit a strategic plan that would show how further sanctions could resolve the issue. We received State's memo in a few days. Although a State Department officer, Rossin sent me a powerful rebuttal of their view, arguing that it was simply more of the same. He warned that we would end up with total sanctions, an obdurate military, worsening internal conditions, a still more hostile Aristide, and decreased domestic and international credibility. We needed at least to make a decision to use force if sanctions fail. Deferring the hard choice between force and a longer-term, lower-profile strategy would only make it harder when, as was inevitable, we must face it. Going State's route would only increase the cost of disengaging when it fails and cause greater suffering in Haiti. Needless to say, I conveyed the same view to the President. At another meeting between the President and his foreign-policy team, on May 7, we went over plans for the possible use of force, but the President was not yet ready to commit to it.

As Rossin predicted, the situation continued to worsen over the summer. Strobe, Sandy Berger, and I continued to urge the President to make the decision for force. By the beginning of the fall, under pressure from Aristide's supporters in Washington and even more from events in Haiti (I saw the President become visibly angry at photos of Haitian citizens whose faces had been slashed because of their pro-democracy views), he was ready to so decide. His political advisors, reading the polls and worried about the upcoming congressional elections, were opposed. The President, to his great credit, disagreed with them and made the decision to go ahead. Planning went forward, with the President's review at various stages, for an invasion in the middle of September. Instructed by our failure in Somalia, Sandy Berger ably led his committee of deputies in the complicated task of planning the integration of a complementary civilian effort.

This decision gave us the leverage we needed to seriously begin to press for a solution that would allow Aristide's return. To help reassure his critics, we urged Aristide to announce that he would only serve out the remainder of his term, although a legal argument could have been made to extend it. My friend Taylor Branch, the Pulitzer Prize–winning biographer of Martin Luther King, Jr., and a friend also of the President and Aristide, had heard Aristide say in an informal conversation that he would do this. We took the opening to gain a formal commitment, which was publicly forthcoming. (Despite rumors to the contrary in Haiti, Aristide met his commitment and stepped down in late 1995, as he had promised, without my leaning on him to do so during a number of trips I was to make there. This is not to say that there were not a number of issues on which I very strongly pressed him even as we sought to support the reconstruction of his country.)

As our planning proceeded, former congressman Bill Gray, whom the President had appointed as his special advisor on Haiti, and I continued to meet with Aristide. We could not tell him when the invasion would take place, but we could assure him that the end was in sight.

The invasion was set for one minute past midnight on September 19.

Meanwhile, with the able staff work of Larry Rossin, we planned a last effort to convince the de facto regime to leave peacefully. At the suggestion of Secretary of Defense Perry, the President approved an effort that would have him call former President Jimmy Carter, asking him to call Cedras, with whom he was already in contact, to tell him that the United States had a plan to resolve the situation peacefully and with dignity. If he agreed to discuss it, General Shalikashvili and I would meet with him to offer the choice of a peaceful departure or an invasion and his subsequent submission to Haitian justice.

Carter spoke twice to Cedras on September 14. It was tough going. Carter was very direct in saying that he did not represent the American government, but that an "irrevocable" decision had been made to invade Haiti unless Cedras and his two closest colleagues were prepared to leave. However, if they agreed to do so, they would be permitted, indeed encouraged, to stay for a period of time to help smooth the transition. Cedras refused, citing a concern that a civil war would follow his departure. The Governor's Island Agreement, he said, was a thing of the past. Carter reiterated the certain prospect of an invasion, supported by twenty-two other nations. He proposed that he lead a group of outsiders to come to Haiti to help manage a transition if Cedras agreed to leave. Cedras picked up on the idea of an outside group coming to help but refused to agree to leave. Carter then made one more try as he ominously summarized for Cedras the position: Carter stood by his offer to lead a group that would come to Haiti to work with a group of its leaders to determine how Governor's Island could be implemented peacefully if Cedras agreed to leave. But Cedras refused to do so. This ensured an invasion. Was this correct? Cedras simply continued to argue that he could not leave, that he was "not a deserter." He was obdurate. They concluded with mutual expressions of faith in the will of God, and an invitation from the former President to Cedras to attend Carter's Sunday school class.

Carter's report of this conversation made it obvious that there was to be no conversation with Cedras for General Shali and me. But that night, the highly respected Senator Sam Nunn told us that he was prepared to join President Carter and Colin Powell in a last-ditch mission to Haiti to try to arrange a peaceful solution. After some discussion over the next two days, in which the Vice President, Chief of Staff Leon Panetta, and I argued for approval of their offer, the President informed President Carter that he agreed that this would be useful. But he emphasized that the sole purpose of the mission would be to arrange Cedras's peaceful departure. (We did not want to allow any wriggling that could erode the position of strength that the planned invasion, now only a few days off, was giving us.)

The next day, September 15, the President made the case to the media for an invasion, showing reporters pictures of the brutality of the regime. (In preparations for this, and for the President's speech the following evening, I had recommended making the case based first on American interests. The President disagreed; the case was strongest, he said, on humanitarian grounds. The American public would sympathize with the plight of those whose faces were getting cut for their beliefs. He was right.) On Friday, the sixteenth, he addressed the nation from the Oval Office, warning Cedras, "Your time is up."

The three Americans arrived in Haiti on Saturday, September 17, and began their negotiations with Cedras. Cedras refused to budge. Carter told Cedras that the President had given them twenty-four hours in which to arrange a peaceful departure. Nunn said that if Cedras refused, he and the whole Senate would support the invasion. And Powell impressively described the full power that would be unleashed on Haiti if their mission failed. Cedras was visibly shaken, but still did not give in. Our ships were moving toward the island.

The next morning, in Washington, the President and his senior advisors gathered in the Oval Office to monitor the progress of the invasion force (due to strike at one minute past midnight) and to receive reports from the three in Haiti, as well as from our representatives from the NSC and State who had accompanied the party and were doing their best to be involved. I spent part of my time with the President. Another part of that day was spent in a couple of visits to the dentist's chair in the basement under the President's residence (near the bomb shelter) to fix a tooth that had chosen that morning to depart my jaw. (I recall hoping it was a sign of Cedras's impending departure.) And the rest of the day was spent with Bill Gray in meetings with Aristide at his hotel room.

Aristide was not happy with us. As Carter, Nunn, and Powell moved during the day toward an agreement that would allow a peaceful entry of the invasion force and a delay of a month before his return, Aristide clearly was worried that during the delay an alternative political arrangement might be negotiated that would replace him as president. It was imperative that we convince him of our good faith. Aristide had all along been ambivalent about the invasion. On the one hand, he privately welcomed it as a solution to the problem. On the other, given the memories in Haiti of the American occupation earlier in this century, he would not publicly endorse another entry of American forces, whatever its purpose. We could live with this ambivalence, irritating as it might be. (He was later repeatedly to express his gratitude, once he saw how popular the initial intervention was with his people.) What we could not live with would be his opposition to the intervention. It would be a mess, and possibly dangerous, if his supporters took to the streets against us as we moved in to remove their enemies in the de facto government.

Bill Gray was eloquent in his arguments to Aristide as to why he could trust us. He would be back in Haiti within a month. In addition to appeals to reason, I made two pledges. I would resign if we broke our word. I also suggested we make the following agreement: If Aristide was not back in Haiti in a month, I would come to his hotel room every morning for months and serve him the coffee we so enjoyed at our meetings. But if — or rather, once — he was back in Haiti before October 15, he would serve me a cup of coffee, preferably with some good Haitian rum. He agreed. (And indeed, a few months later on my first visit there, he ceremoniously delivered a cup of coffee to me at a dinner at his residence.)

As we left Aristide's hotel after our last meeting, I expressed to Bill Gray my surprise at the depth of Aristide's suspicions. He reminded me of the earlier history of American support for Haitian dictators and told me to take a look at the mural in the Episcopal cathedral in Port-au-Prince. I later did so. The altar is surrounded by typically glorious Haitian art. To the left is a representation of the Last Supper. All of the figures are black, save one: a white Judas.

By late afternoon, Carter, Nunn, and Powell were making some progress, discussing the details of an agreement with the Haitian leaders. But, as Rossin reported to us from Haiti, the concessions they were recommending to Washington went beyond what we considered acceptable; for example, there would be no fixed deadline for Cedras's departure. The President held firm on the central issues. Meanwhile, our military commanders were becoming increasingly alarmed. The three Americans did not know that the invasion was about to take place. They had to leave immediately. The President told Carter on the telephone that he had one half hour in which to leave. In fact, elements of the 82nd Airborne were then loading up on their air transports and were airborne when the Haitians, hearing that this was the case, finally came to terms. At around 6 P.M. Carter called to say that we had a deal.

The terms of the agreement were ambiguous and required some further negotiation. And there was some unhappy friction with President Carter over his publicly expressed sympathetic view of Cedras. But our troops were able to enter Haiti peacefully and to a tumultuous reception. One American officer later told me that he had met the air-traffic controller at the airport and had told him what a lucky man he was. If the intervention had been forcible, his unit's tasks would have included "taking out" his new Haitian friend.

Whoever should receive the credit for this diplomatic resolution — and Carter, Nunn, and Powell deserve much — one fact is certain: It would not have happened had the 82nd Airborne and our ships not been on the way. The President's decision to employ force, and not to bluff, had allowed us to gain our end without having to actually use it.

Aristide was returned to power. Cedras and the worst of his colleagues were moved safely to exile. The country is better off today than it was then, however much the critics of the President's policy want to believe otherwise. But in the following years, we were to see how much easier it is to help a nation build the structures of democracy than it is to change a political culture. Elections were held, and Aristide did step down as promised, presumably to run again, but the deep divisions within the political leadership produced a devastating political gridlock. The abuses of human rights are far, far less than they were under Cedras, but political violence does continue. Yet despite its many shortcomings, the international community has given Haiti an opportunity to move forward and claim a democratic future. Whether or not it does so is largely in the hands of the enigmatic Aristide, who has the skill, political power, and inclination to be his nation's Nelson Mandela — but also is bound by the fears and habits that could make him simply another on the sad list of Haitian leaders who could not see beyond their own political base and personal prospects.

Our use of coercive diplomacy in Haiti followed a pattern of the previous June, under far more dangerous circumstances, in gaining an agreement with the North Koreans that froze their dangerous nuclear facilities in return for a promise to help them build safer reactors. (The agreement was actually signed in October.) In this case, also, the President's political opponents strongly denounced his policy. And as with Haiti, President Carter had played a crucial role, meeting with the North Koreans to broker a last-minute deal. Here, too, there had been an unfortunate spat with the Administration in the wake of the diplomatic agreement. We believed Carter's public attacks on our threat of sanctions against the North Korean regime was at least mistaken and probably dangerous. Unnamed Administration officials voiced their unhappiness to the press. Some of the President's image makers also were worried that Carter's role diminished that of Clinton. The press loved the sniping on both sides, which masked the central point. His contribution was beyond question. But surely, while we will likely never know what moved the North Koreans, the threat of sanctions and the movements of additional American military forces to the theater (to counter their threats of a military response to sanctions) made an impression on them. Their history suggests that they understand the language of force at least as well as that of reason and of appeals to our common humanity.

In Bosnia, however, it was not until the following summer of 1995 that we were able, at long last, to successfully marry power to our diplomacy. The history of this period has been written in a number of volumes — often accurately. In particular, Ivo Daalder, a member of the NSC staff working on the issue in late 1995 and 1996 with authoritative knowledge of the subject, has described what happened in his excellent *Getting to Dayton*.[1] I need not recount it in great detail here.

By Thanksgiving 1994, the situation in Bosnia was again in serious decline. Serb forces were in the process of attacking and possibly overrunning the Bihac area. NATO air strikes, severely limited by the UN commanders in Bosnia, were proving ineffective. And we were stuck in a vise. If we acted unilaterally, against the unalterable wishes of our European allies, and took more forceful measures, we faced the worst crisis in the history of NATO. The Serbs would respond by attacking the British, French, and other European troops in the UN peacekeeping operation (UNPROFOR). We would then be blamed for the deaths of our allies' people. If we felt so strongly about doing more, my European friends constantly told me, why didn't we send in our own soldiers and share the risks with them? They knew very well that no one in our Congress, even the strongest hawks, were suggesting U.S. ground troops. So we backed off. My colleagues and I recommended to the President a policy in which, for the sake of the alliance, we would forgo firmer action and simply try to contain the consequences of the conflict within Bosnia.

This was the low point in our approach to the problem. While I have little doubt that in the same circumstances I would again have joined in making this recommendation, I hate the memory of it.

The situation continued to worsen, and by May 1995, as I wrote in a memorandum to the President, our diplomatic efforts through a "contact group" of U.S. and European negotiators were nearly spent. On May 27 the President agreed that NATO should carry out stronger air strikes against Bosnian Serb advances. The problem remained that such strikes imperiled the UN forces on the ground, and indeed, on May 27, the Bosnian Serbs took some UN soldiers hostage. This was a tactical success but a strategic blunder by the Serbs, for it forced new thinking about our approach not only in Washington but in Europe and the UN as well.

The first, immediate issue, on which we were already working, was what to do if our allies asked for our help in redeploying their troops out of the most dangerous areas. Secretary of Defense Bill Perry and General Shali strongly believed that we could not refuse such an allied request. I agreed. In December 1994, the President had accepted their recommendation, in principle.

There is a myth that even by mid-June the President was somehow distant from the decision to agree to go to the rescue, with our ground forces, if necessary. (In the end, we were never asked to do so.) And that he was uninvolved in the subsequent "endgame strategy" that my staff and I developed that summer. This is flatly wrong. I do not know whether he would have acted in 1993 as he did in 1995. Two years of experience as Commander in Chief, of making decisions that could have gone the wrong way, as in Haiti, had toughened him. In 1993, as Sandy Berger, Leon Fuerth (the Vice President's national security advisor), and

I would enter the Oval Office the first thing in the morning for our daily meetings with the President and Vice President, I had often felt as if I had a "B" branded on my forehead, for Bosnia. The President would almost visibly wince when the subject came up, as it did almost every day. There were occasional explosions of anger, for good reason but for no good purpose. By 1995, all meetings with him were far more crisp and presidential. On Bosnia he was clearly in command of the subject, of his government, and of himself. As the Pentagon developed contingency operational plans for a rescue operation, the President was kept informed, and then he gave his approval after being fully briefed on the details by General Shali on June 2. On May 29, I had sent a memo to the President stating that, while no one was calling for such a withdrawal now, Perry, Shalikashvili, and I believed we should provide assistance in redeploying from eastern enclaves to central Bosnia if NATO asked us to do so — provided that we could bring the Congress along. The President wrote on the memo that he agreed, in the terms set forth. He then publicly made this commitment in a speech at the Air Force Academy on May 31. I was struck, when he delivered it, by the notable lack of enthusiasm in the audience for this pledge. And although we emphasized that no such request had been made for our assistance, congressional reaction, even among the Bosnia hawks, was very negative.

The congressional hawks wanted no part of American ground involvement, as our allies were always quick to point out. These hawks wanted instead to lift our participation in the UN arms embargo insofar as it applied to the Bosnian Muslims. This was a painful issue for us. On the one hand, the President rightly felt very strongly that the embargo, which dated back to 1991, was a mistake. It penalized the victim as much as the aggressor. But our allies were somewhere between strongly opposed and apoplectic about our violating the embargo, since, like heavier bombing, such a measure could imperil their troops in UNPROFOR. We had reached an uneasy compromise with the Congress — that we would no longer help *enforce* the embargo, but would not violate it — and had not objected to Croatian violations. (In 1994 we had helped broker a federation between the Bosnian Croats and Muslims that was of fundamental, strategic importance in maintaining any kind of military balance with the Serbs. We could not ask Croatia to imperil it by denying arms to its allies in Bosnia.)

So our diplomatic efforts were going nowhere, UNPROFOR was under assault, our ability to explain our policy, constructed of a series of compromises among conflicting realities, much less gain support for it, was weakening, and most important, the Bosnian Serbs were making new advances while more and more civilians were again being slaughtered.

As I was blessed to have a Larry Rossin on the staff when it came to Haiti, so another Foreign Service officer of extraordinary conceptual skill and bureaucratic bravery deserves much more credit than he has received for the process that led to the Dayton Accords and its peace — an incomplete peace, perhaps, but a peace. "Sandy" Vershbow, the NSC senior director for Europe, was convinced that the situation was unsustainable. He, too, had very reluctantly concluded that we were forced to punt, for the sake of the alliance, the previous Thanksgiving. But he, too, hated it, and he recalls we started thinking about different strategic approaches some weeks later. Now, in the late spring of 1995, it was clear that the ground would be more fertile for such proposals. Furious at what was happening on the ground, frustrated by the restrictions imposed by the UN and our NATO allies, embarrassed by congressional attacks on his policies in both parties, and pushed by his political advisors who reported that Bosnia was hurting his standing on other issues, the President encouraged me to proceed with thinking through what Vershbow and I began calling an endgame strategy. During late June and July, we worked through a new approach, meeting repeatedly in a small NSC group including Sandy Berger (who on this, as on all other issues, brought a brilliant sense of judgment and clarity of mind), when possible Fuerth (who brought a passion and bull-dogged determination to the issue), Vershbow, and Nelson Drew, an engaging, intellectually acute air force officer assigned to the NSC, who was the workhorse in the effort. The group was broadened at the later stages for informal sessions with officials from State and Defense, including Under Secretary of State for Political Affairs Peter Tarnoff. And as we developed the approach, I worked on selling it to my senior colleagues in our regular weekly breakfasts. Madeleine Albright, a regular participant (together with the secretaries of state and defense, the chairman of the Joint Chiefs, and the director of Central Intelligence), was a very valuable ally at the breakfasts, as well as co-conspirator in developing the ideas. And at all times, I kept the President and Vice President informed of the trends in our thinking.

We were under great pressure to deal with the daily decisions required as the fighting worsened during July (including the massacre at Srebrenica), and it was not easy to keep us focused also on considering our strategic approach. I was unable to gain consensus or even clarity in discussions either at the breakfasts or in our formal meetings on Bosnia. In mid July, I informally asked my colleagues to provide their written views on an endgame strategy. Finally, at a formal Principals Committee meeting on August 1, I asked that each agency submit within three days its own written recommendation to the President of a longer-term approach. It should include its view of the desirable "end state" if a withdrawal of UNPROFOR became necessary, as the basis for decisions on a possible new U.S. diplomatic initiative.

Vershbow and I were convinced that the time was ripe, that the situation demanded a new American effort at bringing the conflict to an end. Such an effort, we believed, had to meet several criteria. It had to be made clear to the allies that they had no veto over our approach; we would act with or without them. It had to bring the threat of greater American power to bear, which meant a prior decision to actually use it, if necessary. It had to lay out carrots and sticks for all the parties, including the Muslims, without violating their basic claims, to make it clearly in all their interests to settle.

The key to cutting the Gordian knot was the status of UNPRO-FOR. For years the UN troops had been doing their best, in harrowing circumstances and under very restrictive rules of engagement, to perform an important humanitarian function that we could not easily gainsay. But so long as it was on the ground, the Serbs had a hostage and our allies had good reason to oppose stronger action. In June, in a discussion paper for a meeting of the President and his senior advisors, we had raised the question of whether there was a point at which we would shift our position and encourage UNPROFOR to withdraw: This was to set up a proposal that Madeleine Albright then presented, to her great credit, suggesting that we get the allies to agree both not to stay on the ground beyond the next winter and to arm the Muslims.

Our strategy built on this principle. Unless we were prepared to see the hostage of UNPROFOR removed, threats would lack meaning to the Serbs. In a memorandum to the President on August 5, in preparation for a pivotal meeting of his foreign-policy team with him on August 7, I wrote that his advisors now agreed that if a settlement could not be reached and/or if UNPROFOR's credibility continued to erode, then we should pull the plug, fulfill our commitment to help UNPROFOR withdraw, lift the arms embargo, and move to a post-withdrawal strategy.

"Muddling through," I wrote, was no longer an option. The memo covered the submissions of the other agencies and the action plans for a new approach we had developed at the NSC. My cabinet-level colleagues and I had gone over our papers on August 4, so there would be no surprises.

The memo to the President noted that we all agreed on a new diplomatic effort along the lines of an attached NSC paper, although State had some reservations. There was also agreement that if diplomacy failed and UNPROFOR collapsed, we needed to provide some degree of support for the Muslims and Croats. The memo, and the attached papers from the agencies (which began with a general memo from Albright on the importance of taking action), listed a number of areas of disagreement on the dimensions of that support (State and the JCS had some reservations) and on the nature of a final settlement. Madeleine and I suggested staying with the 50–50 division of land currently proposed, give or take 5 percent. State and Defense argued for "a more limited commitment": The Muslims should settle for the lesser territories they then held, with "some modest adjustments."

The NSC paper urged that, over the next few weeks, we make an all-out effort to get a settlement. If we failed, we should let UNPROFOR collapse and take a number of steps to protect the Muslims and Sarajevo. (No one called for ground troops.) We then presented three papers: a detailed diplomatic game plan; a plan for aid to the Bosnians if diplomacy failed; a modified plan for a settlement and actions to be taken to apply more pressure against Serb president Milosevic if he offered more support for the Bosnian Serbs. The pressures would include air strikes against key supply routes and the bridges across the Drina River.

It was most important that the President approve the strategy of letting UNPROFOR collapse, followed by strong measures to support the Muslims. And to decide that we would pursue such a course alone, if necessary. Such a decision would give us not only a strategy that could work, but also the needed diplomatic leverage with the Serbs — and with our European allies. At a lengthy meeting on August 7, followed by meetings on August 8 and the early morning of August 9, the President agreed and ordered me, accompanied by Peter Tarnoff, to present our plan to the Europeans in their capitals. All concurred save the State Department, which argued that I should discuss only issues of process on launching a new negotiating round, not the substance of our approach.

I had looked forward to such a mission for some time. (In August 1993, I had made a similar trip to Europe, which may have helped soften the ground for the President's Sarajevo ultimatum proposal.) At meetings with Tarnoff and other officials from State and Defense, we carefully went over the draft talking points I would use in Europe. It would be a lengthy, detailed presentation, eight single-spaced pages, as drafted by Vershbow and Drew working closely with Berger and me. The President reviewed them and suggested that I reverse their general order. To get the Europeans' attention, I had proposed that I first give them the details of the forceful strategy on which the President had decided and then to outline our new diplomatic strategy. He thought it would gain a more sympathetic hearing if I began with the diplomatic approach and then spoke of the more forceful strategy. He said that in the end it was up to me. I reflected on his point as our team crossed the Atlantic on August 9, and on the fact that he was the President, and decided that he was right — as he was. In every capital — London, Bonn, Paris, Madrid, Rome, and Ankara, and with the Russian foreign minister at his vacation spot on the Black Sea — the argument that the purpose of our new policy was a diplomatic settlement made much of the difference. They also found appealing the point that our threat against the Serbs — settle or we will support the Bosnians with arms and air strikes — was matched by our telling the Bosnians that if they failed to negotiate in good faith, the deal was off. And in any case, I emphasized, the President has decided. We will pursue this effort with or without you. Indeed, I said, the Congress will likely lift our participation in the arms embargo against the Muslims in any case, and soon, if you don't come along with a new initiative. (The President vetoed such a measure while I was in Europe, on August 11. It was not clear whether we would have the votes to sustain it. Happily, as the new diplomatic effort began, we never had to find out.) Most important, I told my European interlocutors, our chances of success will be much the greatest if we act together.

Sandy Vershbow was right that it would be easier than I thought to persuade the Europeans. There were a number of reasons for this. Clearly, events of the summer had convinced the Europeans they were in a cul-de-sac and that UNPROFOR faced a very grim winter. The massacre at Srebrenica and other Serb atrocities had revolted their peoples (and, thus, voters). President Chirac of France had been urging a NATO ground operation in the eastern areas, a position reportedly not supported by his own military, much less ours. But his strength on the issue helped stiffen the Europeans generally. Even the French seemed to feel that American leadership was needed, and understood the President's determination. (A note on the French: They can be extremely irritating when wrapping themselves in Cartesian logic while opposing common action. But when they decide to act in times of crisis, they can be superb. In this case, we wanted to saddle up, and Chirac did not put Descartes before our horse.)

In addition, the Europeans knew that recent Croatian military successes against the Bosnian Serbs, together with improved Muslim capacities, increased the chances of a diplomatic agreement. And they understood that only an exercise in coercive diplomacy could put an end to the nightmare.

We began our trip in London and I ended it there on August 14 to meet with our assistant secretary of state for European affairs, Richard Holbrooke, who would take over the new round of negotiations. Sandy Berger had warned, in a telephone call, that Dick was hesitant about the mission. Before we sat down with my team and his to go over my meetings and to reassure him on the substance of our approach, I met privately with him. We had joined the foreign service together, had shared experiences and views in and on Vietnam, and I was moved by the moment. This opportunity was what we had dreamed of when we were young, I said. If the effort failed, we in Washington would stand by him and take the blame. But I thought he could succeed. He left, accompanied by General Wesley Clark, who had been an invaluable part of the team traveling with me around Europe, and three exceptional officials: Bob Frasure of the State Department, Joe Kruzel of Defense, and Nelson Drew of the NSC. Five days later, all three were killed in an accident on Mount Igman, outside Sarajevo.

When I got the news, I drove to the home of Nelson Drew to inform his wife, Sandy. When she saw me standing at the door, she knew, immediately, why I was there. An extraordinary woman, she took the news with great bravery, as did her two children. (Both of them, Samantha and Phillip, have since attended the Air Force Academy, where Nelson had taught, which gives Nelson's friends great pleasure.) When I left the house after talking with them for a while, Sandy said to me, with calm intensity: "You have to solve this, for Nelson." As Dick Holbrooke with Warren Christopher proceeded to negotiate, brilliantly, the Dayton Accords, backed by NATO bombing, I often thought of her words, and of Nelson.

3.

Peacekeeping Missions

As in Haiti, coercive diplomacy — diplomacy backed by a clear presidential decision to use force — had succeeded. The agreement at Dayton was signed officially at an elegant ceremony in Paris in December 1995. As I watched the leaders of the parties to the conflict grudgingly and glumly affix their signatures to the documents, I thought about the complexity of the task facing the peacekeeping mission that would help implement the accords. A peace agreement is a piece of paper. It is the peacekeepers who will help a people turn such a paper into real peace, a complicated, onerous, and dangerous task. So the work of the peacekeepers is likely to be more controversial than that of the diplomats.

I was at a conference in late 1999 with a number of academic colleagues who believe, as I do, that the United States must be a leader in international peacekeeping efforts. I was surprised to see how vehement they were in denouncing the Clinton Administration's internal review of "multilateral peace operations" in 1993–94. They considered it an ignoble effort to cut back on our peacekeeping efforts — a response to the furor over the deaths of American servicemen in Somalia in October 1993. There is no question that Somalia reinforced for us the importance of coherently working through our guidelines for such efforts. I recall vividly the pressure that my colleagues and I felt in the wake of Somalia to present such guidelines to the Congress and public. And the study, which was being completed as the crisis in Rwanda erupted, contributed to — but was not central to — our failure to support a large-scale intervention in Rwanda.

But I found it impossible to have much sympathy for my academic colleagues' complaints. As we believe that peacekeeping is important, so we should think through clearly when and how best to pursue it. Quixotic, failed missions serve no one. Neither the UN nor its members have infinite resources, so choices must be made. The debates about those choices will be clearest when their criteria have been agreed.

As the number of such operations mounts, peacekeeping is, predictably, becoming more controversial. Its supporters would do better to show that its purposes and programs make sense, based on careful, consistent analysis, than to denounce instinctively any limits on it. Without such a demonstration, the political will to conduct peacekeeping operations in the future will evaporate — and not only in the United States. It is imperative that a national debate on peacekeeping and "humanitarian interventions" not be a partisan clash of competing doctrines (never intervene vs. near automatic intervention). We need a reasoned debate over how to confront a serious issue we cannot wish away.

Following a year-long interagency review, including intensive consultations with key legislators in Congress, President Clinton signed in May 1994 Presidential Decision Directive 25: Reforming Multilateral Peace Operations. It was the first comprehensive U.S. policy on multilateral peace operations in the post–Cold War era. It concluded that properly conceived, well-executed peacekeeping missions can be an important and useful tool of American foreign policy. It aimed to establish guidelines that would help us use peacekeeping more selectively and effectively than in the past. PDD-25 recognized that peacekeeping is a *part* of our national security strategy, but not the centerpiece.

Yes, as I said in presenting the study at the time, we would like to solve every problem. But neither we nor the international community have the resources, the mandate, or the possibility to make such a difference every time. We have to ask hard questions about where and when we should deploy military personnel. We have to accept that we can rarely solve other people's problems; we can only offer the breathing space in which they can make and preserve their own peace.

At the same time, the policy emphasized that effective, selective peacekeeping serves American and global collective interests — preventing, containing, or resolving conflicts that could otherwise be more costly and deadly, and promoting democracy, regional security, and economic growth. It also enables us to advance U.S. goals without shouldering all the burdens, taking all the risks, and footing all the bills.

We addressed six major issues in the policy review:

1. To ensure that we support the right operations, we developed rigorous new standards to determine when the United States should vote for peace operations and also when we should take part.

2. We committed to reduce the cost of peacekeeping operations — both the U.S. contribution and the cost for the United Nations overall. This was both right and necessary if we were to retain any congressional base for further peacekeeping.

3. We made recommendations to improve UN peacekeeping capabilities. During the Somalia crisis, there were times when people on the ground literally could not reach the United Nations in New York because there was no one to answer the phone. By the time PDD-25 was approved, the United Nations with U.S. assistance was already moving on reforms such as establishing a situation center that allowed them to keep in touch with peacekeeping missions day in and day out around the clock.

4. We clearly defined our policy on command and control of American military forces in UN operations. As General Wesley Clark explained, in presenting the policy with me, "The President will never relinquish command of United States forces. That is inviolable." But "[w]e will be able to place U.S. forces under foreign op[erational] con[trol] when it's prudent or tactically advantageous"[2] — as we have done many times since the Revolutionary War, including in Desert Storm.

5. We created a new "shared responsibility" approach to managing and funding UN peace operations within the U.S. government. (Budgetary arguments in the Administration and jurisdictional disputes in the Congress were to make this impossible to achieve.)

6. We proposed new ways to increase and regularize the flow of information, consultation, and, hopefully, cooperation between the Congress and the executive branch.

PDD-25 was an important step toward more discriminating and effective use of peacekeeping operations. But it did not relieve the enormous pressure that peacekeeping puts on the U.S. Army. There is the cost in flexibility for each of our military units involved. Assuming a peacekeeping operation takes six months of predeployment training and six months to retrain afterward, a single division may find all three brigades tied up for months — one training to go in, one on the ground, and one retraining after it has come out. With only ten divisions in the entire U.S. Army, monopolizing one for a peacekeeping operation puts strains on the force as a whole.

There is the cost in morale, as increased deployments take soldiers away from their families more often, and for longer spans of time. There is the cost in readiness, because without congressional support, peacekeeping resources come out of the operational budget. And there is the cost in skill and confidence, as lengthy peacekeeping operations take time away from soldiers' combat exercises and training.

Some have proposed that in order to deal with greater numbers of "operations other than war," we should dedicate some of our forces to peacekeeping operations only. While the goal is a good one, the proposed solution is probably flawed. For one thing, it would be difficult to designate adequate numbers of troops. Even if two entire divisions were assigned, they would still be overburdened — while our ability to fight two regional conflicts at once would be undermined. Creating two totally new divisions would cost $4 to $5 billion — difficult to justify in this era of competing needs. Moreover, in order to maintain a disciplined fighting force, where morale is high and unity is strong, peacekeeping and humanitarian missions must be a common responsibility of the whole force, no less than deterring conflicts or winning wars. That is why I also strongly oppose the suggestion that our servicemen and women be allowed to decide whether or not they will participate in such missions.

I do believe, however, that steps can be taken to ease the strain on our troops, such as limiting peacekeeping units' deployments to six months, as the navy and air force are already doing. And we need a greater focus on the special kinds of training and skills that peacekeeping operations demand.

In "Training for Peace Operations: The U.S. Army Adapts to the Post–Cold War World," Colonel J. Michael Hardesty and Jason Ellis summarize the challenges well:

Peace operations have different operating principles than traditional combat missions. They lack clear strategic direction, have an expanded scope, rely on limited intelligence, are characterized by political and cultural diversity, involve the coordination of multiple actors, are media-intensive, typically take place in "failed states" with a limited rule of law, employ constrictive rules of engagement, are likely to occur in austere environments, are dominated by small and independent unit operations, demand a visible presence, are set in primarily built-up or urban areas, require close coordination with Psychological Operations and Civil Affairs units, and typically require extensive negotiation skills.[3]

Peacekeepers need a different kind of discipline from combat troops: the discipline *not* to pull the trigger in difficult situations. And they need the grit and gutsiness of war fighters, too, because peacekeeping isn't always especially peaceful. In the first week of the Haiti mission, for example, some armed Haitians at a police station pointed their weapons at U.S. Marines. The Marines immediately returned lethal fire. No one ever tried to challenge them again.

WARRIOR FOR PEACE: MIKE BAILEY

If you think that wearing a UN blue beret in a peacekeeping mission is wimpy duty compared to more traditional military service, consider the career of Colonel Mike Bailey, who repeatedly traveled with me to Ethiopia and Eritrea over the past two years on behalf of the White House and State Department as we tried to help the Organization of African Unity resolve an ugly, destructive border conflict. As we flew back and forth from Africa, I drew Mike out on his experiences in some of the toughest spots around the globe in the 1990s, including Cambodia, Somalia, Haiti, Bosnia, Liberia, and East Timor. He firmly believes that the U.S. military can fulfill its war-fighting and peacekeeping responsibilities simultaneously. And he believes strongly in both.

In 1992, Mike volunteered to serve as a military observer in Cambodia. Seventy-two hours later, he was in Phnom Penh, with only a copy of the Paris Peace Accords and a "Standard Operating Procedures" manual for the UN Transitional Authority in Cambodia as guidance. As an Observer Team chief, he was assigned a 2,000-square-kilometer patrol sector — including a village that had served as Khmer Rouge headquarters in 1975 and had since been recaptured by the government's forces, obliging Khmer Rouge soldiers to sneak back into the village, armed, to see their families.

Bailey was unarmed, which, he says, "crazy as it sounds," served as his protection; it reinforced his neutrality. He began by making overtures to the local Khmer Rouge forces, because he knew that demilitarization would be impossible if they were not part of the process. When the Khmer Rouge local battalion commander agreed to meet, Bailey hopped on an ox cart and rode across their defensive line, even as Khmer Rouge soldiers in the trees trained their weapons on him. After a three-month dialogue, work began for a disarmament site in Bailey's district.

The day the site was activated, Mike told a UN captain to stay with some government troops on the other side of an unofficial demilitarized zone, to make sure that they didn't make trouble. A UN helicopter arrived with four tons of food, and Bailey worked with a dozen uniformed Khmer Rouge who laid down their guns to help unload the bags of rice. The mood was cordial; Bailey's Austrian captain even asked the KR if he could look at one of their weapons, a rare model of AK-47.

Suddenly, Bailey's interpreter signaled in alarm. Twelve of the government soldiers were kneeling behind a dike in firing position. The Khmer Rouge were unarmed, with bags of rice in their hands. The other UN captain, with the government troops, was nowhere in sight. As the government soldiers took aim, Bailey instructed the Austrian to put down the weapon and keep the

Khmer Rouge under control. He then ran straight toward the kneeling soldiers, yelling through his interpreter, "Don't shoot!" As Bailey recalls, "[I] put myself in between the CPP and the KR so that if there was a firefight they'd have to shoot through me. I just didn't want them to start shooting, and I figured that if I ran at them, they might blink, and they would pause and not shoot. It worked."

The government unit was escorted away without incident. But tensions continued to mount. After a UN platoon from Tunisia changed its camp toward the demilitarized zone, the government forces felt emboldened to deploy closer to the zone themselves, blocking the Khmer Rouge from visiting their families in the village. Tension rose. One day, the UN electoral team asked to do reconnaissance over the area in preparation for the elections. Bailey thought he had gained KR approval for the flyover, which he would join. But as their white UN helicopter descended over the KR headquarters, twenty to thirty Khmer soldiers in the trees opened fire.

An American captain from UN headquarters was sitting at the helicopter door. He turned to Bailey and said, "Hey sir, there's something wrong!" A bullet hit above the Australian radio operator's head. Bailey realized the Khmer Rouge were shooting at them. He pulled the American away from the door. A round whizzed by his shoulder. He turned to the British captain and said, "Close the door, tell the pilots we're taking ground fire, and get us the hell out of here."

As Bailey describes that instant years later, "Everybody on the helicopter at that moment said, 'You're the senior American, you're senior. It's our lives — what do you want us to do?'" Bailey noticed all the rounds were going high on the helicopter, so he told everyone to lie flat. At this point, the Russian pilots realized that they were taking fire. As veterans of the Afghan war, Bailey recalls, they did some things with the helicopter he didn't know were possible. By the time they landed safely in the Tunisian sector, the rotor blades had five or six bullet holes. "What I took away from the experience," Bailey says, "was that when people were under fire . . . under duress . . . they turned to the American flag and [said], 'Okay, get us out of this.'"

While Bailey's experiences in Cambodia illustrate the real risks and skills involved in peacekeeping, one of his stories about Haiti shows what lies at the core of his commitment to his work. As the UN chief military electoral assistance officer, one day Bailey performed a spot check for voter registration in Port-de-Paix, far from the capital. A Haitian man was there filling out a card with the help of voter registration officials. When he was done, the man walked outside and said to Bailey's team, *"I can vote."*

"And to me, that's what it's about," Bailey says. "And our soldiers realize that — that you can make a difference. That peacekeeping can make a difference. There's a lot of things that are hard about it. We continue to learn lessons about better ways to do it. But the bottom line is that it makes a difference. It's seeing that guy holding his voter registration card and saying 'I can vote.'"[4]

SHARING THE BURDEN

Certainly, greater international capacity for peacekeeping, on a global or regional scale, would alleviate some of the pressure peacekeeping puts on the United States Army. Without international action, the United States must decide between bearing all burdens and paying all the price — or seeing nothing ever happen.

During his 1992 campaign, then-Governor Clinton supported exploring the idea of a United Nations "rapid deployment force" that could be used for purposes beyond traditional peacekeeping, such as standing guard at the borders of countries threatened by aggression, preventing attacks on civilians, providing humanitarian relief, and combating terrorism and drug trafficking.[5] I still believe this is a good idea — although its time has not yet, apparently, come. The United Nations has, however, taken steps in that direction. Some eighty countries have offered "stand-by" resources that could be readily available for peacekeeping operations, and the Secretary General is creating a core headquarters unit that could be quickly deployed once any new operation is agreed on.

Increasingly, however, we are seeing the development of greater regional responsibility and effort. NATO's role is evolving, with major operations in Bosnia and Kosovo led by the United States. European nations are also establishing force structures that can act, either outside NATO (but in coordination with it) or within NATO when the United States is not taking part.

African nations have taken action through the Organization of African Unity and the Economic Community of West African States and are at the early stages of creating an African crisis response force. In general, these are positive and timely developments, since the current structure of the UN and divisions within the Security Council make the world body an uncertain instrument. There will be times when we must decide that we cannot let people die and refugees see their lives uprooted while waiting for the UN to act, if it can act at all. In Bosnia, the limits on UN forces meant that, in effect, we circumvented the UN secretary general through action by NATO.

But there are also dangers in relying too heavily on regional action. As UN Secretary General Kofi Annan argued in early 1999,

[F]ew others have, or would claim to have, the same operational capacity that NATO has. It is, therefore, unfortunate that in recent years the Security Council has been reluctant to authorize new United Nations peacekeeping operations, and has often left regional or subregional organizations to struggle with local conflicts on their own. That puts an unfair burden on the organizations in question. It is also a waste of the expertise in peacekeeping which the United Nations has developed over the years. . . . It is a paradox that, in technical terms, we are better equipped now that we have only 14,000 soldiers in the field than we were five years ago, when we had nearly 80,000. And if our capacity continues to be underutilized, there is an obvious risk that Member States will no longer give us the resources we need to sustain it.[6]

Moreover, using regional organizations raises a difficult point in international law. The UN Charter explicitly encourages regional organizations to deal with problems in their own neighborhoods, as long as they do so in a manner consistent with the purposes and principles of the United Nations. Such action should be approved by the UN Security Council. The more such authority is circumvented, the more regional groups could start justifying the use of force in ways that are hostile to one another. This would undercut the central principle of the UN Charter and the main hope of Harry Truman and the other founders of the UN: that one central body, the Security Council, decide when the international use of force is justified.

The trend toward more regional initiative and action will and should continue until the UN can act more effectively, through reforms of the UN system and maybe even the Charter, or changes in the conduct of nations around the Security Council table. By the latter, I mean in part that Russia and China must stop acting so often simply as naysayers.

THE CIVILIAN SIDE

"Peacekeeping," to most of us, means military efforts: cease-fires, soldiers, and blue berets. But while the military side of peace-keeping is absolutely *necessary*, it is not a *sufficient* condition for an operation to succeed.

In peacekeeping operations, the *military* mission is generally straightforward: to create a secure environment. In itself, achieving this goal is often far more complicated than it sounds. For example, the line between providing a secure environment and performing local police work is easily blurred. It may be difficult to persuade belligerent factions to give up their weapons, which for them are often their primary means of protection, livelihood, and self-identity. Do we incorporate house-to-house searches into the military mandate? Should our soldiers have the power to arrest and detain?

And even as we answer such difficult questions, we must accept a basic fact: The military mission, on its own, will not achieve a strategic objective. We can send in soldiers to create a secure environment. They can complete their task. The country will nominally be at peace. But that is only a context, not the goal. The goal must be broader: the future of the society itself. In a strategic sense, a peacekeeping operation is more about political progress and economic programs than it is about troops in blue berets.

In most recent cases, the goal of peacekeeping operations has been to help preserve fractured states, such as Bosnia, or to restore the health of states that are corroding from within, such as Haiti. The "breathing room" the military forces provide must be filled with the oxygen of reconstruction assistance. This means everything from reuniting divided families to ensuring free elections, bringing war criminals to justice, and providing basic development aid. Both the UN and the U.S. government are getting better at planning for integrated peacekeeping missions, including civilian as well as military programs. The President has ordered that the kind of political/military planning done before the operation in Haiti be improved and institutionalized. But as the shaky start in Kosovo in 1999 demonstrated, the international community still has a long way to go.

One of the most crucial aspects of civilian assistance is restoring public security; in particular, improving the performance of local police. International civilian police operations are becoming an increasingly important part of peacekeeping missions. Yet the international community's policing capabilities are not yet up to the task. First, there is the lag time between the swift military deployment and the civilian police force's slower arrival. We need to tackle this problem from both ends at once, establishing better means of rapid police mobilization while training the military peacekeepers to manage constabulary functions in the interim. But it must only be in the interim, and a short one, or our troops will be stuck with performing police work for which they are not trained or properly used.

The military peacekeepers must also deal with serious challenges to law and order before local law enforcement is up to speed. International police are generally unarmed, and thus unable to respond effectively to violence. Military peacekeepers, however, rarely have the special training to perform law-enforcement duties such as riot control. One solution is vetting and retraining local forces, but this inevitably takes time. In the interim, crime rates are likely to rise, especially if government security forces have been demobilized or restricted to cantonments. There is also the danger that demobilized forces will not be able to find civilian jobs — prompting them to turn to criminal activity. Retraining and reintegration programs can help to meet this challenge, but people may be reluctant to provide assistance to those who were responsible for previous terror.

In the end, true public security can only be achieved with a functioning local criminal-justice system — including judges, jailers, and appropriate legal codes and penal systems. A long-term, broad-based approach is needed to complement police reform. And this, as with any other meaningful policy, demands resources, both financial and human, and the patience to stay the course. In February 2000 the President issued a welcome directive aimed at strengthening criminal-justice systems and the capacities of civilian police (CIVPOL) as we conduct "complex humanitarian" operations.

All this points up the need — an urgent need — to build up the capacity of the UN and its members to quickly supply the trained police and police trainers who can accompany military peace-keepers. Indeed, a standing UN constabulary that can be moved quickly is a higher priority than a UN rapid-deployment military force.

4.

The Purposes of Peacekeeping

We are making progress at thinking through how to do peace-keeping. But we will not get it right until we have addressed, far more carefully, the question of its *purposes*.

Certainly, our first purpose in humanitarian interventions is simply saving lives. But without defining success, and a reasonable timeline on which to achieve it, the President will not be able to offer the public, Congress, and our servicemen and women a clear idea of when we can say, "Job well done. It's time to come home." It is not enough simply to say we have no choice but to act, that the alternatives to intervention are horrible. That is, in effect, what we have done in Kosovo. I believe we were right to intervene. But we did so without a clear political solution to the problem as our goal. It was a *response* to events — not a strategy that can shape them.

This is what happened in Vietnam. Our troops were sent to defend South Vietnam from the Communist north, a worthy goal. And so long as our forces were there, they succeeded in doing so. They did what we asked of them in military terms. But the only way to achieve real success in Vietnam was to leave behind a government in Saigon that could survive on its own. And this our military could not accomplish. Indeed, the more we did for that government, the more it was seen by too many Vietnamese as a "puppet" of the United States. Yet as it thus ceded the banner of nationalism to the communists, the more it needed our help. This was a vicious circle we were never able to break.

In Kosovo, because of the strong feelings of our European allies and the Russians, the international community has implied that Kosovo will remain a part of Serb-dominated Yugoslavia in some undefined status. Many doubt very strongly that the Kosovars will ever accept Serb sovereignty. If that is true, and I believe it is, then at some point the international community will either have to change its policy or see its peacekeepers in Kosovo become a permanent occupying force opposed to the wishes of the people it went there to save.

In Somalia, the Bush Administration intervened to save lives — and the intervention did so. We should be proud of that. But in 1993 we in the Clinton Administration inherited a situation without a strategy or timetable. And sadly, as we struggled with the issue, we probably made an ill-defined mission worse.

I have enormous respect for General John Shalikashvili. I know of no chairman of the Joint Chiefs of Staff who was more sympathetic to the need for peacekeeping operations. I went with him to Haiti in December 1995 to spend Christmas with our troops there. At a number of meetings with them, in groups of twenty or thirty, he told them they were tough troops, trained to do tough work. "But today," he said, "is Christmas. Take a step back. Look at what you've done. You've saved the lives of thousands of people. Your mothers would be proud." I could see these soldiers look a little embarrassed at the praise, but they also seemed very proud of themselves as the general's words sunk in.

General Shalikashvili supported peacekeeping, but with the right caution. As he has observed,

> [T]he difficulty lies in distinguishing between helping — narrowly defining our interests and our involvement — and on the other hand, getting caught in someone else's hatreds, prejudices, and intrigues. And even when we enter with the best of intentions, if we are not extraordinarily cautious, there is always this impulse to bring more than relief — in fact, to bring solutions. Largely, it becomes a matter of expectations. In war we expect victory. But in peacekeeping and humanitarian operations, what do we expect? At what point do we declare an endpoint and return home?[7]

Our troops deserve an answer to this question when we send them off on any enterprise that does not involve our vital interests. (If the interests are "vital," we should simply be prepared to fight in their defense for as long as it takes.) I do not mean here that there simply should be an "exit strategy" in case of failure, although one there should be. The proper "exit strategy" is one that also is based on a definition of "success." Over the years, in almost every case of peacekeeping, the general goal has been to put a stop to a slaughter and then preserve the state in which it was taking place by healing its political and economic wounds.

That is a worthy ambition. It also is seldom achievable in any reasonable span of time, since that healing can be the work of generations. Nor should the international community take on the responsibility of making a society whole. It can help. Establishing military security, instituting economic-development programs, supporting elections and viable democratic institutions is a start. But it is beyond our capacity to put a country back together. In the end, the future of a broken society lies in the hands and hearts of its people.

So the logic is clear: We must limit our military mission to giving such societies "breathing space" — a reasonable period of calm, combined with some economic and political progress, before they again take responsibility for managing their own affairs. That is something we, the international community, *can* do. If we reach farther, and set as our goal the full healing of a shattered nation, we condemn ourselves either to defeat or the near perpetual occupation of a society that will develop habits of dependency, or grow to resent our presence, or both.

I am not suggesting we become so rigid that we set only short deadlines. If America's interests demand that we leave troops on the ground for an extended period of time, we should be ready to shoulder the burden. And if there is a reasonable case for extending a deadline, it should be done. But I continue to believe, as I first made plain in a speech on Bosnia in March 1996, that the alternative to this "tough love" policy underscores why it is necessary: Without limiting our efforts, we will take on responsibilities that are not ours and create a plethora of unsustainable dependencies around the world.

After a reasonable period of time, the "breathing space" created by the military peacekeepers should end. If the operation has succeeded, civilian international programs can continue into an indefinite future. If the security situation again erodes, and even an extended "breathing space" did not allow a new beginning, then we should think the unthinkable. There will be cases in which the legacy of bitterness, the accumulated blood debts, are so large that two or more peoples simply cannot live together in one state. I believe the evidence is overwhelming that this is the case in Kosovo. After all that has happened, it is a romantic illusion to believe that the Kosovars will ever accept peacefully the sovereignty of Serbia.

In a very few cases, the international community should work not to hold a state together, but to oversee and assist in a peaceful separation.

For most governments today, and for most American national security analysts and practitioners, it is unthinkable that peace-keeping operations should have as their goal the peaceful separation of a nation. Our European allies oppose entertaining the notion of ultimate independence for Kosovo, for example, because of the precedent the further dismemberment of Yugoslavia could set for the rest of the Balkans. The Russians and the Chinese hate the thought, because an independent Kosovo could be an inspiration for separatists opposed to their own rule — in Chechnya, for example, or Tibet. The Organization of African Unity has held dear its doctrine of opposing the separation of states, with only rare exception, because it fears any encouragement to the civil wars that are racking that continent. African nations inherited colonial borders that reflected the competition of the colonial powers far more than any considerations of ethnic or economic viability. Redrawing those boundaries now would affect almost every African nation — an immense, if not impossible task. And in every area, there is the fear that new "mini-states" could not survive economically.

All these are good, or at least understandable, reasons for sticking with current boundaries, for trying to do what can be done to avoid the separatist tendencies that fracture states and kill so many people in bloody civil wars. The presumption should always be in favor of keeping states together. But it should only be a presumption. We need to think clearly and carefully about how to define limited exceptions to the rule.

Such exceptions have been made before. Admittedly, the history of partitions is a checkered one. The carnage when Pakistan and India separated was terrible. The division of Ireland was followed by generations of conflict that haunted both Ireland and England. But we cannot know whether the history of such partitioned areas would have been worse still if a different path had been followed. And the fact is that, recently, the international community has again crossed the bridge of approving and assisting in a partition: in East Timor.

The realities of a new world require us to consider entertaining peaceful separation as a policy goal in *certain limited cases*. You can envisage these realities if you will take a moment to imagine three very different maps of the world as it has become.

First, the familiar map we see in our atlases: a map of sovereign *states* with internationally recognized borders.

Next, imagine a map not of states, but of self-defined *nations*. By nations, here, I mean those groups of people who think of themselves as living in distinct communities to which they owe their first loyalty. Examples of such peoples: many Kurds, Kosovars, Quebecois, Tibetans, Chechnyans. Some may actively be pursuing independence, some not. But there are many around the world. Global communications reinforce both their tendency to find strength in their separate identities against cultural invasions and their ability to support that tendency through appeals to their kin abroad for money and political support.

The third map traces real *economic entities*. This map is even more different from the traditional map of states. For example, in many ways, Silicon Valley outside San Francisco has closer ties to Taiwan (both as supplier and as competitor) than it does to, say, Iowa. As the forces of globalization continue to erode the ability of governments to regulate commerce and protect their economic borders, the only thing constant about this map will be the fact of its change.

One trend is clear: Globalization not only ties geographically distant entities together; it makes it possible for smaller and smaller areas to become economically viable, if their people are well enough trained in the ways of the global economy. (After all, even an individual can conduct global business over the Internet. So can small nations. Tiny Tuvalu does nicely by selling its area code to "sex chat" phone services.) A self-defined nation that wants to become a state does not need a large internal market to survive. If it is talented and trained enough, the world is its market. Today, through modern communications, any small nation can become a Singapore even if it lacks access to the sea. What the three maps tell us is that in this new era of globalization, more and more peoples will not only wish their independence, but will be able realistically to imagine and work for it.

For all the reasons cited above, their dream should not automatically be supported. The international community should work to hold states together — through the promotion of the democratic systems that can reconcile the competing interests of such groups; through diplomatic efforts to resolve internal tensions and conflicts; and through peacekeeping where it will be effective. But there will be times when this is impossible or wrong. How do we determine such exceptions to the rule? What questions should we ask in defining them? Here are a few:

- What is the scope of the humanitarian crisis that the pressures for separation have caused? How are our interests affected?
- Is reconciliation still possible, in a practical sense? Have all diplomatic means been tried and failed, or at least considered?
- Has a state's behavior become so repressive that it has lost the right to sovereignty over its component parts?
- Would allowing a state to break up unleash further ethnic bloodshed in the new state between a new majority and new minority?
- What if ethnic separation has already occurred? When do we accept a de facto state of affairs as de jure?
- Would the new entity be democratic? Would it be viable, economically and militarily?
- What effect would allowing separation have on neighboring countries? What effect would it have on the region?
- What role should and could the international community play in guaranteeing the independence of the new state against revanchist attacks by its previous ruler? (The good news here: It is probably easier for the international community to deter such attacks across a border than to prevent interethnic conflict within a single sovereign state.)

There is no perfect calculus for determining when a separation or partition is justified. Each case must be evaluated on its own merits, and against its own strategic backdrop. But a roster of questions we ask every time can help us make wiser decisions. Ethnic conflict is not going away. When we are sure two peoples cannot live together, we should consider helping them live peacefully apart.

The current approach is, I believe, unsustainable. We must make the effort, even take the time, to firmly establish a clear, strategic goal that defines "success" before rushing in with troops to solve the problems of conflicted societies. The desire to stop the carnage as urgently as possible should be a spur to such strategic thought, not a substitute for it. In the process, exceptions to the current rule of supporting the sovereignty even of states like Yugoslavia should be considered.

The current course could be disastrous: a growing number of peacekeeping garrisons scattered around the world with no end in sight. This would turn the UN and other peacekeeping bodies into new colonialists. And it would lead to a revolt (not literally) within the American military against the burdens they would be asked to bear. (Even our fictional Colonel Lanny Jones would be pushed beyond his limits.) This would reinforce all those who are already skeptical of American leadership in supporting the UN's efforts. It must not be allowed to happen.

But the critics and opponents of peacekeeping will never be convinced that they are wrong unless we do peacekeeping right — on the civilian side as well as the military. This means, above all, getting it right when it comes to defining our purposes in such efforts. If we try to do too much, establishing it as our mission to do for others what they must ultimately do for themselves, we will saddle ourselves with a definition of *success* that can never be achieved. For the sake of our interests and for the sake of peacekeeping, we must size our ambitions to our resources and our real responsibilities.

In short, we must use our heads when dealing with societies whose ethnic hatreds have produced the worst horrors of the late twentieth century.

But in the end, this is an issue that must engage our hearts, as well. Our response to it will not only affect those societies; it will help to define our own. If we as a nation act only on the narrowest calculations of national interest in the face of such horrors — if we dismiss efforts to redress such wrongs as mere "social work" — we will have diminished ourselves.

As Franklin Roosevelt once said, "Governments can err. Presidents do make mistakes. But the immortal Dante tells us that divine justice weighs the sins of the cold-blooded and the sins of the warm-hearted on different scales. Better the occasional faults of a government that lives in a spirit of charity than the consistent omissions of a government frozen in the ice of its own indifference." That is why the mistakes of Rwanda, where we did too little, should weigh with those of Somalia, where we attempted too much. And it is why I am proud that, for all the problems, the United States was at last able to take the lead in putting a stop to the fighting in Bosnia in 1995.

CHAPTER FIVE

The Perils of Weakness

MEMORANDUM OF CONVERSATION:
CALL BETWEEN PRESIDENT AND
PRESIDENT YOO OF SOUTH KOREA

(U.S. and Korean interpreters. Consecutive translation. Notes by Situation Room.)

October 6, 2005, 9:00 P.M.

President: Good morning. I appreciate your taking my call.

President Yoo: I am always happy to speak with you.

P: Before we discuss the crisis there, let me tell you how sorry I am that our Red Sox lost again in the playoffs today, despite the fine pitching of Chan Ho Park. I hope it wasn't his last chance to win the World Series. Thirty-two years isn't that old, but maybe he shouldn't have signed with our Boston team.

Y: We were disappointed. As you say there in America, we will wait until the next year.

P: I regret that we have so much to be concerned about this year. How did your talk with the Chinese president go? I'll call him after we speak, as well as the Japanese prime minister.

Y: He is, of course, very, very worried. A collapse like this in North Korea has been our nightmare, China's and ours, and now it's on us.

P: And a nightmare for us and the Japanese, too. The North Korean missiles aren't aimed at China.

Y: Yes, but millions of refugees are.

P: I can't say that we should be sorry when any Communist regime goes down, and especially this one. But this is the worst way it could happen. What do you understand the Chinese are going to do, based on your talk with their president?

Y: He said that they will refuse to allow the refugees to cross their border. Certainly not any military units escaping the fighting. He said there has been one clash already with North Korean soldiers trying to get across the border into Tumen.

P: Yes. I have just been briefed and see on my map that Tumen is across from where hundreds of thousands of Korean civilians are massing in the hills. We believe that there could be more fighting in that region if their Sixth Corps retreats farther north. This would be easier to follow if there were only two sides in this civil war.

Y: That is why the Chinese are reinforcing all along their border with Korea but mostly in the North. And it is not far from the Korean border with Russia.

P: And you? What are you now preparing to do? Any new thoughts since yesterday?

Y: As I said yesterday, it is much harder for us than for the Chinese. Our people will not like it if we fight off the refugees. And any fight with their soldiers trying to escape over the DMZ could lead to a war. But we will be swamped if we open the border.

P: Yes.

Y: What is your latest information on what is happening? The destruction of the radio and TV transmitters in the coup attempt makes it harder for us to know. We aren't even sure where Kim Chong-Il is and whether he survived. It really is chaos. Violence in Pyongyang. Fighting still as the units of the sixth and fifth and first corps that failed in the coup try to survive. But we don't know yet who is in charge of their enemy. As we agreed yesterday, no one is in charge of the country.

P: Our information during the day (or night, there) is much the same. Some more fighting, very murky, mass movements of people. Our intelligence people are sharing with yours what we have. Harder to see, of course, at night. We are doing our best to monitor the missile sites. Luckily, there doesn't seem to be fighting at Yongbyon or other nuclear places. But this is very dangerous. The threat by the second corps commander a few days ago to use missiles somehow was confusing. Use them against us if he isn't saved? Against Pyongyang somehow? Against us if we intervened? Whether or not it made sense, it is dangerous.

Y: I agree.

P: How do we tolerate this? What do you think the Chinese are thinking about whether to intervene?

Y: [Pause] Intervene?

P: Yes.

Y: I think, as you will discover when you talk to him, that they will oppose any intervention diplomatically. What would they do militarily? I don't know.

P: Maybe they don't, either.

Y: They do know they want the situation resolved. But don't know how.

P: As I emphasized in our talk yesterday, this is very, very dangerous. If, because of the Chinese and Russians, who do remember 1950, we can't get the Security Council to do more than authorize humanitarian relief, and we don't go beyond simply warning the North Koreans not to take military actions beyond their borders, it could get more dangerous still. More fighting, more refugees, more famine. Have you reflected on my suggestion that our people get together urgently to share and develop planning if or when (maybe soon) we need to intervene?

Y: Yes. We are reviewing our own planning first. I will let you know when we are ready. We welcome your moving the carrier task force closer. But this is very difficult with our public. I hope you will keep it as quiet as possible.

P: We will. But it's hard to hide an aircraft carrier. Especially when even the press has satellite photos.

Y: We are friends. May I ask you a direct question?

P: Yes. Yes, we are friends. And yes, please do.

Y: Are you recommending an intervention?

P: I can't do that until you and we go through joint planning on such a difficult undertaking. We are well aware, for example, that it could lead to some kind of reunification, or at least your responsibility for affairs in North Korea, which would be extremely expensive with costs you can't now afford, even with our limited help.

Y: Limited?

P: We would see. Anyway, we need to do such planning together. And then with the Japanese and others, including at the UN.

Y: As worried as our people are about the situation now, stories that we were doing such planning could make a big public backlash. That would make an intervention impossible even if we decided we need to do it.

P: Well, let me ask you a direct question. Are you saying you would need an American call for an intervention to help sell such a proposal to your people? [Pause] I can't do that, because of our own Congress and public. This must be done together, if it is to be done.

Y: [Pause] No. I agree we must act — I mean *decide* — together. Somehow.

P: OK. We'll continue to work here on the options. For intervening and what to do if we don't. Let us know when you are ready to have your planners sit down with ours, very quietly.

Y: If they can do it quietly. I heard about the *Washington Times* story yesterday . . .

P: I know. But we would try to keep it quiet. We know this is the most dangerous time for you since 1953. It is for us, too, at least since Cuba and the missiles in 1962. We'll talk again tomorrow morning, or the end of today Seoul time, if not sooner. OK?

Y: Yes. Good-bye.

P: Good-bye. And good luck, my friend.

Conversation ended at 9:43 P.M.

■ ■ ■

The Cold War is over. The Soviet Union is gone. Communism and Fascism are dead or discredited. But human nature, and thus the basic nature of relations among states, remains unchanged. Power still matters, and diplomacy disconnected from power usually fails.

This, I know, is not a novel observation. In antiquity, Thucydides set out with graphic horror in the Melian Dialogue the weakness of diplomacy without the backing of force. The sound arguments of the Melians for preserving their independence provided no defense against an Athens bent on subjugation. Without the power to back their positions, Melos's men were put to the sword; women and children were sold as slaves.

The same arguments many centuries later in Europe were answered by Hitler and his policy by Panzer, and in the Pacific by Pearl Harbor. After World War II, farsighted statesmen like Dean

Acheson worked to keep that lesson in the American mind. Acheson and other wise men knew that the United States needed all the instruments of diplomacy and power to defend vital interests and prevail over the long haul in the Cold War. It was Acheson who coined the phrase, "negotiate from a position of strength."

Maintaining traditional balances of power remains the bedrock of national security policies. As Henry Kissinger has observed, "Whenever peace — conceived as the avoidance of war — has been the primary objective of a power or a group of powers, the international system has been at the mercy of the most ruthless member of the international community."[1]

Of course, a tunnel-vision preoccupation with a balance of power can lead to escalating arms races and deepening suspicions, as in the case of India and Pakistan. (A nuclear war between the two is such an obvious, and possibly immediate, nightmare that I did not include it in this book.) But the absence of such a balance can be just as dangerous.

Maintaining balances of power demands that policy makers adhere to a strategic view of American interests. Zbigniew Brzezinski argues in *The Grand Chessboard* that, "for America, the chief geopolitical prize is Eurasia" — the world's largest continent, home to three-quarters of its people and "most of the world's politically assertive and dynamic states."[2] It is vital that the United States remain closely tied to the western region of the crucial Eurasian land mass. At the same time, we must work to bring its "middle space" — that is, the former Soviet Union — closer to the west; allow no other power to dominate its south; and maintain a balance of power in its east, especially Northeast Asia.

These basic interests drove U.S. policies throughout the Cold War and should continue to do so now. They are the reason to ensure that NATO, the linchpin of security between the United

States and Europe, is revitalized and enlarged in ways that encourage Russian engagement with NATO now — and hold open the possibility, down the road, even of Russia's joining the alliance.

They are the reason to remain engaged and defend our interests in the Persian Gulf, even when others in the international community may base their policies on shorter-term commercial interests. They are the reason to maintain American forces in Northeast Asia and the Pacific at current levels and to work to develop nascent regional security arrangements. It is not just that power matters. Power is the language that others understand best.

Of course, the greatest geopolitical threats before us are still, for the most part, potential and even avoidable. But it is wrong to dismiss as mere spoilsports or alarmists those pessimists who predict them.

1.

A Dangerous World

Consider these facts:

In recent years, China has embarked on a swift, extensive, and expensive military modernization, energized by the Gulf War's revelation of the People's Liberation Army's technological inferiority. Estimates of China's annual military expenditures run as high as $87 billion — ten times more than official statistics report — and a growing economy may only deepen China's military purse. Key elements of the buildup include a Taiwan invasion force and an improved capacity to attack U.S. aircraft carriers, the expansion of China's rapid-reaction force from fifteen thousand to two hundred thousand troops, new fighter-bombers, blue-water ships, and enhanced range for its aircraft, submarines, and mobile-launched missiles.[3] Twenty missiles in China's arsenal have a 13,000-kilometer range — enough to strike the United States, not to mention allies abroad.

Along with the intensification in spending has come a sharpening of military rhetoric — exacerbated by the firm U.S. decision in 1996 to respond to Chinese exercises near Taiwan by sending two aircraft carrier groups to the region. This forceful warning flag rankled Chinese military leaders, who resented American interference. In the words of General Mi Zhenyu, vice-commandant of the Academy of Military Sciences in Beijing, "For a long time it will be absolutely necessary that we quietly nurse our sense of vengeance. We must conceal our abilities and bide our time."[4]

Meanwhile, in their book *Unrestricted War*, Colonels Qiao Liang and Wang Xiangsui advocate unorthodox means of confronting U.S. power — from terrorism to computer plagues — often in combination.[5] Another book, *China's Grand Strategy: A Blueprint for World Leadership*, was ultimately recalled and banned by Chinese authorities because they feared its chest-thumping nationalism would stoke fears of a "China threat" abroad.[6] Aggressive rhetoric has been matched by a willingness to act, at least within China's neighborhood. In January 1995, China seized Mischief Reef, a disputed atoll claimed by the Philippines. In March 1996, more than 150,000 troops took part in major military exercises in the Taiwan Strait — provoking the U.S. response described above. Viewing its relationship with Taiwan as solely an internal matter, China refuses to renounce the use of force across the strait. At the beginning of 2000 the People's Liberation Army issued some of the most bellicose language yet in threatening Taiwan. Such assertiveness abroad may be enhanced in coming years by domestic concerns about the stability of the state, and the replacement of a dying national belief in Marxism with a Chinese nationalism that rulers can exploit.

In some ways, the potential strategic threat from Russia is the reverse of that presented by China.

While China is building its conventional military forces, Russia's are in shambles. The Red Army's glorious domestic image was badly tarnished by the Chechnya debacle in the mid-1990s and the reports of shabby, hungry Russian conscripts too poorly trained to prevail. Sensitive military installations have had their electricity turned off for overdue utility bills. Meanwhile, competition among senior military officials has damaged the chain of command, as demonstrated in June 1999 when a column of Russian troops sped into Kosovo, breaking promises the foreign minister had made hours before and exposing high-level disarray.

As a result, and especially with the perceived threat from an enlarged and active NATO, Russia's military doctrine shifted to include an increasing and dangerous emphasis on nuclear weapons, including a turn away from the previous policy of "no first use." As President Yeltsin said in April 1999, "Our nuclear forces were and remain a key element in the country's strategy for ensuring national security and military power."[7] Although the more than sixty-eight hundred Russian strategic nuclear warheads are presently detargeted away from the United States, it takes only a matter of seconds to retarget them at American cities.

Two key factors make this nuclear reliance especially disturbing. First is Russia's decision to develop or modernize thousands of short-range, tactical nuclear weapons. This casts an ominous shadow over any future regional disputes with NATO or others. Moscow had unilaterally pulled back its tactical nuclear weapons in 1991. Their redevelopment reflects Russia's increasing anxiety about its vulnerability in the face of American military might — an anxiety that could result in meeting a conventional threat with a nuclear response. (It is worth noting that this mirrors

America's own doctrinal reliance on nuclear weapons in the 1950s in order to get "more bang for the buck.")

Second, and most disturbing, is the danger posed by Russia's keeping many of its nuclear forces on hair-trigger alert, which it does, arms expert Michael Krepon explains, "to compensate for weaknesses in Russia's conventional forces, for gaping holes in the old Soviet early-warning network, and for the vast launch readiness of U.S. nuclear forces."[8] It is, Krepon warns, "a recipe for disaster." Mistakes already have been made, as in January 1995, when Russian forces thought a scientific rocket launched from Norway was an American assault — activating President Yeltsin's nuclear "football."[9]

While a return to Communism in Russia seems improbable, nationalist sentiment is likely to grow. An opinion poll taken in April 1999 found that more than seven out of ten Russians believed their country was excessively dependent on the West.[10] Feelings of anti-Americanism were strengthened by the 1999 NATO bombing of Serbia. One Russian political analyst remarked that "anti-Americanism really may be becoming the Russian national idea that we have been searching for."[11] The history of patriotism in mother Russia is admirable; a future of growing Russian nationalism could be dangerous in the extreme.

Three "backlash states," North Korea, Iraq, and Iran, pose a different kind of challenge.

In each case, the threat could be alleviated by internal change. The North Korean system clearly doesn't work and eventually will be replaced. Saddam Hussein will not rule Iraq forever. There could be a new revolution in Iran, or more rapid evolutionary change. But, in the meantime, all three pose serious threats to their regions and our interests. Of greatest concern in all three states is the development of long-range missiles. Relatively cheap and difficult to shoot down, they are the rogue nations' weapon of choice.

North Korea has built modified copies of Soviet Scud-B missiles with a range of some 210 miles. In 1993, it tested the No Dong, with an 800-mile range. Then in 1998, it caused an international stir by testing the Taepo Dong 1, a three-stage missile, over Japan. The Taepo Dong's range and capability caught American intelligence agencies off-guard, especially when it became clear that with minor modifications the missile could reach Alaska or Hawaii. Indications that North Korea was preparing to test a more potent Taepo Dong 2 spurred American efforts to address the issue through a revitalized bilateral dialogue. George Tenet, director of Central Intelligence, testified before Congress in February 1999 that a three-stage Taepo Dong 2 could at some point deliver large payloads anywhere in the United States.[12] Ask yourself what a President should do if such a missile were about to become operational. Nothing, and let it alter the balance of power between us? Or take it out, and risk a bloody war on the peninsula?

President Clinton lifted long-standing U.S. restrictions on trade, travel, and banking with North Korea — and North Korea agreed to freeze long-range-missile test launches while talks were ongoing with the United States. But leaders in Pyongyang continue to refer to the United States in rancorous terms. In the foreign minister's words, North Korea has the right to defend itself against the "hostile power politics of the United States and its subordinating forces."[13]

Moreover, as former Secretary of Defense Donald Rumsfeld pointed out, after chairing the Commission to Assess the Ballistic Missile Threat to the United States, "[W]hat happens in North Korea also is important with respect to other countries. . . . We can be certain that North Korea will offer that capability to other countries, including Iran. That has been their public posture. That has been their private behavior. They are very active marketing ballistic missile technologies."[14]

Iran, for its part, is also working hard on its ballistic missile and WMD programs, in particular two hybrid liquid-fueled missiles, Shahab-3 and Shahab-4. These missiles will be able to target Cairo, Ankara, and all of Israel. The Rumsfeld Commission concluded in 1998 that Iran had the technical capability and resources to fire an ICBM-range ballistic missile within the next five years. In addition, Iran is seeking sophisticated missile components that could be used to produce ballistic missiles that could reach the United States. Extensive imports from other nations, such as Russia, China, and North Korea, have strengthened Iran's missile muscle. According to some estimates, with fissile material from foreign sources, Iran could develop a nuclear weapon in only one to three years."[15]

Iraq had a large and active ballistic-missile program under way before the Gulf War. Of the nine known sites, eight were either demolished in the war or had their missiles and development technologies destroyed by UN inspectors. But the knowledge and skills, as well as some of the equipment and materials, remain in Iraq, permitting a relatively swift revival of a long-range ballistic-missile program. Senior American officials estimate that, left unchecked, Iraq could develop an ICBM capable of reaching the United States within the next fifteen years. In the meantime, Iraq has continued development of short-range missiles. It is believed still to have stockpiles of chemical and biological weapons that could make any missile, whatever its range, more lethal.

So what should we do about these threats? Obviously, we must pursue all possible nonproliferation efforts and also make sure that America retains the military might and technological edge to deter and, if necessary, defeat a foreign enemy. But we also must accept that in this new age, some bad actors may not be deterrable. That is why we should develop capable theater missile defenses (for the protection of our forces as well as friends and allies in foreign theaters) and a national missile defense (NMD) that can protect our people against a limited ballistic-missile attack.

The threat of ballistic missiles puts more than America's shores at risk. It can thwart our capacity to project conventional force, which puts all of our interests at stake. Ask yourself: In 1994, would we have gone to the brink with North Korea if we had known Honolulu or Anchorage might become the target of a nuclear missile?

We need to have the shield and strength to protect our people and resist ballistic blackmail. But it is an extremely difficult undertaking. A national missile defense must have the ability to detect an incoming missile. Then it must launch an interceptor missile armed with a "kill vehicle" to destroy the enemy warhead in midflight, most likely by seeking to collide with it. As journalist Peter Maass has observed, "This task is akin to hitting the tip of a bullet with another bullet, except that the cost of missing the target by even a fraction of an inch is the loss of a U.S. city under a mushroom cloud, or a cloud of anthrax spores or the smallpox virus."[16]

We are on the right path to developing such a system, with a budget request of $10.5 billion for NMD through 2005. Deployment should proceed *only* insofar as the program is technologically viable. And, of course, an NMD will likely need to be expanded and strengthened as the ballistic-missile threat evolves in the coming years.

In theater missile defense, despite a number of setbacks, the Defense Department is continuing tests of the theater high-altitude-area defense, and bolstering the navy's theater-wide program to speed deployment of an upper-tier system by 2007. As Secretary of Defense William Cohen said in January 1999, "We are affirming that there is a growing threat and that it will pose a danger not only to our troops overseas, but also to Americans here at home."[17]

While all these dangers are real, we should also remember that these geopolitical threats can easily be overstated.

Some analysts believe China's military is "not very good, and not getting better very fast," — and that shortcomings in hardware, training, and mobility constrain its potential danger to American interests.[18] They point out that even the highest estimates of China's military spending are merely a fraction of our own, and that while China may have twenty long-range nuclear weapons, America has more than six thousand available for deterrence. It is also true that China has seldom acted militarily beyond its borders.

As for Russia, despite the inevitable setbacks and frustrations, our engagement has produced real benefits for our people — deactivating thousands of nuclear warheads, removing hundreds of tons of weapons-grade uranium to safe storage, and helping prevent sensitive weapons technologies from falling into the wrong hands. As National Security Advisor Sandy Berger has said, "The only way to lose Russia is to give it up for lost."[19]

North Korea is so destitute that it relies on international generosity to feed its people — including humanitarian shipments from the United States and our allies. So, despite its provocative rhetoric and actions, permanently antagonizing the United States and the West would not be in North Korea's self-interest. Moreover, its military, though dangerous and large, is a primitive force using outmoded equipment. The North Koreans must know that in any conflict on the peninsula they could inflict great damage but would lose — and possibly lose everything.

Iran has lost the galvanizing fervor of the Islamic Revolution. Its military expenditures pale in comparison to our own, as well as to those of its regional neighbors. And the election of President Khatami, as well as a Parliament dominated by moderates, has made it possible at least to contemplate an evolutionary normalization of our relations. Iraq, meanwhile, has already paid a dev-astating price for aggression beyond its borders and must know it would again.

In addition, the United States, in cooperation with like-minded nations, can largely monitor and control the sales of advanced technology goods and services provided by Western firms to potentially hostile nations. Of course, this system is not fail-safe. We still will face unpleasant surprises. But it strengthens our hand in preventing rogue states from augmenting their high-tech arsenals. In any case, all of the threats I described are *potential* threats, not preordained. We can influence their likelihood by the policies we pursue. But we need to think about these and other geostrategic threats in another way. Because, paradoxically, the greatest dangers we face to the security and well-being of our citizens may flow not from the *strength* of potential enemies but from their *weakness*.

BALANCES OF POWER;
IMBALANCES OF WEAKNESS

In an age when your military adversary can also rank among your biggest trading partners, and when your military allies double as your fiercest economic competitors, does America want weak global neighbors or strong ones?

DAVID SANGER
New York Times, May 2, 1999

David Sanger's question goes to the heart of a critical quandary. In the global economy, America needs strong partners to pur-chase our products and promote our prosperity. At the same time, we do not want them to be so strong that they run our busi-nesses out of business. And neither do we want the profits reaped by strong economies to be used to fortify military forces that could someday be used against us — in particular, by emerging powers like Russia or China. We want other nations to be strong enough to act as reliable partners, but not so strong that they can shrug off America's influence.

Sanger concludes that:

> Washington wants China, like Russia, to be strong on Washington's terms. Washington wants to encourage China's economic strength and discourage military strength; it wants nations to independently find their own way to a market economy — as long as it runs strictly according to Western rules. In short, Washington wants strong economies run by leaders who will shrink their military power and act weakly beyond their border.

His sober prognosis is that "Washington is not likely to get what it wants."[20]

Sanger is right. But he doesn't take the argument to its even more alarming conclusion. The fact is, a great nation with a weak economy can be more harmful to our interests than one that thrives. Its weakness can drive it to build a more dangerous and unpredictable (read: nuclear) military. Its weakness can create a popular receptiveness to nationalism that can breed destructive anti-American policies.

So if the first responsibility of our government is to defend our citizens from the direct threats that foreign adversaries may pose, in the post–Cold War world, we need to look at those threats through a prism not just of strength but of a number of dangerous weaknesses:

- the weaknesses of the real and potential foes discussed above, which spawn the disturbing kinds of military and other action that should be — and are — at the center of our agenda.

- economic weakness abroad, which most threatens the short-term security of our people. Japan's ability to pull itself out of recession, or Brazil's success in surmounting financial difficulty, is more important to our citizens' daily lives than what happens in war-torn Kosovo.

- weaknesses within states, as discussed in chapter 4, present some of our greatest national security challenges. Three potential cockpits for such conflict could be the next "Balkans": the Caspian, Colombia, and Indonesia. Each is in an important area in geopolitical terms. Each has large natural energy reserves. And each is suffering from the fractures and fissures of internal weakness.

- the weaknesses of our allies and friends, which can have serious national security implications. The growing gap in our military capabilities means both unequal burden sharing and the necessity that the United States play more of a leadership role in some foreign crises than is healthy.

- and, the weaknesses of international institutions — in their structures, missions, or ways of doing business — which can defeat our efforts to deal with global problems on a global basis.

2.

Real and Potential Adversaries

RUSSIA

In retrospect, the turning point in Russia's current troubles was the hasty and massive effort to privatize state-owned enterprises. Convinced that doing away with old structures was the best insurance against a return of Communism, reformers rushed to sell off state firms with little regard for who got them or for how much. In the initial phase of the program, beginning in early 1992, majority control of most large enterprises fell into the hands of insiders — which, while shoring up inefficiencies and preserving traditional interests, at least prevented old-guard managers from blocking market reforms altogether.

The second phase of the program, in 1995, had far more dele-terious results. Anxious for support from powerful bankers in the 1996 election, the government approved a policy of "loans for shares," in which a handful of the bankers, who had made their fortunes following the liberalization of the Soviet, and then Rus-sian, economy, traded loans to the state in exchange for shares in some of Russia's most profitable enterprises. In this manner, a posse of young tycoons won enormous influence at bargain-basement prices — gaining controlling interests in oil companies, nickel producers, mass-media outlets, and more.

Holding companies were created to monitor the new enter-prises. But no one monitored the monitors. Ten or so corporate bosses were allowed not only to amass huge personal fortunes and exercise unhealthy influence over government but also to take enormous sums of money out of the country, placing these funds, among other places, in the New York Stock Exchange.

"Loans for shares" was a defining moment in the money and power grab of Russia's oligarchs — a very generous term by which the Russian kleptocracy is described. It created a small cadre of extraordinarily wealthy men with the means and the motive to impose their will on Russia's beleaguered government forces — what former *Financial Times* Moscow Bureau Chief Chrystia Freeland calls "crony capitalism in its most naked form."[21] With their ostentatious riches and rapacious appetites for power, the kleptos symbolize the worst excesses of capitalist profiteering and greed. Citizens of Moscow ruefully joke, "Everything the Communists told us about communism was a complete and utter lie. Unfortunately, everything the Communists told us about capitalism turned out to be true."

How could this happen? Let me be clear on a first point: Russia is the responsibility of the Russians. The current debate over who lost Russia misses the mark. No one lost Russia because no one ever possessed Russia. But we — that is, all those who correctly want a Russia that is strong, outward looking, and democratic rather than weak, nationalistic, and uncertain in its political institutions — made mistakes in our approach. We offered too little assistance too late. What we did provide, we targeted mostly on economic reform, focusing on the officials and institutions who would implement them rather than on cultivating public support for their success. We had too much faith in "shock therapy," and not enough concern for its social consequences. We calculated that Russia needed a market first, and that democratic institutions would naturally be strengthened, because owners of personal property would demand the rule of law to protect it. As Michael McFaul has noted sardonically, this was the second time in the twentieth century that economic determinism had failed Russia. With hindsight, it's clear that the reform policies encouraged and supported by the United States and the West were debilitated by weaknesses of the Russian government, legal institutions, and civil society that granted the kleptos and cryptokleptos an open invitation to plunder.

Perhaps the most difficult challenge in promoting reforms in another society is to effect change in its political culture. Certainly Russia, with its legacy of tyranny, its lack of democratic experience to draw on, and its politically disengaged populace, posed an unusually difficult case. But we did too little to try. Indeed, when President Clinton encouraged Boris Yeltsin to pursue a modern reelection strategy in 1996 — relying on television, political consultants, and other such tools — we were reinforcing Yeltsin's dependence on the oligarchs, their wallets, and their leverage. This had the dual disadvantage of increasing the kleptos' political influence while undercutting the role of civil society as a link between Moscow elites and the people. Moreover, the extensive role of state-owned and private television in supporting the Yeltsin campaign served his reelection but undercut the independence of the fourth estate overall. In 1999, for example, the government created a ministry to oversee the media, and announced new plans to stifle what it termed "aggression" by the press.

We were right to want to see Yeltsin win. He was running against Communist Party leader Gennady Zyuganov, hardly a committed democrat or economic reformer. And on a number of occasions over the years, the personal tie between Boris and "Beel" was invaluable in achieving progress on arms control and other issues over the opposition of Yeltsin's subordinates. Other personal relationships also have paid off in important ways. The regular consultations between Vice President Gore and Prime Minister Chernomyrdin until 1998, when the prime minister was sacked, were useful in working through detailed issues and unsticking technical logjams. Deputy Secretary of State Strobe Talbott has been a crucial American emissary, able to use his personal ties as well as deep knowledge of Russia and its history in allaying Russian concerns while advancing American interests such as NATO enlargement.

But none of us saw at the time how destructive our nearly exclusive focus on economic reforms and the President's emphasis on U.S.-style political campaigning could be in the longer term. (Not that reliance on television, pollsters, and political consultants is enhancing the quality of American democracy either.) The collusion between the reformers and the kleptos ultimately gave the latter the clout they needed to seize the reins from the former. Said leading reform economist Aleksei Uliukaev, "We were Frankenstein, and they are our monsters. It was our single biggest mistake."[22]

Having fallen on the country's resources, the kleptos then fell on each other as they jockeyed for position. They also fell on the reformers — using their back-door influence and media channels to debilitate or remove those officials they did not like. We should hope that, over time at least, the kleptocrats fall altogether.

All this, combined with pervasive corruption and a generally inefficient government that is unable to propose or pass the kind of laws that any well-run economy must have, has produced a Russian economy that is stunningly weak. Russia's GDP contracted an estimated 43 percent in the 1990s, including a 5 percent drop in 1998.[23] Today its GDP is only a few times that of Switzerland — though its population is twenty-one times as large. Foreign investment is very low, and trade flows have been tiny for a world power. In August 1998, Russia devalued the ruble and suspended repayment of its billions of dollars in foreign debt. Recovery in 1999 and 2000, fueled by increased industrial exports and rises in global oil prices, was limited but prevented disaster.

Russia's economic weakness has been largely discounted in global financial markets. Yet the noneconomic consequences of this weakness are not only dramatic but dangerous. It has eroded Russians' faith in their fledgling democracy and its institutions, and crippled the emergence of a vibrant civil society that could represent their interests to the state. While a revival of Communism appears unlikely, the rise of nationalism and nationalists seems likely — in part because of the diminishment of whatever faith Russians had in themselves. The popularity of Prime Minister — and then, at the time, Acting President — Vladimir Putin's war in Chechnya in early 2000 clearly revealed the thirst of the Russian public for any "success" that would compensate for this sense of weakness. Putin's statements suggesting that Russia and Russians needed stronger leadership than could be provided by a Western-style democracy captured well the mood of frustration and self-doubt. His suggestion that a large increase in military spending was necessary not only to meet external and internal threats but also to boost the economy shows how dangerous this sense of weakness can be.

Hopelessness breeds a psychological reaction — a tendency to lash out, to scapegoat, to pin blame on the United States and others for Russia's ills. Around every corner, Russians see a plot to kick them where they are hurting and keep them down, be it NATO enlargement, our efforts in Kosovo, or the terms of IMF loans. These suspicions get in the way of cooperation on other international issues. They provoke Russian grandstanding not only diplomatically but in bizarre and even dangerous ways, such as the madcap dash into Kosovo by a convoy of Russian-armed vehicles — all to compensate not only for real but also for imagined weaknesses relative to the West.

Another alarming consequence of economic weakness is the inability to properly prevent "loose nukes" and other components of weapons of mass destruction from falling into the wrong hands, as discussed in chapter 1. Without money to properly safeguard sensitive sites, or resources to redirect nuclear weapons scientists to civilian pursuits, Russia's nuclear sector is frighteningly vulnerable to the big-dollar lure of corruption. Economic weakness has also made it difficult for Russia to pursue arms-control measures that are in their interest as well as our own, since implementing arms-reduction agreements carries a short-term price tag in the billions of dollars, even if the long-term savings are greater.

Criminal organizations have exploited the vulnerabilities of Russia's underpaid and underequipped law enforcement. A familiar tale has Russian police taking city buses to catch armed criminals fleeing in luxury sports cars.

Meanwhile, the Russian military has badly decayed; a 1999 study by the State Department described sharp cuts in Russian army, navy, and air force training exercises, deep reductions in sea duty and flight time, and debilitating shortages of new equipment. Tight budgets and a tottering ruble mean the Russian state can neither afford to maintain current forces nor reduce them.[24]

Thus, a cash-starved, proud, and insecure state has relied increasingly on the one tool it can count on to bolster its international security and standing: its massive nuclear arsenal. Which leads to the risks and threats described at the start of this chapter.

CHINA

While the rhetoric in Washington in 1999 and 2000 recognized Russia as weak, much of it portrayed a China on the brink of becoming a rival superpower, a hostile state bent on stealing our nuclear secrets to reinforce its drive to achieve a dominant strategic position in the Pacific if not beyond.

This is not the first time the United States has gone to extremes in its popular portrayal of China. From the belief that the People's Republic and the Soviet Union were working hand-in-glove during the 1950s (just as the Sino-Soviet split was emerging) to the belief that it was China more than the USSR that had to be contained in Vietnam (never mind two thousand years of Chinese-Vietnamese enmity), to the near euphoria of the Nixon opening (never mind the destruction caused by the Cultural Revolution), to the current fears, again, of a hostile mainland, we have always had trouble seeing China and its people in all their complexity. We must do so now, or the prophecy of Chinese hostility will become self-fulfilled. And the fact is that China's weaknesses, as with Russia, are as dangerous as its strengths.

In a March 1999 article called "China's Choices," *New York Times* columnist Tom Friedman wrote, "You worry that China is a car about to run us off the road. I'll worry that it's a car with 1.3 billion people going 80 miles an hour toward a speed bump, with wheels that could come off at any moment."[25] Could such a crash occur? Improbable, yes, but possible, and it could have terrible economic consequences. It could trigger a new Asian economic crisis, with ripples across the globe. Even a Chinese devaluation of its currency could spark competitive devaluations in the region. The last Asian economic crisis was a financial crisis. This could, through Asia-wide devaluations, become a trade war as well.

If you were a Chinese economic official, you would have a lot to worry about: a banking system that has reached insolvency and remains far too dependent on government loans; excess production subsidized by the state; huge and mounting government debt; some of the world's worst environmental problems; growing unemployment and unequal income distribution, with no social safety net; and, despite government claims, economic growth that, after some boom years, is modest and slowing. *The Economist* remarked in late 1999 that despite China's claim of a 7 to 8 percent growth rate, when one subtracts for statistical exaggeration, production of excess, shoddy goods, and increases in the labor force, "it is clear that the economy is hardly growing at all."[26]

Government leaders have proclaimed the need to reform inefficient state enterprises and the financial sector. But slow growth makes such overhauls hard to afford. And real reform has to overcome challenging obstacles, such as a bloated bureaucracy, declining foreign investment, the lack of a legal framework that could encourage such investment, a sclerotic leadership, and pervasive corruption. Moreover, as China scholar and U.S. official Kenneth Lieberthal points out, the Chinese Communist Party —

"overloaded at the top and gridlocked below" — is hardly in a position to pull off such a complicated feat.[27]

Without such reform, the long-term prospects for China's economy are not nearly as optimistic as the conventional wisdom suggested as recently as the mid-1990s. The consequences of a sinking Chinese economy could go far beyond the regional and global economic waves and ripples that would be, in themselves, bad enough. President Clinton noted in a speech on China, in April 1999, that a weak China could become the center of a zone of instability in Asia: "[W]e have seen the first danger signs: free-wheeling Chinese enterprises selling weapons abroad, the rise in China of organized crime, stirrings of ethnic tension and rural unrest, the use of Chinese territory for heroin trafficking, and even piracy of ships at sea. In short, we're seeing in China the kinds of problems a society can face when it is moving away from the rule of fear but is not yet firmly rooted in the rule of law."

If you were at their Beidaihe retreat on the sea with the Chinese leadership as they wrestled with their economic problems, you might, but only might, hear them honestly address a central dilemma that goes something like this: *Without economic reform, we cannot sustain the growth needed to cope with a burgeoning population. But without a social safety net, which we cannot afford to build, such reforms as the restructuring of the state enterprises will not only create greater unemployment but risk accelerating social and political instability.*

Already, some thirteen to fifteen million urban Chinese are unemployed — which doesn't include the three to four million who are laid off each year from inefficient state-owned firms.[28] Meanwhile, millions of rural unemployed Chinese are streaming from the countryside, where they see no future, to the cities, where no future is guaranteed. There are signs of labor unrest — from cotton-mill workers staging a sit-down strike in the small city of Changde in Hunan province to steelworkers blocking a railway line at Jiangyou in Sichuan province. Activists report that thousands of similar small protests take place each year. The restless army of the unemployed gets new recruits each day. The gap between coastal areas and the hinterland is growing as well. (This has particular resonance with the more nationalistic of the Chinese, as it recapitulates the nineteenth-century contrast between the wealth of the foreign concessions on the coast and the poverty in the rest of China.)

There are two ways for China to resolve its dilemma, and neither is in America's interest. The first is to generate the growth that is needed to carry out reforms by stepping up exports — with unfair subsidies if necessary. This will aggravate our relations by increasing our already enormous trade deficit with China. It is one reason why China's accession to the World Trade Organization, and its trading rules, is so much in our interest. The other way, which also is being pursued, is to institute economic reform as best they can while cracking down on consequent social and political dissent. This deterioration in China's human rights record, documented by the U.S. State Department, could be a poison in our relations for years to come.

In 1993, President Clinton had a long talk about China with Prime Minister Kiichi Miyazawa of Japan, together with my old friend Ambassador Takakazu Kuriyama and me, over sushi in a Tokyo hotel. Miyazawa offered an interesting lens through which to view China's transformation. Instead of assuming that Chinese leaders fear democracy because they will be voted out of power, Miyazawa suggested the authorities' greater fear is the historic threat of disunity or dismemberment. This historic preoccupation with unity and stability, as much as the desire to preserve their own power, is why the Chinese government continues to repress and punish political dissent.

I tried to use this emphasis on stability to our advantage when I visited China in 1996 to launch our "strategic dialogue." Before my trip, I was briefed by a group of CIA analysts and other China experts. They all made the point, like Miyazawa, that unity and stability are at the core of Chinese concerns. As I flew to Beijing, I made notes to myself to use as a strategic overview — the opening salvo in my meetings with Chinese officials, which became known, not entirely sympathetically, by the meetings' notetakers as my "strat rap." My key point in the rap was that our strategic purpose, like theirs, is regional stability. Strategic engagement between the United States and China, the American presence in the Pacific, and the positive global role that America wants to see a strong China play all serve that purpose. When I met with Chinese military leaders, who were very concerned about our deepening ties with Japan, I found that the argument that worked the best was the undeniable fact that the U.S.-Japan relationship since World War II has contributed very strongly to stability.

The Chinese preoccupation with unity is evident especially with regard to Taiwan. In many meetings, my Chinese interlocutors worked from talking points, rarely straying from scripted positions. When it came to Taiwan, however, each became personally engaged. Canned presentations gave way to heated, heartfelt discussion. (All the more reason for us to be very firm in our opposition to any use of force across the Taiwan Strait.) Their intense reaction is shaped both by the memory of humiliating concessions exacted by the West in the nineteenth century and by the self-perception of China as the centuries-old Middle Kingdom. There is a vivid contrast between China's long-standing sense of self as the center of the civilized world and the reality of its weakness. This disconnect helps explain China's sense of grievance and its determination never to allow the West to push

it around again. It drives Chinese leaders toward intense preoccupation with the classic chessboard of international relations,
power, and geopolitics. In strategic dialogue, Chinese officials
make Metternich sound like a fuzzy-minded One-Worlder.
When we seek a constructive Chinese role at the United Nations
Security Council on, say, an African issue that is not in their
immediate, specific interest, it is very tough going. China's own
preoccupations make such support extremely unlikely.

China's reaction to the stupid but accidental bombing of their
embassy in Belgrade during the Kosovo crisis in 1999 was a perfect illustration of this combination of sense of grievance and narrow calculation of interest. Chinese officials seemed genuinely to
believe that the United States had made a decision to strike their
embassy, even though it was patently not in our interest to do
such a reckless thing. But they also used the incident to put the
United States on the defensive and to whip up support for the
regime in Beijing.

The leadership took advantage of that incident because they
need to use every possible occasion to reinforce their legitimacy
with a people whose faith is shaken. Another example is the
reported $4 billion they spent on the heavily choreographed
pageantry, pomp, and parades surrounding the regime's fiftieth
anniversary. Like the Russians, the Chinese are experiencing a
gradual erosion of faith, whether in a central ideology or in
themselves. Part of the problem stems from the party's loss of
legitimacy following the Tiananmen crackdown and the collapse
of the Soviet Union. In addition, the government's credibility has
been damaged by its inability to clamp down on corruption.
Attempts to reinvigorate the study of Marxism have failed to
inspire enthusiasm. Appeals to tradition and nationalism are
risky; the Falun Gong spiritual group that has been giving the
leadership such heartburn since the spring of 1999 drew some of

its popularity from the government's emphasis and support for traditional culture.

In the end, the legitimacy of the system and the leadership depend on delivering a better life, as the regime, to its credit, did in earlier years in greatly reducing poverty (although at terrible political cost). As a weak economy undercuts the legitimacy of the regime, China's leaders will rely all the more on power and repression to maintain their grip. And that means China's military.

The Chinese military, already anxious about its inadequacies in the face of American superiority, has been aggressive in hawking advanced-weapons technology to states like Pakistan and Iran to earn much-needed cash. Weak central control within the government over its subsidiaries has contributed to destabilizing arms sales. On top of this, the regime's growing insecurity will make it more receptive to military demands for greater resources, despite difficult budget constraints. More insular and suspicious of the West than most of the political leadership, the army's increased influence is not good news for the region or the United States.

Thus, as with Russia, it is the underlying weakness of China that will produce both the behavior and the military posture that could challenge our interests. For both, a sense of their own weaknesses leads to an emphasis in their foreign policies on classic balance-of-power diplomacy as they seek to limit the influence of the American "hegemon." It is striking that most other large nations, with a greater sense of their own strength (and a history of closer ties to the United States), take a different view of "the hegemon." But as we enter the twenty-first century, Russia and China bring with them a nineteenth-century view of international politics. Condemning them to oppositionist irrelevance on the most pressing issues facing the international community, this approach will not serve them well.

NORTH KOREA

Few nations outside Africa can make Russia's economic problems appear relatively manageable. North Korea has the dubious distinction of being one of them.

The *juche* ideology (literally, "self-reliance") that drives North Korea's economic policies has led to gross autarkic inefficiencies and sustained hardship for its people. Despite recent claimed improvement, North Korea's economy has been in basic decline since 1990, when it lost most of its trading partners as Communism crumbled in the USSR and Eastern Europe. It runs large, systemic trade deficits with its few remaining trade partners, and trade volumes are shrinking overall. Its gross domestic product shriveled 30 percent from 1991 to 1996. Its annual budget for 1999 was less than half what it was in 1994. North Korea is not a member of the World Bank, the International Monetary Fund, or any other regime that would make it eligible for multilateral loans and assistance. Even former friends like China and Russia are reluctant to give aid after North Korea defaulted on billions of dollars of debt in the early 1990s.

Economic mismanagement results not only from the incompetence and perverse priorities of North Korea's leadership; it is inherent in the system. Economies run by state bureaucracies just don't work, especially economies run by *bad* state bureaucracies. Annual famines in North Korea, which have killed an estimated two to three million from 1995 to 1999, as well as the repression the regime relies on to maintain its hold on power and its irresponsible policies abroad, have cost it legitimacy not only in the eyes of the world, but by some accounts in the eyes of its people. The immediate consequences of this perilous state of affairs are evident in North Korea's starving citizens and missile tests. Even more important is the longer-term crisis it almost certainly will create. The less legitimate the regime (and this regime deserves less allegiance, perhaps, than any government on the globe), the greater its reliance on the army and other instruments of state repression.

Where will this lead? Abroad, to a combination of positive diplomatic maneuvers and desperate actions, each designed to compensate for economic weakness. At home, to more repression, and still more, until the system collapses.

Actions abroad include, most seriously, the development and sale of dangerous weaponry. According to the Commission to Assess the Ballistic Missile Threat, North Korea "is a major proliferator of the ballistic missile capabilities it possesses — missiles, technology, technicians, transporter-erector-launchers and underground facility expertise — to other countries of missile proliferation concern," including Iran, Pakistan, and others.[29] There has been some debate in Washington over Pyongyang's August 1998 testing of the three-stage Taepo Dong I over Japan. Some argued it was designed to intimidate Japan, South Korea, and other regional actors. Others thought it was to blackmail the United States into offering cash to prevent further tests. Still others believe that North Korean missile tests are kind of an advertising campaign to promote its weapons' sales abroad.

All these theories are probably true. If so, Japan was more angry than intimidated. But the United States, with Japan, South Korea, and others, was still forced into concessions. However American officials may deny it, they did give in to blackmail in agreeing to a relaxation of U.S. sanctions against North Korea in return for a pledge to suspend missile launches — at least for a limited time.

This is a very unattractive spot for America to be in. But the critics who attacked this concession had little to offer in the way of a better alternative. Our nation was faced with a classic, strategic threat — long-range ballistic missiles — whose root cause was

North Korea's weakness, not its strength. In addition to peddling weapons, North Korea has resorted to a panoply of criminal activities to generate cash: selling narcotics, counterfeit American $100 bills, bootlegged cigarettes, alcohol, and more. North Korean diplomats have been caught in illicit activities, from trafficking cocaine to selling heroin to smuggling methamphetamine and tens of thousands of bogus dollars. According to the U.S. Congressional Research Service, North Korea's criminal behavior produced some $86 million in 1997.[30]

But the most important ramification of North Korea's weakness is its longer-term consequence: the collapse not only of the regime but of the system itself. It is hard to predict precisely when this will happen. Korea is known as the Hermit Kingdom — a reference to the peninsula's long history of isolation. The current regime in Pyongyang makes the previous Korean "hermits" look like gregarious exhibitionists. Based on limited, anecdotal evidence, some of our analysts have been predicting for many years that collapse was only a few years away. I believed them a few years ago and it has not happened — yet I continue to believe that it could come sooner rather than later.

No one should lament the passing of the corrupt and cruel North Korean system. But no one should believe that the collapse will come without real dangers — dangers of which the South Koreans are very aware. The most important question is not *when* the system collapses but *how*. A so-called soft landing is possible, in which Marxism in North Korea goes the way of its comrades in the former USSR and Eastern Europe: relatively peacefully. Some in South Korea hope for a version softer still, in which there is a gradual evolution of the regime in its economic and international policies and even in democratic directions. (The last seems especially improbable.) More alarming, and perhaps more likely, is the "hard landing," in which a desperate regime in Pyongyang, facing growing popular opposition and uncertain of its control of the armed forces, creates an international crisis to rally nationalist sentiment — perhaps by creating massive refugee flows south or into China; perhaps through a new missile crisis; or perhaps even through a military confrontation of some kind with South Korea and its allies.

A prospect that should concern us at least as much is the prospect of a North Korea that some day becomes a kind of Asian version of Albania in early 1997: a near anarchy in which contending military and less organized forces vie in increasingly violent ways to succeed a collapsing or collapsed regime. Refugee flows and the possibility that the fighting could spill across the North's borders would present the South, other neighbors, and us with very difficult decisions, including the question of whether or not we should intervene.

We should not try to prop up the regime. In any event, it would be difficult to do without massive resource transfers, and probably not even then. We must be absolutely direct and firm about our security ties to South Korea and our refusal to let the North Koreans drive any diplomatic wedges between us. But limited and growing economic ties of the kind the South Koreans have advocated make sense, especially if they are used as leverage for more responsible (or rather, less dangerous) North Korean behavior.

Why? Two reasons. First, the weaker the North Korean economy, the more likely the collapse of the regime will be sudden and violent. Second, the weaker the North Korean economy, the greater the costs of eventual reunification, which sooner or later will become a real option. The costs of reunification will be much greater proportionately than they have been for Germany. Estimates now range from a few billion dollars to some three trillion dollars, with most in the range of half a trillion to a trillion and a half. And, of course, the stronger the South Korean economy is at the time, the better Seoul will be able to bear such costs without large-scale assistance from the international community, including us.

Thus, as with Russia and China, it is North Korea's weakness more than its strength that helps generate very real threats to us now and could produce still greater crises in the future.

IRAN AND IRAQ

This same point — the peril inherent in our opponents' weaknesses — applies to our dealings in the Persian Gulf.

While the main Iraqi threat to American interests is Saddam Hussein, overall, Iraq's international behavior is influenced by a sense of historic grievance and accumulated wrongs — from its semicolonial past to the lingering impact of the Iran-Iraq War and Desert Storm. This does not mean Iraq's outrageous actions are justified, but it is a reality with which America must deal.

In Iran, meanwhile, the drive to export its brand of Islam through extremist means (that are by no means in accordance, ironically, with the best tenets of Islam) is driven not only by classic messianism. It also is inspired by a fear of the West — fear not so much of our arms as of our good ideas and our idea of the good life.

As a leading Middle East scholar pointed out at one of the Thursday morning breakfast meetings I held with outside experts on various topics, we should remember that when the Iranians called us the "Great Satan," they were not referring to a warrior. Satan did and does his best work with the insidious power of the tempter. That is why the hard-liners in Teheran worry most about the West. And it is the desire of the Iranian people, like all others, for personal freedom, as well as the temptation of Western goods, that will ultimately loosen the grip of those who fear both.

3.

Economic Weakness Abroad

Take a look at your daily newspaper — or the lead stories on the nightly news. Most mornings and evenings, the headlines are dominated by reports of carnage of one kind or another or worthy, diplomatic efforts to prevent or end such bloodshed. Military confrontations. Plane crashes. Peace talks. Events that draw the camera lens and seize the imagination.

It is not surprising that this kind of story monopolizes the news. But, except in the case of a large-scale war that involves the United States, they are not the national security issues that most affect the immediate lives of our citizens. International economic policy is no less a part of our "national security" concerns than traditional geopolitical concerns. This is becoming more true all the time as globalization succeeds in tying our everyday lives to the global marketplace. A bureaucratic decision about a foreign exchange rate can have a far greater impact on the life of an American than the drama of an ethnic conflict. Slobodan Milosevic's brutality had little bearing in the late 1990s on the daily lives of hog farmers in the American heartland, for example, but Asia's economic woes cost them tens of thousands of dollars, as dwindling demand among Asian consumers drove pork prices down to the ground. Wheat, apples, and other agricultural goods piled up on American docks. The collapse of Asia's market led to a 30 percent decline in our nation's farm exports to the region, putting at risk the livelihoods of entire rural communities. When countries like Russia, Japan, and Indonesia reacted to zero or negative growth by unfairly subsidizing their steel exports, which they dumped on the American market, it cost American industry dearly. In one year, the United States experienced a 500 percent increase in the imports of hot-rolled steel from Japan and a 300 percent increase in the import of hot-rolled steel from Russia. And all this foreign hot-rolled steel meant that American businesses — and the employees they were forced to lay off — got burned.

While we most certainly face a threat of competition from strong economies abroad, and while we must continue to oppose unfair trade practices by our competitors, it is the *weaknesses* of other economies that can have the most damaging effects on our people's security.

JAPAN

It wasn't so long ago that Japan was seen as a menacing economic powerhouse. American analysts and firms fretted about how to compete with, and emulate, the Japanese juggernaut. At the turn of the century, with Japan's economy only just starting to pull out of years of decline, the picture is very different, but the peril for our nation is still real. The United States has a clear and large stake in a strong, open Japanese economy. Already, Japan is our second- or third-largest export market after Canada. We sell as much to Japan as to the United Kingdom, Germany, and Italy combined. Almost 20 percent of our agricultural exports go to Japan, supplying nearly 40 percent of Japan's agricultural imports overall. Japanese-affiliated enterprises in the United States have created more than 756,000 American jobs, second only to those created by British-affiliated businesses.

A growing Japanese economy would provide a still greater market for American goods, buy still more food from American farmers, and create still more American jobs. Although more progress is needed, the trade agreements the Clinton Administration has reached with Japan are as much in our interest as they were difficult to negotiate. Overcoming resistance in the Japanese bureaucracy is not easy. During the 1993 G-7 Summit meeting, Robert Rubin, then the head of the National Economic Council, Bo Cutter, his able deputy, and I privately met in a Tokyo hotel room with a senior representative of Japan's Foreign Ministry. Together we negotiated the Framework Agreement, which governed subsequent talks on economic issues. The Foreign Ministry official had approached me to set up these talks with the approval of the prime minister. We reached agreement after two days' talks and the prime minister approved the deal. Late that night, we were told, an official of the hard-line Ministry of International Trade and Industry, furious that he and his colleagues had been circumvented and at the concessions the Japanese had made, got in a brief fistfight (or at least shoving match) with a Foreign Ministry official in the lobby of our hotel.

Our stake in Japanese growth, however, goes well beyond our own exports. As the second-largest economy in the world, Japan's continued recession through the 1990s sent tremors far beyond its shores. In particular, its tepid consumer demand and tightened access to credit retarded economic recovery throughout the rest of Asia. Japanese imports shrank as anxious consumers snapped shut their wallets. Japanese banks — once the motor of the region's growth — restricted their lending operations, calling in loans from Southeast Asia and cutting back regional investment.

If a new shock somewhere, such as a large correction in the U.S. stock market, provides a new setback to the Japanese economy, with resulting pressure on the value of the yen, China might feel obliged to devalue its currency as well to compete with Japanese exports. This could spawn a series of competitive devaluations, and trade wars from Jakarta to Seoul. At best, Japan's economy is moving from recession to longer-term stagnation or very slow growth. Once seen as the leader of Asia's economic "flying geese," it now is finding it must beat its wings harder —

and still is drifting along toward the middle of the formation. (For a while in the late 1990s, it looked as if the whole flock might head south.)

Japan's system of protections against the outside world and linkages among its bankers and businesses served Japan well into the mid-1980s — but it is neither efficient nor well suited to the demands of a globalized economy. And when Japan's foreign markets shrink, as they did during the Asian economic crisis of the late 1990s, weak consumer demand at home gives its products precious little domestic market to fall back on. Weak demand is the downside of the extraordinary discipline of the Japanese people in their very high desire to save for the future. In the late 1990s, they were caught in a psychological trap. As the economy failed to recover, they became all the more concerned about the future and thus unwilling to save less and spend more. In any case, an aging population consumes less than a younger one — and there are more Japanese over sixty than under fifteen. At the same time, the Japanese were doing well enough that they did not demand that the government act more aggressively to reform the economy.

To increase demand (and to improve the ruling party's electoral fortunes), the Japanese government in the late 1990s pumped a number of infusions of cash into the economy. This helped produce very modest growth of roughly 2 percent in the first quarter of 1999. But without basic reforms of its outmoded system of corporate cartels, of its banking and regulatory systems, and of its barriers to foreign imports, prospects for sustained future growth are dim. Fiscal stimulus cannot by itself create recovery. The Japanese government should not confuse priming a pump with fixing it. Of course, fixing the pump will be hard to do. The reforms will be costly, both financially and politically. Breaking up the cartels and achieving greater efficiencies will mean serious layoffs in a country with a weak social safety net — something no elected leader wants to face. Thus far, a weak political will has meant a weak economy. This is not in Asia's interest; neither is it in America's.

BRAZIL

Already burdened by enormous debts (the result of years of huge budget deficits), Brazil was battered in the 1998 Asian financial crisis when investor confidence plummeted in emerging markets, including its own. Apprehensive investors yanked $35 billion out of Brazil. In one day alone, Brazil's stock market took a dizzying 16 percent dive.

To stem the crisis, President Fernando Henrique Cardoso announced a package of austerity policies, including higher interest rates, more taxes, and tens of billions of dollars in federal budget cuts. His efforts earned the approval of the United States, paving the way for a $41.5 billion loan from the International Monetary Fund — with firm American support.

During the crisis, as the IMF rescue package was being assembled, I ran into Treasury Secretary Robert Rubin. As we chatted about old times, I recalled how, at our morning senior staff meetings in the White House, we would sometimes ask him what the effect of one event or another might be on the stock market. He would invariably lean back, smile Delphicly, and do his Chauncy Gardner impersonation, saying, "Oh, the market goes up, it goes down, it goes up, it goes down."

As he smiled (Delphicly) at the recollection, an aide rushed up to his side. Secretary Rubin turned to him, and with real concern asked, "How is the market doing?" As the aide replied and they discussed the implications of the news, I realized that he was asking not about the Dow Jones, but about the Brazilian stock market. This is the reality of life in the era of globalization. Secretary Rubin, like President Clinton, understood that a strong Brazilian economy is in America's national security interest. And while the President put his comments in positive terms, saying, "A strong Brazil makes for a stronger United States," the clear corollary is that a weak Brazil could hurt our people at home.[31] How? It could curb American exports, crimping prosperity and chipping at jobs. As Latin America's largest market, with more than half of its people, Brazil is the engine of regional growth. If its economy started to sink, it could pull down its neighbors as well. Not only would we lose our eleventh-largest export market — one of the few with which we run a trade surplus — we would see demand dry up throughout a region that buys 20 percent of American exports. And that could put a lot of our people out of work. A Brazilian setback could also have devastating effects on U.S. private lenders. Both Citibank and BankBoston, for example, have loaned billions of dollars each to Brazil; American enterprises have invested billions more. It could rattle American businesses, some two thousand of which operate in Brazil. Globally, a major panic in Brazil could spark a new contagion, prompting jittery investors to pull their funds out of emerging markets around the world, destroying Asia's incipient recovery, and risking a global recession.

In the late 1990s, President Cardoso struggled to put in place the reforms that could help Brazil deal with the crushing debts that are so threatening to its future and to our interests. He did it right, warning voters that he would carry out such reforms before he gained reelection. But a weak political base and plunging popularity ratings — reaching all-time lows in the single digits in late 1999 — made it impossible to carry out his program as planned. Strikes and protests by truckers, farmers, educators, and others further complicated President Cardoso's hand.

At the turn of the century, Brazil did not face a new collapse. But, as in Japan, either a weak political base or a weak political will was reinforcing economic weakness. The negative effects that are likely to ensue threaten citizens not only in São Paolo but also in St. Paul.

4.

Weaknesses Within States —
The Next Cockpits of Conflict?

Strong nations cooperate to the harmony and wealth of the world. Weak nations are a perpetual cause of disturbances and perils.

ANATOLE FRANCE

When I was national security advisor, every morning a briefer from the Central Intelligence Agency would go over the latest intelligence with me before we went to meet with the President. (Well, *most* mornings, when we were not already knee-deep in a crisis. On other mornings, I would make do with reading the President's daily brief plus the CIA and State Department's Intelligence and Research daily briefs that got wider distribution.) From time to time, as we talked about a new attack on a village in Bosnia or an incident somewhere in, say, Sierra Leone, I would ask if he or she could tell me the name of the obscure provincial capital we would be discussing a year from then.

There are three potential candidates that I believe we are likely to hear much more about in the coming years: Aceh, Ambon, and Irian Jaya in Indonesia; the Ferghana Valley in Central Asia; and San Vicente del Caguan or any one of a number of towns in southern Colombia.

The possibilities of growing conflicts in Indonesia, in the vast area from the southern Caucasus through the Caspian Sea area to

Central Asia, and in Colombia are very real. And while these hot spots are very different in their nature, they are similar in several key respects: Each is an area of geographic importance. Indonesia incorporates seventeen thousand islands from the Strait of Malacca out into the Pacific Ocean. The "Eurasian Balkans" girdle the southern reaches of the Eurasian land mass. Colombia, a mere three-and-one-half-hour flight from Miami, borders Panama, Venezuela, Brazil, Peru, and Ecuador. Each is rich in energy resources. Upheaval in any of these places can affect our lives through their impact on energy markets alone. In each, internal weaknesses are the root of problem.

INDONESIA

Why should what happens in Indonesia matter to us? For starters, it is the fourth-most populous nation in the world. It is the largest Muslim nation — though only some 30 percent of Indonesians are practicing. It sits astride crucial sea lanes in Southeast Asia, home to important American allies. Its preoccupation with internal affairs could damage the already weak ability and willingness of the Association of Southeast Asian Nations (ASEAN) to act in dealing with regional crisis, which would mean more pressure on the United Nations and the United States to fill the gap. Its collapse could spawn legions of desperate refugees, especially among its Chinese population. American companies are heavily invested in Indonesia's petroleum resources, which produce approximately one million and one-half barrels of crude and condensate oil a day.

Against tough odds, Indonesia successfully managed the transition to democratically elected government in late 1999, albeit not through direct elections. But daunting problems persist, starting with its economic weakness, including rampant poverty. The number of people living below the poverty line nearly quadrupled in the last years of the century, reaching about 140 million — that is, two out of every three Indonesians. Barely half of Indonesia's children were enrolled in school, down from 78 percent in 1997. Unemployment had reached record highs.[32] Meanwhile, the state had budget shortfalls in the billions of dollars, and owed billions more in foreign debt.

Economic weakness exacerbates fissures in Indonesia society — with increasingly violent results. Disgruntled poor have occupied land, raided agricultural fields and farms, and stormed state-owned teak plantations, cutting down valuable trees. There have been attacks against Christians by Muslims, and against Muslims by Christians, including gruesome assaults in the Molucca islands and in East Java. Resentment of the Chinese population, whose members have both a disproportionate and a central place in the economy, has led to arson and other forms of violence against Chinese merchants and entrepreneurs. Continued economic trouble could provoke a return to the *Year of Living Dangerously.* If that happens, with an exodus of the Chinese population, the Indonesian economy will only further decline.

Still more dangerous than simmering social disorder are the separatist efforts that are likely to intensify with the precedent of East Timor. With thousands of islands making up its disparate archipelago, and two hundred million citizens speaking more than three hundred languages and dialects, Indonesia has not been dealt an easy hand in developing a strong sense of nationhood.

In Aceh, for example, where guerrillas have been fighting against Jakarta's rule since the 1970s, tens of thousands of citizens have been emboldened by East Timor's experience to rally in the streets for their own referendum on independence. Organized independence forces include students, human rights groups, Muslim leaders, and the armed Free Aceh Movement — which declares it is ready to fight for liberty if necessary. They complain about decades of neglect and abuse from the government: massive human-rights violations and the ransacking of natural resources, including oil and gas.

President Abdurrahman Wahid has suggested that he would be willing to support some sort of referendum, while saying that this is his own opinion and not the government's policy. The military has been ordered to reduce its presence in the turbulent province. But army leaders have made it clear they do not support independence. As the deputy commander of military operations said, "Aceh is like Indonesia's oldest son. It is very hard to let your oldest son go."[33]

Meanwhile, in restless Irian Jaya — a mineral-rich province bordering Papua New Guinea — demands have mounted for independence since the fall of the Soeharto regime. Like their cousins in Aceh, Irianese separatists complain that the central government plundered the rich bounty of the province while leaving its people to suffer, and that discriminatory policies and oppressive enforcement by the military resulted in numerous human-rights abuses that date back thirty years.

The question is: If there is no tangible progress on all these fronts, how long will the Indonesian military wait before stepping into the fray? Smarting from perceived humiliation by the West over East Timor, the military has the motive and the means to seize control. A military government would be a defeat not only for democracy in Indonesia but for stability in Asia and for America's interests there.

THE "EURASIAN BALKANS"

What Zbigniew Brzezinski has called the Eurasian Balkans are a group of states that sweep across the southern core of the Eurasian land mass.[34] They have the good fortune to sit on an unusually large slice of the world's energy and other natural resources. But they are also unstable countries in transition, with self-centered leaders, ethnically diverse populations, and artificially crafted borders. Stretching from the Caucasus (racked by conflict in Chechnya) through the states surrounding the Caspian (with its lucrative oil resources), through Central Asia and the former Soviet "Stans" (where newly independent states are struggling to maintain freedom from Russian dominance while facing attacks from Muslim militants), the Eurasian Balkans will likely be a source of more than one crisis in this century.

The multiple weaknesses throughout this geostrategically important region are drawing the attention and ambitions of major powers — Turkey, Iran, China, Russia, Europe, and the United States — much as during what Rudyard Kipling called the Great Game between England and Russia during the nineteenth century. These six powers are competing not only for influence, but for oil and potential control over the pipelines that will carry the "black gold" to the west.

The stakes are far higher than the attention this area has received either publicly or within the government — though in 1999 it was the setting and subject of the James Bond film *The World Is Not Enough*, suggesting, in the words of the *New York Times*, that the region "has come of age." The Caspian region may have reserves of almost 200 billion barrels, as compared to 260 billion in Saudi Arabia, or roughly equal to those in the North Sea. (This energy wealth does not necessarily mean that the Caspian states will find their economic troubles solved; indeed, other developing nations have found that oil revenues can push up their exchange rates and make most other exports less competitive.) The United States has an important stake in promoting the development and free flow of Caspian oil and gas to world markets, and to supporting the interests of American energy titans such as Chevron, Exxon, and Mobil. At the same time, we have a stake in limiting excessive Russian or Iranian involvement and influence.

Meanwhile, continued instability in this region affects broader U.S. interests. As we work to build a peaceful, undivided, democratic Europe, and as we try to extend the peace of western Europe to the east, we will have to grapple all the more with such conflicts as Nagorno-Karabakh and other Eurasian Balkan family feuds. The Caucasus and Central Asia are rife with internal fissures that complicate every issue. Political institutions are weak; the leaders of Azerbaijan, Turkmenistan, and Kazakhstan, for example, are all former Communist apparatchiks. There are competing territorial claims over borders and Caspian waters, and internal disputes among the varied pieces of the ethnic quilt.

In this region, one of the least democratic in the world, there is little transparency in official business. Bureaucracies are corrupt, with officials skimming and stealing at every level of government. According to *The Economist,* "In Kazakhstan, for instance, a $500m cash payment made by Mobil for some of its shares in the Tengiz oil field allegedly never reached the budget. . . . In Azerbaijan, virtually all public positions that involve the collection of money must be bought. The job of a tax inspector, for instance, might cost about $50,000 up front." Meanwhile, miserably paid midlevel officials supplement their salaries by demanding bribes for everything from health services to passing grades on university exams.[35]

Although corruption is a problem in Georgia as well, it is an exception in the quality of its senior leadership. Eduard Shevardnadze is a widely respected, experienced leader. But Georgia fought, and lost, a war with its rebellious Abkhazia province in 1992–94. Despite outside peacekeepers, no political agreement has been reached and violence periodically flares. The region of South Ossetia has also resisted central control, resulting in the deployment of a Russian-led multinational peacekeeping force, mediation by the Organization for Security and Cooperation in Europe (OSCE), numerous refugees, and continued dissent about the region's status within Georgia. The restive regions of Ajaria and Javakheti could also decide for independence. And ongoing trouble in Chechnya means trouble for Georgia's leaders, as Muslim separatists could decide to help their brothers across the border.

Hostility between Armenia and Azerbaijan remains high, in the aftermath of their bloody war over Nagorno-Karabakh (a mostly ethnic Armenian area within Azeri borders). Azerbaijan, with its rich oil resources, has been assiduously wooing the West; Russia has responded by arming Armenia, which does little to mitigate tensions.

One of Central Asia's hottest danger zones is concentrated in the densely populated and ethnically mixed Ferghana Valley, a region the size of Ireland that includes parts of Uzbekistan, Kyrgyzstan, and Tajikistan. Citizens there have watched in dismay as corruption and mismanagement have driven down their standard of living since the collapse of the USSR. All three parts of the valley include forces opposed to their government, which has sparked political repression that in turn has stoked resentment. Few mechanisms exist to manage competition for natural resources. Economic crisis has made the region vulnerable to narco-traffickers — one of the few enterprises in which different ethnic groups are working together. Given all this, it is hardly surprising that the region is the object of and susceptible to the pressures and rivalries of outside powers — Russia, Iran, Turkey, China, the United States, and Europe.

Some forces in Russia would like to ensure that Russia is the only route through which Caspian oil and gas can reach world markets, with all the attendant benefits that would imply. The United States, for its part, says it wants to ensure free and fair access to the region's energy resources — but the subtext is to avoid permitting either Russia or Iran more leverage over the Caspian region's riches. The United States has pushed for a pipeline through Turkey, and Turkey is certainly keen to expand its influence in the region. But American and European energy companies are leery of the price tag attached to a Turkish pipeline, which is higher than other routes. Iran wants its share of Caspian wealth to help build up its economy, and it supports a pipeline to one of its own modern ports. But the United States and Russia share concerns about strengthening the regional influence of radical Islam. Even agreements over routes will not end the competition for influence with the states over whose territory the oil flows.

And it is not surprising that this is an arena in which various Muslim militant movements are fighting to gain control (while competing among themselves). Religious zealots based in Afghanistan have started to spread throughout Central Asia and the Caucasus, hoping that economic hardship will make radical appeals more popular. In Chechnya, Dagestan, and elsewhere, Muslim rebels have taken on Moscow. In the Ferghana Valley, armed gangs of Islamists have seized villages and hostages and fomented unrest against government forces. Such radical Islamic activism is setting off alarm bells in Moscow and Beijing, who fear its spillover into their territories. And it should be setting off louder bells than it has in Washington and throughout Europe.

Complicated enough for you? Unhappily, the region is as dangerous as it is complex.

COLOMBIA

Colombia's weaknesses are all too evident. Two well-entrenched left-wing guerrilla groups, the Revolutionary Armed Forces of Colombia (FARC) and the National Liberation Army (ELN), control some 40 percent of the country and command perhaps twenty thousand troops. Private militias and right-wing death squads have filled the government's security vacuum with violent repression. Both sides have ties to the drug cartels that produce about 80 percent of the world's cocaine and some 75 percent of the heroin that ends up on American streets. Economic woes compound Colombia's fragility, with unemployment as high as 20 percent, the worst recession since 1931, dozens of major companies and thousands of small businesses going under, and mounting national debt. In August 1999, Colombia suffered a devastating setback in an era of globalization: Moody's Investor Service lowered its country rating by a full two notches.

As in the areas above, our stake in Colombia includes energy resources, both in Colombia and its neighbor Venezuela. It is not too much of a stretch to say that Colombia is in some ways a problem like Vietnam — but a Vietnam with oil and gas. A Vietnam the size of Texas, New Mexico, and Arkansas combined. A Vietnam in our backyard.

The grasping tentacles of Colombian narco-traffickers have poisoned countless American lives and desperately weakened Colombia. Judges have been killed. Politicians have been intimidated or bought. Meanwhile, the guerrillas have reaped their own profit from the drug harvest, providing protection to the narco-traffickers' crops or charging tolls on airfield strips to the tune of $30 million to $100 million a year, or more.

Colombia's problems have also infected its neighbors, spreading the germs of a regional crisis. Panama has absorbed about two thousand Colombian refugees. Its Darien region is threatened both by the FARC, which uses it as a rear-guard supply area, and paramilitaries who sweep into the region in search of guerrillas (and also to advance their own economic interests). In recent years, more than one hundred Panamanians have been driven from their homes, while coastal villages have been subjected to boycotts enforced by illegal militias. Venezuela's populist leader, Hugo Chavez, is sympathetic to the guerrillas. But while his stance has roiled relations with the Colombian government, it has not prevented Colombian rebels from crossing the 1,500-mile border and kidnapping, terrorizing, and extorting Venezuelan citizens. Nor did it prevent the FARC from murdering three American human-rights workers in Venezuela in March 1999. As a result, some Venezuelans in the border regions are now paying Colombian paramilitaries for protection. Guerrillas also cross the border into Ecuador to run guns, hide kidnapping victims, and regroup after military operations. In 1998, an Ecuadorian congressman accused of being an arms supplier to the FARC was assassinated in Quito, presumably by someone affiliated with Colombian paramilitaries, and Colombian guerrillas have kidnapped several Ecuadorian businessmen. Peru and Brazil have both increased their troops on their border regions, and President Fujimori — known for his hard line against Peru's Shining Path — has been openly critical of Colombian President Andres Pastrana, who has taken a more conciliatory approach.

With the stakes so high, the United States is becoming more engaged in finding a solution, as we should be. A military solution is unlikely. But so is a negotiated solution, unless another source of weakness is corrected: the weak bargaining position of the government. In November 1998, President Pastrana withdrew army troops from a rebel-dominated area the size of Switzerland — a goodwill gesture intended to pave the way to durable peace talks. The military, however, was vehemently opposed; the minister of defense and at least ten generals handed in their resignations. The insurgents, for their part, have shown little willingness to compromise; they reportedly responded to the government's good faith by increasing their list of talking points from 10 to more than

100.[36] Talks had barely struggled off the ground before they began to falter. "Farclandia" is now under rebel control, to the dismay of some local residents. "Our greatest fear is that the peace process falls apart, the paramilitaries come in here and accuse us all of being collaborators, and kill a lot of people," said one.[37]

The Colombian military is demoralized, debilitated, and burdened by a history of human-rights abuses. In July 1999, U.S. Drug Czar General Barry McCaffrey wrote to Secretary of State Albright, "Intelligence assessments have identified numerous deficiencies in training, force structure, leadership, mobility and communications which must be corrected if the government of Colombia is to mount credible counter-drug operations."[38] In eighty separate instances, FARC leaders rallied hundreds of insurgents to attack army troops and defeated them almost every time.

Washington is beginning to build up the Colombian military. By 1999 Colombia was the fourth-largest recipient of American aid worldwide (with more than $300 million a year), and the third-largest beneficiary of security assistance. Military aid could be increased to as much as $1.4 billion over three years, probably including a squadron of new helicopters, a package of excess equipment from the Pentagon, and training for Colombian soldiers and police. The United States already was training Colombia's first elite anti-drug battalion of 950 soldiers and 200 police officers.

But for much too long, the Administration saw Colombia as a drug problem rather than a regional security problem. (As with the Eurasian Balkans, I wish I had given it more attention.) This issue needs more national debate than it has received — preferably nonpartisan, as unlikely a prospect as that might be. The ghosts of Vietnam are likely to be present at the debate. But rather than find absolute analogies to the problem in our previous experiences in Vietnam or Central America, we should learn practical lessons from them: We should become more involved, preferably working with neighboring and other governments in the region, in building up the army in order to create incentives for the FARC to negotiate and to reduce incentives for right-wing groups to operate. But we should learn from Vietnam the danger of crossing the line between assisting another government and taking over from it responsibilities that are its and its alone. When we do so, we undercut the standing of the government with its own people (as we did in Vietnam) and encourage it to let Uncle Sam do the heavy lifting (as we did in Vietnam). We should not, therefore, go beyond the supply of material, training and trainers, and intelligence. We need to help the Colombian government overcome its weaknesses — not attempt to replace its weakness with our strength.

AFRICA

Indonesia, the Eurasian Balkans, and Colombia present some of the most difficult cases of internal weakness before us. But they are by no means the only ones.

Consider the plight of vast areas of Africa. While the number of states moving toward democracy offers some hope, there are cases of real economic progress, and the continent showed economic gains in the 1990s, the average annual growth in Africa from 1965 to 1997 was well below that in any other region.

Too many African nations lack the kind of institutional infrastructure (modern telecommunications systems, for example) that will allow them to take advantage of, much less fairly compete in, the global markets of the twenty-first century. And thus, when it comes to the information revolution, most of the people on the continent are electronically disenfranchised.

When I was accompanying General Shali on a trip to visit our troops in Haiti, our helicopter flew over an isolated village on top of a hill. It was only 20 miles or so outside the capital, but with no roads and telephone lines, it could have been on the other side of the earth. As we looked down on the children playing in a small dirt square in the middle of the village, the sergeant sitting in the door of the helicopter pointed at them and said through the intercom, "They don't have a chance." Thinking of their physical isolation, I agreed. "No chance," he went on to say. "None of them are learning how to use a computer."

This applies to most of Africa as well. There are more Internet hosts in Bulgaria than in all of sub-Saharan Africa (minus South Africa) combined. As we enter the age of e-commerce and what will become e-government and even e-education, with all the efficiencies that implies, Africa could be left farther and farther behind, in spiraling e-deficit.

The barriers to African development are not only economic. The HIV/AIDS crisis in many countries is stunning in its toll; 22.3 million adults in sub-Saharan Africa have HIV, more than half of whom are women. That amounts to nearly 70 percent of all the infected people on the planet. Life expectancy in southern Africa, which rose to fifty-nine in the early 1990s, is expected to diminish to forty-five in ten years. And with 10.7 million "AIDS orphans" in sub-Saharan Africa, the virus is also taking a devastating toll on the survivors.[39]

In addition, civil wars (and competitions and conflicts among states) help prevent the kind of economic integration we see proceeding in every other region of the world. Angola is a terrible case in point. Rich in natural resources, a healthy Angola could provide the final piece of a thriving southern African region. But personal ambitions and accumulated blood debts have torn the country to shreds in a civil war that has claimed some three hundred thousand lives over the past decade and one-half.

When I visited the small city of Kuito in the central highlands of Angola in 1994, almost every building was heavily damaged by shells and machine-gun fire. Tens of thousands of refugees were crammed into a camp outside the city. The hospital was full of the civilian victims of the fighting. No one knew how many were buried in the surrounding countryside. A few miles from the outskirts of Kuito, I found the perfect, infuriating metaphor for the waste of Angola's natural riches. Across a lovely field, the mango trees were laden with fruit. But no one could pick them, I was told. The field was full of land mines.

During much of the 1990s, Africa was growing at a rate of 4 percent or so. There are numerous stories of economic progress. Mozambique, like Angola a former Portuguese territory torn by civil war, had grown at roughly 12 percent a year since finding peace in the early 1990s before the devastating floods of 2000.

The United States is helping, but we can do much more if we overcome the attention deficit disorder in Washington that produces occasional visits to the region by our most senior officials but too little of their sustained engagement in between, and occasional new African trade and development legislation but too few resources. If we do not, we will continue to bear some responsibility for weaknesses in Africa that challenge our hearts, our consciences, and, in some cases, our important interests.

5.

Weaknesses Among Friends

Weaknesses within stronger key allies and friends may not presage their collapse or descent into serious instability, but can damage their ability or willingness to work with us in defense of our interests.

Saudi Arabia, one of America's key allies in the Middle East, has long relied on its petroleum riches to subsidize extensive benefits for its people, and perpetuate the Saud family's hold on power. Yet temporary declines in world oil prices, combined with the kingdom's high population growth, forced the government to tighten its belt — including by raising domestic gasoline prices, cutting back on government services, and reducing military purchases from the United States. Even though the economy is encountering difficulties, the Saudi government has thus far resisted serious economic reform, such as direct personal taxation and large-scale privatization, in an attempt to limit calls for popular control of the government. Moreover, the leadership cannot afford to accept foreign assistance, whether from governments or corporations, especially when radical fundamentalists already accuse them of selling out to the West and defiling the heartland of Islam. At the turn of the century, the internal political situation in Saudi Arabia was, happily, as calm as at any recent time. But it was coming at a cost: deferred reforms and de facto accommodations with Iran, in order to head off Iranian troublemaking within the kingdom.

In recent years, America's relations with Mexico have reached a new level of mutual respect and a sense of common cause. But weaknesses in Mexico, including crime, corruption, and the inability to prevent intimidation of officials, are preventing the kind of cooperation on drugs that we must have to protect our citizens. "[The] sophisticated, organized criminal groups from Mexico have eclipsed the drug-trafficking criminals from Cali and Medellin, Colombia, as the greatest law-enforcement threat facing the United States today," said Michael Horn, DEA chief of international operations, in 1997 congressional testimony. Some 70 percent of the cocaine on America's streets makes its way here via Mexico. And while seizures of drugs are up in recent years, the volume of trafficking is, too.

Corrupt senior agents in Mexico's antidrug forces are part of the problem. In 1997, Mexico's own drug czar, General Jesus Gutierrez Rebollo, was arrested for taking kickbacks from Amada Carrillo Fuentes, one of the country's most powerful drug lords, with charges pending. In 1998, three senior agents of an elite Mexican police force trained by American officials reportedly failed lie-detector tests concerning their contacts with drug traffickers. On several occasions, American intelligence and law-enforcement officials have supplied their Mexican counterparts with specific information about the whereabouts of drug kingpins, only to have the Mexican police fumble the intelligence while the traffickers roamed free. Meanwhile, the drug cartels employ increasingly sophisticated counterintelligence to target and exploit law-enforcement vulnerabilities and elude antidrug operations. (At the same time, we need to recognize better the fact that for every sale of drugs, there is a buyer as well as a supplier. The ultimate solution to our nation's drug problem lies here in the United States, not in Mexico, Colombia, or Burma.)

A different kind of weakness affects our interests in Europe. The growing gap between our military capacities and those of our NATO allies means more than just our taxpayers bearing an unfair share of our common defense burden. Kosovo showed how our military might creates a dependency on the U.S. that requires our taking over diplomatic responsibilities that should have been European. (Every time I check a map, the Balkans remain in Europe.) Over Kosovo there were some eight hundred American aircraft — more than double the rest of NATO's contribution. Only the United States had the stealth fighters and bombers to make such an air campaign feasible. Only the United States had sufficient precision-guided weapons to sustain the action. Had a ground invasion become necessary, most European troops could not have been swiftly deployed without the aid of

American C-17s. So our nation, which was providing the lion's share of the intelligence, ordnance, and manpower, called the shots in terms of strategy. That bred frustration in Europe as the bombing campaign dragged on.

But it also gave our allies an important, if unpleasant, wake-up call. "In Kosovo, we have come face-to-face with the European future, and it's frightening," said George Robertson, now NATO secretary general, in May 1999. Catching up will require billions of dollars — and deep reserves of political will. As U.S. Defense Secretary Cohen put it, "NATO countries spend roughly 60 percent of what the United States does and they get about 10 percent of the capability. That has to change."[40] Let's hope our allies act on President Eisenhower's observation: "Weakness cannot cooperate with anything. Only strength can cooperate."

6.

Addressing a World of Weaknesses

In the meantime, faced with a world of weakness, what is our nation to do?

We must help other nations to deal with economic difficulties, including IMF bail-out programs when necessary. This is not easy. Indeed, we could conquer the military of almost any nation on earth more easily than we can fix its economy. But we must try, out of self-interest. And we must work to draw weak economies and weak nations into the global community and global economy through policies of constructive engagement without giving up our efforts to deter dangerous behavior. Such engagement means more than just regular contacts between foreign ministries. It must include reaching out to the forces within society, the institutions and individuals, most likely to be hostile to

America and our interests. The more isolated they are, the more likely that they will pose problems for us down the line.

For engagement to work, however, it must take into account not only political and economic factors, but also psychological ones. Trumpeting America's indispensability may make us feel good at home, but abroad it raises hackles, among our friends as well as potential enemies. So toning down our rhetoric would be prudent. But relaxing our strength would not. There are still rogue states. We still face real threats. We still need to maintain our naval dominance in the Pacific, our troops on the border of North Korea, our presence in Europe and elsewhere.

And even as we subdue overheated rhetoric, we should also sharpen our message. Proclamations of "partnership" and the pretense at a symmetry of short-term interests creates illusions that, in the end, produce disillusion, not diplomatic gain. China and Russia are *not* our partners. It is disingenuous to pretend they are. The utility of our strategic dialogue with Beijing is to help us cooperate in areas where we can — and to inject clarity in dealing with the many areas where, as yet, we cannot. It was very important that we made clear to Russia from the start of the process that NATO enlargement was on track and would happen, with or without Russia's blessing. To the degree that Russian leaders made opposition to NATO enlargement a test case of their international power, to that degree they would appear all the weaker. This would hurt them at home as well as abroad. It is equally essential that Russian leaders understand now they cannot force NATO to deny the Baltic states entry into the alliance, if they meet the criteria for membership. To say the Baltic states could not be members of the alliance because they were once part of the USSR would violate NATO policy and be a moral obscenity. These nations did not ask to be incorporated by force into the Soviet Union. What they have built in democracy since reclaiming their independence they have a right to keep in security. Any European nation that meets the criteria for membership, including the Baltic states and Russia herself, must sooner or later be allowed entry.

Finally, we need to recognize that the United States, for all our strength, cannot manage others' weaknesses alone. We need to work cooperatively with international institutions — which, alas, are often weak or lagging themselves in addressing the challenges posed by globalization. From the IMF and World Bank to the United Nations and more, America and its partners must help adapt our international institutions for the demands of the twenty-first century.

In the end, the likelihood of our success is a question of political will in Washington. It is much easier conceptually to understand the danger of foreign might than foreign frailty; much easier to rally public and congressional support for policies dealing with the obvious threat of strength than the less obvious menace of weakness. Consider, for example, this tub-thumping speech by Senator Thad Cochran in support of national missile defense:

> Will we, or will we not, commit in a meaningful way to defending ourselves against limited ballistic-missile attack? Will we tell the world the United States will not be subject to blackmail by ballistic missile? Will we tell our citizens they will not be hostages to the demands of those nations who seek to coerce the United States?

Now try to give the same speech about some of the weaknesses discussed above:

> Will we, or will we not, commit in a meaningful way to defending ourselves against Japan's lagging economy? Will we tell the world the United States will not be subject to instability in the Ferghana Valley? Will we tell our citizens they will not be hostages to the demands of our militarily deficient NATO allies?

It doesn't bring the audience cheering to its feet, does it?

And yet, imagine the world we are seeking to build, a world very much in our interest. It is a world of democracies that respect the rights of their peoples and a world of free markets that are open to American goods. A world of stability, within and among nations. Ask yourself what poses the greater threat to this vision's realization: the strength of the enemies of such a world order, or the accumulated weaknesses that are producing so much world disorder?

To help address those weaknesses, we need resources. And even at a time of unparalleled budget surpluses, it is an annual battle to fund our already very modest foreign-affairs account — a battle we continue to lose. Which brings us to the sixth and final nightmare, a nightmare not for the future but for today: the political culture of contemporary Washington, D.C.

CHAPTER SIX

The Sixth Nightmare:
Washington, D.C.

FM AMEMBASSY F*****

TO SECSTATE WASHINGTON

19 JANUARY 2003 0930Z

FROM THE AMBASSADOR

NART — THINGS FALL APART

SUMMARY

1. I MET TODAY WITH PRESIDENT J***** TO DISCUSS THE
GOVERNMENT'S PLAN FOR MOVING FORWARD IN THE
WAKE OF THE LEGISLATURE'S DRAMATIC REJECTION OF
THE REGION'S NUCLEAR ARMS REDUCTION TREATY (NART).
THE PARTISAN POLEMICS THAT DROVE THE TREATY TO
DEFEAT HAVE ONLY BEEN AGGRAVATED FURTHER BY THE
VOTE, WHICH THE PRESIDENT INTERPRETS AS A PER-
SONAL ATTACK. CAUGHT UP IN ITS DOMESTIC POLITICAL
GAMES, HIS COUNTRY WILL BE A LESS DEPENDABLE
PARTNER FOR THE US IN THE YEARS AHEAD.

PRESIDENT J*****, DENOUNCING PARTISANSHIP, PLOTS POLITICAL REVENGE

2. I SAW THE PRESIDENT THIS MORNING AT HIS COUNTRYSIDE RETREAT. SURPRISINGLY, J***** WAS IN HIGH SPIRITS, VOLUBLE AND ENERGETIC, DESPITE THE LEGISLATURE'S OVERWHELMING REJECTION LAST WEEK OF ONE OF HIS SIGNATURE FOREIGN POLICY ACHIEVEMENTS — THE NUCLEAR ARMS REDUCTION TREATY (NART).

3. J***** DESCRIBED THE MOOD THAT HAD LED TO THE NART'S DEFEAT AS ONE OF "POISONOUS PARTISANSHIP — THE WORST I'VE SEEN IN MY CAREER." HE NOTED THAT REPRESENTATIVES OF THE OPPOSITION MAJORITY PARTY, AFTER 18 MONTHS OF DELAY, HAD SCHEDULED THE NART VOTE IN A DRAMATICALLY COMPRESSED TIMETABLE. THEN, DESPITE CLEAR SUPPORT OF THE PUBLIC FOR THE TREATY, MEMBERS OF THE OPPOSITION HAD MADE IT THEIR MISSION TO KILL THE NART — IN THE PRESIDENT'S VIEW, "TO GET ME POLITICALLY."

4. J***** POINTED OUT THAT LEADERS OF THE OPPOSITION HAD FORCED THE DOOMED VOTE EVEN AFTER A MAJORITY OF THE LEGISLATURE — INCLUDING MANY MEMBERS OF THEIR OWN PARTY — HAD FORMALLY REQUESTED IT BE POSTPONED.

5. "THEY GOT WHAT THEY WANTED, IN THE SHORT TERM," J***** OBSERVED. "BUT IF THEY TOOK AWAY MY NART, THEY GAVE ME A POWERFUL POLITICAL TOOL. I'LL TURN IT BACK AROUND ON THEM IN NEXT YEAR'S PRESIDENTIAL CAMPAIGN — AND HAMMER THEM WITH IT HARD. THEY'LL PAY THE PRICE OF RECKLESS ISOLATIONISM AT THE POLLS."

COMMENT

6. THE PRESIDENT'S VERSION OF THE NART DEBACLE IS ACCURATE BUT INCOMPLETE. WHILE THE MOST CONSERVATIVE OF HIS OPPONENTS BEAR THE LION'S SHARE OF RESPONSIBILITY FOR THE NART'S DEMISE, LEGISLATORS IN HIS OWN MINORITY PARTY ALSO CONTRIBUTED SUBSTANTIALLY TO THE CURRENT ATMOSPHERE OF PARTISAN RECRIMINATION AND MISTRUST. IN PARTICULAR, THEIR PERSISTENT NEEDLING OF THE OPPOSITION LEADER BACKFIRED BY RESULTING IN THE HASTILY SCHEDULED NART VOTE — A VOTE THE PRESIDENT'S PARTY HAD REPEATEDLY DEMANDED, BUT FOR WHICH THEY WERE UNPREPARED.

7. CENTRIST MEMBERS OF THE LEGISLATURE, ON BOTH SIDES OF THE AISLE, HAVE BEEN REPEATEDLY OUTMANEUVERED BY THEIR RESPECTIVE PARTY'S MORE EXTREME FLANKS. LEGISLATORS ONCE KNOWN FOR THEIR FOREIGN POLICY LEADERSHIP KEPT A STUBBORNLY QUIET PROFILE IN THE BRIEF RUN-UP TO THE VOTE. THE BIPARTISAN CONSENSUS ON THE COUNTRY'S FOREIGN POLICY, INCREASINGLY FRAYED IN RECENT YEARS, MAY SOON BE BEYOND REPAIR.

8. WHATEVER THE MERITS OR DEFECTS OF THE NART, THE FACT REMAINS THAT A TREATY OF PRIME NATIONAL — AND INTERNATIONAL — SECURITY CONCERN FELL VICTIM TO DOMESTIC POLITICAL POINT-SCORING. WITH BOTH PARTIES DETERMINED TO WIN THIS "GAME" AT ANY COST, THE POLITICAL ARENA HERE IS LIKELY TO BECOME EVEN ROUGHER AND EVER LESS RELATED TO THE SUBSTANCE OF ISSUES IN THE MONTHS AHEAD.

9. THE NART VOTE, AND THE POLITICAL HYSTERIA THAT IS BOTH ITS CAUSE AND EFFECT, REPRESENT A SAD

CHAPTER IN THIS COUNTRY'S DEMOCRATIC HISTORY —
AND IN ITS RELATIONS WITH OTHER NATIONS. IN THIS
ENVIRONMENT, IT IS NOT CLEAR TO ME THAT WE WILL
BE ABLE TO CONDUCT SERIOUS BUSINESS WITH IT ON
ANY OF THE PRESSING ISSUES ON OUR BILATERAL AND
REGIONAL AGENDA — AT LEAST UNTIL THE ELECTIONS,
AND POSSIBLY EVEN BEYOND.

LAFLEUR

1.

The Comprehensive Test Ban Treaty —
Bipartisanship Gets Nuked

American officials in Washington receiving a cable with these
words would probably shake their heads in dismay and wonder
at such a hapless government. At least, they might console themselves, it couldn't happen here. But of course it did.

President Clinton became the first world leader to sign the
Comprehensive Test Ban Treaty (CTBT) on September 24, 1996,
at the UN General Assembly. Decades after Presidents Eisenhower
and Kennedy first planted and nurtured the seeds of a nuclear
test-ban treaty, and after two and a half years of tough negotiation at the Geneva Conference on Disarmament, many in 1996
believed the CTBT was a historic milestone toward reducing the
nuclear threat and building a better, safer world. By banning all
nuclear tests for all time and setting up a sophisticated international monitoring system, the CTBT aimed to constrain nations
with nuclear weapons from building more advanced and lethal
arsenals, while preventing nonnuclear states from developing
such weapons of their own.

Reasonable people can argue about the specifics of the treaty. As the President himself emphasized, the Clinton Administration believed the treaty would benefit from a number of safeguards and reservations and had invited the Senate to add more. But whatever the substance of the CTBT debate, the process by which the treaty went down in October 1999 was shameful in the extreme, and symptomatic of a Washington in which partisanship has come to supersede policy — and even the national interest.

So what happened? There is plenty of blame to go around. The Administration, despite its strong support for the treaty and repeated calls for ratification, failed to lay the necessary groundwork with skeptical (and sometimes hostile) Republican Senators. Democrats in Congress, fueled by partisan zeal themselves, as well as the belief that the CTBT was a good campaign issue for them, taunted the Republican leadership for blocking the test-ban treaty.

On September 8, 1999, Senator Byron L. Dorgan of North Dakota accused Republican Majority Leader Trent Lott of letting down the Senate and the world by not bringing the CTBT to the floor. Throwing down the gauntlet, Dorgan, a serious man, insisted that until Lott allowed consideration of the treaty, he would obstruct Senate business. The Republican leadership responded with a jujitsu move: They agreed to the vote, and the Democrats were caught empty-handed. It turned out that a small, committed group of Republicans, led by Senator Jon Kyl of Arizona, had been rustling up votes against the treaty for almost a year — and had more than enough to block its passage.

According to *New York Times* reporter John M. Broder, "Democrats did not see the opposition to the treaty hardening in large part because relations between the parties are so bad that Democrats and Republicans often do not talk to each other about pending business. The White House's legislative affairs operation likewise did not detect the looming disaster for the President, according to a senior Administration official."[1]

Consequently, Senate Democrats pushed aggressively for the treaty, and when Senator Lott suddenly announced that he would bring up the CTBT if the Democrats agreed not to block the Senate's routine business, they felt they had to agree to his timetable or risk looking like cowards or hypocrites. Yet Lott had his finger on the fast-forward button. The treaty was to be rushed to a vote in less than two weeks, with scant time for the hearings and thoughtful debate that such an important issue surely deserved.

Caught by surprise, the Administration soon realized it did not have the votes to prevail. Frantically, it tried to persuade Senator Lott to accept a face-saving compromise. Senator Lott, under pressure from hard-line elements in his party, insisted the President guarantee he would not bring up the treaty again before his term had expired — a condition President Clinton would not accept. An eleventh-hour phone call to Senator Lott in which the President asked him to delay the treaty vote for national security reasons was rebuffed.

On Wednesday, October 13, 1999, the Senate voted down the CTBT 51–48 — a decisive, humiliating defeat. It was a highly partisan moment. It is statistically improbable that this was a vote on the merits: Not a single Democrat found the treaty's imperfections serious enough to warrant a negative vote. Only four Republicans found it worthy of support. It was the first time the Senate had rejected an international accord of this magnitude since the Treaty of Versailles.

Certainly, the specific provisions of the treaty were open to argument. It is wrong to accuse those who opposed the CTBT on its merits of being isolationist or simply partisan. But it is not wrong to accuse those members who insisted on adhering to the speeded-up, slapdash process, and who expressed their clear desire to deliver the President a failure at any cost, of sacrificing America's national interest for narrow, partisan advantage.

Why, for example, if Republicans had questions about the treaty's provisions, did they refuse to listen to possible answers? The State Department, National Security Council staff, and Department of Defense all had briefing teams ready to go up to Capitol Hill at a moment's notice to discuss the treaty in detail. Only one Republican agreed to meet with such a team. He voted for the treaty — which he probably would have done anyway.

Why, when sixty-two senators — from both parties — understood that holding the vote would be a diplomatic disaster and requested in writing that the vote be delayed, was the CTBT still hustled down the gangplank to the Senate floor?

Why, when more than 80 percent of the American people supported the treaty, were Senate Republicans so determined to destroy it?

Why did a body that prides itself on being the greatest legislative and deliberative institution in the world forgo extensive hearings and serious debate, resorting instead to puerile barbs, such as Senator Jesse Helms's outrageous characterization of British Prime Minister Tony Blair's strong support for the treaty, in which he imagined that Blair ended a conversation with Clinton saying, "Give Monica my regards"?

Why? Because in the end, a handful of Republicans cared more about their hatred of the President than about their undoubted love for their country. Because moderate Republicans were too tired, or weak, or careless, to stand in their way. Because Democrats had helped to poison the well with no antidote at hand. It was reckless, thoughtless, embarrassing behavior. The American people, and the world, deserved better.

The Senate vote had important and far-reaching consequences, despite the President's assurances that the United States would continue to abide by the treaty's terms and would uphold the moratorium on nuclear testing first declared by President Bush in 1992. It undermined our leadership on nonproliferation, weakening our leverage in persuading states like Russia and China to ratify the treaty — or India even to sign it. If India doesn't sign the treaty, neighboring Pakistan surely will not, which, given the contemporaneous military coup in Pakistan, does not bode well for stability. It undercut our relations with our allies, complicating their ability to rally support for the treaty at home and leaving the unmistakable impression that America cares only about itself. As the President said, with regard to Britain, France, and Germany, "We say, 'O.K., you guys are with us every time we need you — the Gulf War, the Balkans, always in NATO. But you ask us to do something for your common safety? Go take a hike.'"[2] It damaged nonproliferation efforts already under way, by implying that the United States lacked steadiness and political will. As one frustrated arms-control expert complained, in discussing the impact of the Senate vote on the global-inspection regime of the International Atomic Energy Agency, "Not only has the Senate said no to an added line of defense against proliferation; it has also weakened a potent defense barrier we had already constructed."[3]

Ironically, as the *New York Times* observed, "[S]ome of the worst fears expressed by treaty opponents may now be more likely to come about. . . . These include nuclear weapons development by countries that have not yet signed the treaty, erosion of America's current lead in weapons technology and secret low-yield testing by Russia or other nuclear powers."[4]

I believed the CTBT was a good treaty when it was signed, and I continue to believe that now. It isn't flawless — but the treaty's opponents were making the perfect the enemy of the good. On the issue of its verifiability, the treaty would have established a far more extensive international sensing system to detect tests than is currently available. It would have given us the possibility of on-site inspections. It would have provided a much stronger framework for bringing international pressure to bear on suspected cheaters. And at the end of the day, an American safeguard in the treaty would have permitted us to withdraw from the regime if we had evidence — which we currently do not — that we were unable to maintain the reliability of our nuclear deterrent. If there were problems in the treaty, the Senate could have fixed them. That is what the advise-and-consent process is supposed to be about.

2.

The Great Democratic Divide

There is nothing new in the politics of personal destruction. Thomas Jefferson, one of our most revered national heroes, was taken to task in the press for his alleged liaison with Sally Hemmings. Grover Cleveland's illegitimate child with Maria Halprin gave his Republican opponents fodder for one of the most memorable campaign ditties of all time: "Ma, Ma, where's my Pa? Gone to the White House, ha ha ha." (Democrats got back with a tune of their own when Cleveland won: "Hurrah for Maria! Hurrah for the kid! I voted for Cleveland, and I'm damned glad I did!"[5])

But seldom before has such virulence so trivialized serious issues. As Washington observer E. J. Dionne has written,

> The United States has fallen into a politics of accusation in which the moral annihilation of opponents is the ultimate goal. It is now

no longer enough simply to defeat, outargue or outpoll a foe. Now, the only test of victory is whether an adversary's moral standing is thoroughly shredded and destroyed. A political rival or philosophical adversary cannot be simply mistaken, foolish, impractical or wrongheaded. He or she has to be made into the moral equivalent of Hitler or Stalin, the Marquis de Sade or Al Capone.[6]

McCarthyism was more evil than what we are facing now, but it was part of a debate about an issue of great consequence: how to pursue a Cold War in which our very existence was at stake. The yellow press, led by William Randolph Hearst and Joseph Pulitzer, was irresponsible in the way it worked to drive us into the Spanish-American War, but the issue at hand would help define America's role in the world. Today, as in the CTBT debate, politics has become an end in itself, not a means of deciding great issues. All that matters to most of the participants, most of the press, and too much of the public is who wins and loses, not what the game is about. And it *has* become a game.

America is not alone in this. The modern politics in which political consultants have become more important to candidates' fortunes than political constituencies, in which polls are more important than beliefs in shaping not only their speeches but how they dress and who they say they are, in which tearing down the other guy's character and platform is more important than establishing your own has infected all the world's great democracies and most of the emerging ones, as we have seen so dangerously in Russia.

The result is the same everywhere: a deepening cynicism about government, one that transcends the healthy skepticism through which a public endeavors to hold its leaders accountable for their actions. The kind of cynicism we are seeing today breeds apathy and damages democracy. Opinion polls suggest that the favorable opinion Americans had of their government has declined steadily over the past four decades. In 1999, the Council for Excellence in Government found that while just 6 percent of adults say they feel very connected to their federal government, 29 percent — almost five times as many — feel very disconnected. This Great Divide between the public and the government is present elsewhere as well. In eleven out of fourteen mature democracies, including Britain, Canada, and Germany, surveys indicate that confidence in parliament has dropped. Trust in politicians has fallen from Italy to Japan.[7]

It is ironic that as the idea and even practice of democracy have swept most of the world in the past generation, and could spread even further in the next, the great democracies are in a position to triumph abroad, yet are losing their democratic vitality at home.

This is all too true of the United States. The Great Divide between the public and government here is vividly illustrated by our participation — or lack thereof — in the most important civic function: voting for elected officials. Of twenty leading, mature democracies, we rank next to last in electoral turnout.[8] Perhaps one reason for this dismal ranking is the sour taste recent campaigns have left in voters' mouths, with negative advertising becoming the norm and every forum or political event an opportunity for invective or argument.

The press plays into Americans' ever-dimmer view of government by focusing heavily on negative stories. During the 1992 election, more than 80 percent of network news stories on the Democratic party were unfavorable, as were 87 percent of stories about the Republicans. Nine stories out of ten about Congress were bad; stories about the federal government in general were 93 percent negative. In addition, as Harvard's Thomas Patterson points out, journalists exaggerate the extent to which politicians renege on campaign promises — which, during campaigns, they cynically portray as transparent ploys for votes. Analysis of recent administrations shows that presidents largely uphold their campaign pledges, except in cases of conflict with Congress, changes in conditions, or a higher priority commitment. Yet press coverage focuses on broken promises and on issues that require negotiation with Congress, portraying compromise as failure or retreat rather than a natural part of American democracy.[9]

Our political games are damaging our democracy not only in the long run. In the short run, as with the CTBT, they are making it almost impossible to conduct serious national business. It took years to come up with an agreement to pay our back dues to the United Nations. Meaningful advances on our trade agenda have been stymied by the President's inability to secure "fast-track" negotiating authority. Domestic issues from health care to campaign finance reform have been held hostage to partisan posturing. It may seem to some, with the Cold War over and our economy going like gangbusters, that our nation can afford irresponsibility and indulge in politics as an end in itself. That cannot be right. We must not let these be the years the locusts ate. We must not squander today's opportunity to shape tomorrow's world.

Polls show the public understands, better than do many in Washington, a point made forcefully by noted Texas philosopher Molly Ivins:

> Politics may not touch our lives, but government sure as daybreak does. . . . Back in the real world, where many parents are trying to support their children by working more than one minimum wage job; where working mothers are often caught between

aging parents who need long-term care and children who need day care; where the median income is a little more than $40,000 a year for a family of four, with half the people in this country living on less than that and lots of them on a whole lot less than that; where there is no such thing as affordable housing for the people who are not in the upper part of our hourglass economy — back in *that* world, what government does makes a big difference.[10]

Yes, the public looks at politics across a Great Divide of distrust and disdain, but that doesn't mean it doesn't want serious government, or to be led by serious politicians. A majority of government respondents to a recent survey by the Pew Research Center for the People and the Press said they believe the public wants federal programs cut back, when in fact 57 percent of the public, asked the same question, favored an activist approach to government.[11]

At the same time, this public has been reared on television and is caught up in the glitz and glamour of a culture of celebrity. As Czech novelist Ivan Klima has said, "We have a new God. The new God is called Entertainment." A burgeoning entertainment industry now seems to include Washington as much as Hollywood. It embraces our news producers and even the government itself. The line is blurred further as what historian Michael Beschloss calls "celebrity candidates," from Donald Trump to Warren Beatty, are floated with more or less seriousness in the presidential political pond.

Government officials undergoing daily scrutiny of their personal lives come to feel that their purpose is more to be good entertainment than to serve the public good. In some ways, they even bring it on themselves when they allow celebrity to become a value; the point is to be famous — it doesn't matter why. Take, for example, this dubious joke by President Clinton at the 1999 annual White House correspondents' dinner:

You may have seen a list compiled by the Newseum of the top 100 news stories of the century — everything from putting a man on the moon to the polio vaccine, ranked in order of importance. I don't mind telling you, I made the Newseum list — something about the events of last year, number 53 — 53! I mean, what does a guy have to do to make the top 50 around here?[12]

The President's punch line was followed by laughter and applause. But it is no wonder that political parody is almost a lost art — not just because our politics have become absurd almost *beyond* the point of parody, but because the politics already have become a form of show business.

It is hard for any citizen to be a passive consumer of television entertainment, in which the line between reality and docudrama has been blurred, and to be moved at the same time toward serious political activity. We cannot expect good, democratic government if we see politics as a spectator sport (and often enough a brutal, degrading one at that) rather than what politics in a healthy democracy must be: the vehicle for debating and deciding great issues, and the means by which we hold our leaders accountable and shape their actions. In our growing disdain for the disgrace that our national politics have become, we are diminishing the lifeblood of our democratic system.

It is popular to blame our plight on historical factors, for example, the high expectations of government engendered by the New Deal, expectations that no single government in an age of globalization can meet. Or the press. Or the politicians in Congress and the White House. Or the political consultants who pander to the politicians yet dominate their campaigns. Or a passive public. Or the money that has supplanted popular participation as the key to political success.

The blame, of course, rests with all of the above — with all of us.

3.

It's Your Turn

My view of all this is particularly colored by my experience as President Clinton's nominee to be the director of Central Intelligence after I had served as his national security advisor during his first term. After months of unpleasantness during the winter and spring of 1997, in which I was accused of various offenses, including membership in and even helping to found organizations of which I had never heard, I pulled my nomination. It was not the attacks themselves, although however much you tell yourself otherwise, they always do sting. I bowed out when it became clear that the chairman of the Senate Intelligence Committee had no real intention of bringing the matter to a vote in any foreseeable future, perhaps because, according to our Congressional Affairs office, there were more than enough votes to approve the nomination.

I should note here my gratitude to the number of Republicans who went beyond party loyalty and supported the nomination, notably Senator John McCain and former Senator Warren Rudman. I got to know and admire McCain when we privately met a number of times in the fall of 1996, with the approval of the President and Senator Dole, to go over the decisions the President would be making on Bosnia and other issues. That way, there would be no surprises for McCain or Dole and they could avoid uninformed statements or positions that could have made it more difficult to resolve issues both Senators cared deeply about. It was a commendable example of putting the national interest ahead of partisanship in the context of a tough political campaign.

I was very sad when I told the President of my decision and that I appreciated his support (and his clear desire that I continue the fight — in part, I hope, on the merits, and in part, I suspect, to avoid giving an opponent this modest victory). But as I left the White House at the end of that grueling day, I swore to myself not to show any bitterness. Indeed, I have now developed a retroactive affection for the chairman, since life is so enjoyable as a *former* government official. (Many years ago, when asked what his ambition was in life by the examiners who would decide whether he could join the Foreign Service, a young man who was to become one of our most distinguished career diplomats replied, "To be a retired Ambassador.")

During my ungainly dismount from the government, I often comforted myself, as I have tried to do with more than one colleague who has had to endure a public pummeling for some sin, real or imagined, with the thought that, in the end, it wasn't personal. Just business. Just the business of the press and politics. I recalled for them a scene from the movie *The Paper*. An urban official's career has been ruined by one of the paper's columnists. Drunk and despondent, the official finds the journalist in a bar and angrily asks, "Why me?" The columnist, unshaken by a pistol the official aims at him, snarls back, "Because you work for the city . . . it was your turn."

In today's government, almost everyone gets his or her turn. And usually for political reasons.

I had never met the chairman before he made my defeat his cause. At the time, the *Wall Street Journal* ran a piece reviewing the history of his political differences with the President and Vice President. The piece described the unpardonable affront that in retaliation for his switching parties to the Republicans, the

White House had failed to invite him to a ceremony honoring the National Champion football team from his home state of Alabama.

I had three particular regrets at the end. One was that I could no longer serve in the government. Another, more important: that my experience, and similar experiences of other nominees, might discourage talented men and women from a career in public service. The third was that no one had asked me, during the Committee's hearings on my nomination, whether I had anything to do with Charles Trie, the owner of a Chinese restaurant in Little Rock who helped raise hundreds of thousands of dollars for President Clinton's legal defense fund. I was prepared to pause for a moment, and then reply with apparent spontaneity, "Senator, you are Borking up the wrong Trie."

Borking is a term that entered the American lexicon in the wake of President Reagan's failed 1987 nomination of Robert Bork to the Supreme Court. The left, which opposed Bork's stances on abortion and affirmative action, led the charge in bringing him down through what many considered a heavy-handed, cheap shot–riddled public opinion campaign. The Borking Wars, in which each side tries to pay the other back for previous injuries, are our domestic political version of the actual blood debts that have perpetuated so many self-destructive conflicts abroad.

Actually, the phenomenon goes back well before Bork. I can well recall the satisfaction of my friends on the Senate Foreign Relations Committee staff as they tried to find all the damaging information they could on Henry Kissinger and other Nixon Administration appointees. They were driven by a combination of ideological opposition over the Vietnam War and partisanship pure and simple. They were Democrats. The Republicans held the White House. And they hated Richard Nixon, as so many

Republican staffers and members have hated Bill Clinton. Texas Democrat and Speaker of the House Jim Wright, who was forced from office in 1989 by an investigation into his financial dealings led by Georgia Republican Newt Gingrich, described the mood as "mindless cannibalism," and called for an end to a period in which "vengeance becomes more desirable than vindication." Yet, a few years later, when Gingrich became Speaker, Wright's party immediately launched an ethics investigation into him.[13] I was not thrilled when I heard some of the younger staff members in the White House say that my treatment would someday be avenged when "they" tried to get similar nominations through a Democratic Senate. Somehow, this cycle of tit for tat must end. We all must say, "No Mas."

It is not only that the use of holds on nominations damages the ability of the Congress to do its business in the necessary spirit of compromise. It is not only that they are aesthetically displeasing. They are another example of the growing tendency to sacrifice substance for political or personal ends. It is American interests that must ultimately pay the price. We lost the talents of Richard Holbrooke as Permanent Representative to the United Nations for nearly a year, even though when his nomination finally made it to the floor, he was confirmed by an overwhelming 81–16 after merely thirty minutes of debate. Other important nominations were held up at the end of 1999, including the nomination of John Holum as under secretary of state for international security and arms control. Holum had assumed his new position, on an acting basis, as part of the State Department reorganization championed by Senator Helms. But then the Senate wouldn't move his nomination up or down — and tried to block his ability to do his *substantive* work in the meantime. Senator Lott wrote the President in September 1999 to complain about Holum's having led the U.S. delegation in meetings to discuss the START III and ABM treaties with Russia (alleging that Holum's role, as an unconfirmed official, was both legally and politically untenable), and warned that, as a result, it was even less likely the Senate would take up his nomination anytime soon. The President replied with a letter underscoring the legal speciousness of Lott's allegations: "I have been assured that Mr. Holum has consulted closely with Department of State attorneys as to what activities are and are not permissible and has followed that advice. I further understand that all aspects of Mr. Holum's work in Moscow, which were undertaken in his role as Senior Adviser and not in his capacity as Under Secretary designate, were consistent with past practice."

Collateral damage in the nation's Borking Wars, the delays in the approval of a Dick Holbrooke, John Holum, Brian Atwood, Peter Burleigh, or many other talented American public servants damage the nation's business. It is not a game.

4.

The Congress, the White House, the Press, the Public

THE CONGRESS

Both journalists and Democrats have referred to the attitude of the Senate and House leadership as isolationism. In my view, this is not really the case. Isolationism, as in the 1930s and 1940s, represents a coherent view of the world. Its defeat in our debates and decisions of the late '40s and early '50s made it a word of opprobrium to be used for political purposes against the critics of a President's policies — by Nixon against his Democratic opponents on Vietnam, by Clintonites against their opponents in the late 1990s.

I think what we are seeing in Congress is less isolationism than insularity and carelessness — carelessness in its most literal sense: not caring about consequences. You see that carelessness in the battle that was waged over paying our arrears to the United Nations — a battle that went on so long we almost lost our vote in the UN General Assembly. You see it in the efforts to slash our already very modest international affairs budget. In 1999, for example, Republicans endeavored to carve more than $2 billion off the President's request, including funds for Middle East peace, Russian denuclearization, and 40 percent of our aid to Africa. You see it in the refusal of congressional Democrats, no less than Republicans, to grant President Clinton the fast-track trade-negotiating authority that presidents of both parties have enjoyed since the mid-1970s, and that enables us to continue the work of opening markets to American exports. You see it in Republican leaders' refusal (with some Democratic support) to allow the Pentagon to close unneeded bases, and save money that could be put to far better use in this time of budgetary restraint.

As Senator John McCain told the *National Journal,* "Fewer and fewer members of Congress today have any real interest in national security issues, and they don't appreciate that we live in a less dangerous, but far less predictable, world. That's led to an incredible increase in pork barreling in the defense budget and a lack of concern for its impact on the men and women in the military."[14]

Committed internationalists have retired or been replaced, and their inheritors have a different point of view. "I've been to Europe once — I don't need to go again," House Majority Leader Dick Armey has boasted. Armey also says he hasn't set foot off American soil since 1986.[15] Some members of Congress apparently don't even hold passports.

The current Republican chairmen of the House and Senate committees with primary authority over foreign policy and national security — Benjamin Gilman, Floyd Spence, Jesse Helms, and Strom Thurmond — have an average age of eighty. Republican Senator Richard Lugar, former chairman of the Senate Foreign Relations Committee, describes one of the consequences this way: "In fairness, Chairman Helms hasn't been feeling well, but the truth is the Committee hardly meets anymore. Back in those days [the mid 1980s], I would travel around the world at the President's request, helping take care of crises in the Philippines or Guatemala, or being on hand for the transition to democracy in Latin America or South Africa. That just doesn't happen anymore.[16]

Newt Gingrich was an internationalist, however partisan his behavior. He discussed with the President a number of times his desire to get younger members of the House abroad to acquaint them with foreign realities and get them engaged in world affairs. I believe he was a patriot who, in the end, would support what he thought was right. But his poll-tested Contract With America, the manifesto of the 1994 Republican revolution, barely mentioned national security concerns. That was not where his activist followers' interests lay.

Much of the trend is also attributable, I believe, to the increasing influence of young staff members, Democrat as well as Republican, who came of age professionally as foot soldiers in these political wars and now are achieving power as mid-level officers. They are the ones who write the questions and comments that you see busy and/or careless senators and representatives reading, sometimes obviously for the first time, on televised C-SPAN hearings. They are also the ones who draft the endless onslaught of letters to the White House, State Department, and elsewhere, demanding the internal documents on almost every decision of which they disapprove, in the hopes of finding embarrassing material that can provide ammunition for their next attacks. As a consequence, Administration officials are starting to put less in writing. They are careful about being too candid with Congress — they know not to lie, but they know also not to volunteer too much information to those who might be their enemies, because what you say or especially write can and will be held against you in the court of some congressional staffer's computer disk, and used or leaked in the most damaging way.

This is bad for how business is done within the executive branch, and — more important — between the Executive and Congress. Less written down means more room for misunderstanding and mistakes. Moreover, the constant specter of a suspicious Congress can have a chilling effect on what Administration officials say or do. Before I made one of a number of trips to Haiti in the late 1990s as an unpaid special envoy, I was told that the Senate Foreign Relations Committee staff wanted to see all my memoranda of conversation. In Haiti, I made the points that I had planned with Haitian leaders, and when I returned I provided the memoranda as instructed. Still, it was strange to have staffers hostile to Administration policies present, in effect, in the room. It goes beyond any interpretation of powers given by the Constitution to Congress.

Worse still is when congressional staff members go abroad and actively undercut our foreign-policy efforts. It is more than unseemly. Foreigners are all too quick to exploit such divisions. Yet on November 5, 1999, at a public ceremony in Bogota attended by many senior Colombian officials, the remarks of two House staff members sent to represent their absent bosses were highly partisan attacks on the Administration's antidrug efforts. One suggested that the Republican Congress was a better supporter of Colombia than the Administration. According to an internal State Department memo, their remarks included "completely false statements." In an understandable, slight departure from the customarily judicious tone used within the State Department, the memo noted that, "We do not believe that a Colombian ceremonial occasion is the place for political grandstanding by official U.S. representatives." As the memo urged, Secretary Albright sent letters of protest to the congressmen concerned. The point of the story is not to pass judgment on the judgment of the staffers. It is that, creatures of the culture on many staffs in the Congress, they apparently saw nothing wrong in taking our partisanship abroad. A perfect example of our highly imperfect times.

The Constitution is an "invitation to struggle" for power over the making of national security policies. This is a good thing. But without some basic level of trust, "struggle" descends into "war." In times of war, the Executive refuses to cooperate. Not as a decision, but as a daily habit for the sake of survival. And in a time of partisan war, members of Congress avoid all the more taking responsibility on a tough decision lest, should things go wrong, it be held against them by their political opponents.

When the Executive does not consult with Congress, members are all the more likely to lash out at the Administration, sacrificing our national interest on the altar of partisan advantage. It is a vicious circle that serves no one.

This is one reason why it is time — indeed, past the time — to reform the War Powers Resolution, which requires the President to inform the Congress when deploying American forces abroad in harm's way. If the Congress does not act within a few months, the troops must come home. In its current form, it simply doesn't serve its purpose. Beyond all the constitutional arguments, no President likes it, because it requires congressional action and complicates the ability of the President to move quickly in a crisis.

The Congress doesn't like it because it requires that its members take responsibility. The result has been that its provisions have only been triggered once, and then (regarding Lebanon) in a way that made it almost meaningless. The Resolution needs to be strengthened to force each side to act in accordance with its purpose: shared responsibility when we send our young men and women off to take life and shed their own blood. This is in the interest of Presidents: If the Congress is forced to share responsibility at the start of such enterprises, the more likely it is to be supportive when things get rough.

The partisan wars are also bad for how Congress does its own business. Whenever I have asked any of the growing numbers of senators and representatives who left the Congress on their own steam why they gave up their seats, most included their frustration and even anger at the deepening inability of an institution they loved to get things done. Men and women like Senators Warren Rudman, Nancy Kassebaum, Alan Simpson, Sam Nunn, and David Boren and representatives like Lee Hamilton, whatever their ideological views, knew how to compromise and work across the aisle. In that sense, they were the necessary center of the process. The center is not holding, and, as Yeats went on, "The best lack all conviction, while the worst are full of passionate intensity."

With all our governing institutions conducting business so badly, it's no surprise the nation's business simply is not getting done. We have no agreement on a plan to save Social Security or fix Medicare. We have no meaningful health-care reform. There is no coherent view of foreign-aid programs because the Congress didn't manage to pass a Foreign Aid Authorization bill from 1985 to the end of the century.

All sense of proportion seems to have eroded: Some senators, for example, attempted to take advantage of emergency funding legislation for our troops in Kosovo to attach a variety of anti-environmental riders — including an effort to block the Fish and Wildlife Service from listing the Alabama sturgeon as an endangered species.

THE WHITE HOUSE

It takes two to tangle, and the Congress is not alone to blame. Every White House is highly political, or should be, if it wants to get things done. President Carter's apparent disdain for politics hurt his ability to lead the Congress and the country. But in the Clinton White House, politics was too often seen as an end in itself.

At the 8:30 A.M. senior staff meeting, held every morning in the office of the Chief of Staff, I engaged in almost daily battle with the President's political staff, notably one of the Deputy Chiefs of Staff, the engaging Harold Ickes, over the relative weight to be given political considerations when they conflicted with our substantive goals. I well recall the look the political advisors would give me, as if I had somehow just fallen off the turnip truck, when I would argue for a policy that might entail some short-term political pain.

I almost never discussed politics with the President. Indeed, at my request, the President instructed me never to meet or discuss national security polling numbers with Dick Morris, the strategic advisor the President increasingly turned to in the run-up to the 1996 campaign (and who George Stephanopoulos later memorably described as the "dark buddha whose belly Clinton rubbed in desperate times").[17] The President understood that it could lead not only to bad national security policy but would be bad politics as well if his national security advisor appeared to be basing his advice on the polls. Morris felt differently, as he later wrote, "The charade, carefully preserved by Lake, that foreign policy in a democracy could or should be determined without regard to 'politics' was, in my view, nonsense."[18] (One of the few times I ran into Morris was when he was leaving the President's family quarters. As he left, I heard him say, "Good night, Bill." It was the only time I ever heard anyone, other than the President's wife, call him by his first name — and a sign of how seriously Morris took the office to which he had helped his clients aspire. Morris, for his part, claims that this particular meeting — in fact, our first — was the only time I didn't give him my "evil-rodent look."[19])

Like sex in Victorian times, the political implications of our national security decisions are seldom discussed in the polite company of the President's foreign policy advisors. (Also like sex in Victorian times, that doesn't mean it isn't on their minds.) No doubt, President Clinton was driven in part by calculations of political advantage. He is a great and natural politician. He loves people. He loves politics. He's been running for something all his life. But I believe that he learned, as we all have, or should have, that on national security issues, what succeeds best politically at home is not today's headline, but success abroad the day, or month, or week after.

This wasn't the case in October 1993, when we dispatched the USS *Harlan County* to Haiti, as discussed in chapter 3. We pulled the ship back in part because we had not prepared properly to react forcefully if the permission we had been given to land were revoked. For that, I was at fault. But we also withdrew because the President's public relations advisors were urging him to do so, to get beyond the story and remove a symbol of American weakness. We removed the symbol — and, in so doing, we also confirmed the weakness. Almost a year later, many worried that intervention in Haiti would be unpopular. This time, President Clinton held firm. He knew that if the intervention went well, as it did, his standing as President and Commander in Chief would rise — as it did. There is no question that the President's support for the Bosnia initiative in 1995 was driven not only by his horror at the suffering abroad and damage to our interests, but also by the sense that the ongoing conflict was starting to damage him at home. And there is no question that for political reasons Morris urged the President to act. I am glad that he did. So the President grasped the nettle, and the United States led NATO in bombing the Serbs to the bargaining table and forging the Dayton Accords. But I believe that if it had been the Clinton of 1993 and not the Clinton of 1995, he would have been far less likely to approve a plan that contemplated the use of unilateral force, should diplomacy have failed.

The President Clinton of 1995 recognized that the best politics is usually to find the best policy. That was not the ethos of his White House overall. But I believed it important that the National Security Council staff concentrate on policy. I believe it still should be the case. There is no way any office in the White House can be hermetically sealed off from politics. Political considerations in this (or, likely, any future) White House will never lack for representation. But the National Security Council staff needs to resist taking up that mantle as well. It should be made up of as many career officials as possible, with as much carryover between administrations as can be managed. Its experts should be good (but not necessarily gray) bureaucrats who know how to get things done and how to fight for their views, and who are serving the national interest more than the political interests of their President. Of course, the President needs men and women who will fight for his agenda. A mix of career public servants and political appointees is healthy. But a political appointee whose main credential is work on national security issues in political campaigns will have learned to think about national security issues in a partisan context. The effect of his or her advice is likely to be to lengthen the period of time during which a President, at the outset of a term, tries to make policy on the basis of campaign rhetoric rather than international reality. The world does not change every four or eight years, and sooner or later it always will force a new President to adjust the positions taken during the partisan heat of an election campaign.

Sooner is better than later.

The National Security Council must, of course, be deeply involved in preparing the President for press conferences and speeches. Likewise, with such great demands from the press, the national security advisor needs to talk to reporters and be "out there." I did on occasion give speeches and appear on TV talk shows, but, in retrospect, not often enough. I didn't want to seem to be competing with the secretary of state. I had admired the way some of my predecessors had worked effectively behind the scenes. This discreet posture was my picture of the way to do my job, and I now believe it was a mistake. Especially in the fast-paced confusion and change of the post–Cold War world, the President needs all the help he can get in explaining his policies to the nation. Even so, in public statements, the national security advisor should avoid taking partisan positions. It can diminish his or her credibility, and only adds to the distrust and division between the Executive and Congress.

THE PRESS

If either the press or the officials with which it deals were to blame for the spiral of mistrust between them, the problem would be easier to resolve. This is not a case of public servants setting out every day to manipulate or deceive the press because the officials are inherently lowlifes or "the truth is not in them," as my grandmother used to say of congenital liars. Nor is it a case of evil or callous reporters setting out every day to pry into and even ruin the lives of their prey, or to refuse to take the word of even honorable officials. Of course, some officials and some reporters would make you want to escape into shark-infested waters if they were your only companions on a desert island. But my friends on both sides — officials and journalists alike — are genuinely good people. Good people who genuinely come to hate one another, at least at times.

Why?

Within the government, the ethos of dealing with the media has certainly changed. When I was a young foreign service officer working on Vietnam in the 1960s, I would take what opportunities I could to spend time with reporters like Murray Marder of the *Washington Post*. I did it to learn from them. Marder knew more about the negotiations on Vietnam than almost any U.S. government official. I didn't have to worry in such conversations about whether he would use any betrayal of ignorance on my part against me or my colleagues. Today, with very few exceptions (Tom Friedman of the *New York Times* is one), it is hard to have a free-ranging conversation with a reporter, a conversation in which you can trade ideas and admit that a policy may or may not succeed, even off the record. Most will seize upon any admission of government fallibility like a great white shark tasting blood.

In earlier days, what to say to the press was generally the last item, if it was present at all, on the agenda of government meetings. Now it is, or should be, always on the agenda. And too often, the question is not, "How much can we tell them?" It is how best to discipline the officials present and their press spokespeople into a united front against the enemy. Why? Survival, both personal and official. Senior officials know that if they do not try to spin stories themselves, their colleagues will. Reporters will use these various spins to put their own, generally negative, twist on the resulting stories. Thus more spinners are hired in all the departments. More political consultants are given senior jobs to protect the flanks of the senior officials. And partisan fury is further fueled, as all of this contributes to what has become a four-year campaign for the next presidency.

Reporters, meanwhile, as the objects of this dizzying spin-fest (which need not be untruthful, in the narrowest sense of honesty), have lost any confidence in the word of most of the officials with whom they deal. (For the more cynical reporters, good spinning has become the object of admiration and even positive pieces about the spinners. The reporters know they are being had, but at least the spin provides a good story.) Competitive pressures in a much larger press corps make them less willing than they were in the previous generation to settle for a positive story, even if it happens to be true.

In short, the ethos of the Washington press corps has changed. Two examples help show what I mean.

In 1993, one of the best White House reporters called me about some rumor of a failure by the State Department to act on a presidential instruction. I called the State Department, double-checked the answer, and called the reporter back to report the good news: The instruction had been carried out and, miraculously, the approach was working! The response? Okay, the story would be dropped. "Wait a minute," I naively replied. "Why not a story on this modest success?" "Not my job," I was told. The reporter was there to find out what we were doing wrong, not to report it when we got it right. "Isn't it news — big news, even," I asked ironically, "when the government does something that's working? Isn't 'news' something new and perhaps important, good as well as bad?"

"No," I was told. "Our job is to hold you accountable for what you do wrong." This reporter almost never erred. This was a highly respected reporter. And this conversation illustrated a fundamental problem. Decisions on which stories to print or air ought to be based on some effort to present what is *true*, whether good or bad. The truth, as written by human beings, can never be objective, but it can be *the* objective. In the war between government officials and the press, truth has become the most important casualty.

Here's the second example: Through a series of mistakes and my own inattention, for a considerable period of time I failed to divest a number of stocks that might have been affected by government decisions. I had said I wanted them sold rather than held in a blind trust. I thought they had been sold and when I learned I was wrong, I divested them right away. The White House counsel referred the matter to the Department of Justice, as required.

Later, when I was nominated to be the director of Central Intelligence, Bob Woodward of the *Washington Post* received a tip about the matter. He called me, and I referred him to the lawyer I had hired to deal with the investigation. Woodward called me back to say he thought the story was [expletive deleted], and he wasn't going to use it. His tipster (at the lower reaches of the FBI, I was later told by someone else) then called a Woodward-wannabe, who handled the matter differently. I was given a chance to deny a charge of malfeasance. But no independent judgment of the truth or importance of the matter would be made, and the story was aired, to my mortification. (I later settled the case, extremely reluctantly, to avoid an expensive trial. My mistake did place me in violation of the law, even if, as the Justice Department agreed, there was no evidence that my violation was intentional.)

Woodward's approach was fundamentally different from that of his up-and-coming imitators. Remember the scene in *All the President's Men* where the editor, Ben Bradlee (Jason Robards), grills Woodward and Bernstein (Robert Redford and Dustin Hoffman) about the veracity of their sources, i.e., the *truth* of the story, before he will print it? Today, the job definition of the mainstream investigative reporter is easier: Take the charge, call the alleged miscreant and get the denial or explanation, and print both. Let the reader decide which is true.

The effect of all this is very serious. One result, of course, is the damage done to individual reputations. More important is the effect on the confidence of the public in both government and the press. Perhaps most important, and also least recognized, is that government officials are becoming *less* accountable for their actions. After a while, all officials who come under assault for their personal or official actions (and that, after all, is most senior officials), develop a thicker skin. They experience a kind of psychic numbing. One starts to feel, Whatever I do, I'll get hit. And it's not just me. Everyone is getting it. So I should try not to take it as seriously as my wounded pride tells me I should. If almost everyone is accused of something, the allegations stick to almost no one. If the press judges so many officials guilty, the public will lose track of who actually is, while within the government, officials themselves become, or try to be, almost indifferent to the assault. The result, paradoxically, as the press presses its attacks, is that it increasingly is failing to carry out its primary function: to accurately describe and hold the government accountable for its actions, so that the public may make its democratic decisions on an informed basis.

Reporters don't blame their problems only on the spinning and lies of our officials. Indeed, they know something is wrong with their own estate, and the best of them often write about it. What is wrong? In part, it is what Bill Kovach and Tom Rosenstiel of the Committee of Concerned Journalists call a Mixed Media Culture, in which tabloid trash and serious journalism have converged as never before. As they explain, our fourth estate now consists of

> a newly diversified mass media in which the cultures of entertainment, infotainment, argument, analysis, tabloid and mainstream press not only work side by side but intermingle and merge. It is a culture in which Matt Drudge sits alongside William Safire on *Meet the Press* and Ted Koppel talks about the nuances of oral sex, in which *Hard Copy* and CBS News jostle for camera position outside the federal grand jury to hear from a special prosecutor.[20]

Kovach and Rosenstiel conclude that the Mixed Media Culture — with its "continuous news cycle, the growing power of sources over reporters, varying standards of journalism, and a fascination with inexpensive, polarizing argument" — is eroding the core function of journalism to provide a truthful account of the day's events and, in so doing, is contributing to the public's sense of disconnection — not reducing it.

The emergence of CNN and the twenty-four-hour news cycle may be particularly important. The written press is no longer able to compete on breaking news, so it tends to explain more than simply report. Editorials masquerading as news. In any case, reporters also feel less inclined to disguise their own views. In the old days, if I wanted to know what a reporter really thought on policy or politics, I would need to catch him or her at an unguarded moment of inebriation. Today, all I need to do is watch him or her on a television talk show. *Newsweek* even offers incentives to its reporters to appear on radio and TV.[21] Happily, this tilt toward punditry is not true of all reporters by any means.

Bob Kaiser, senior correspondent at the *Washington Post*, points out that even he does not know the political views of Dan Balz, the paper's excellent political reporter.

The Internet also is playing a role, with the largely unregulated cyberterrain providing fertile soil for rumor and gossip to take root. With no overarching editors to filter content, individuals like Matt Drudge can set up shop and share whatever anonymous scoop or slam or sleaze they please — in Drudge's case, with roughly a million reader hits on his Web page each day. The result is what Kovach and Rosenstiel call "a kind of Gresham's Law of Journalism," in which bad allegations crowd out good stories. Heightened competition among so many media sources drives mainstream journals that would not ordinarily run an allegation to go with the story once it has broken somewhere else; in other words, the story, not the content, *is* the story. Once that barrier has broken down, garbage enters the mainstream.

In 1964, J. Edgar Hoover attempted to ruin Martin Luther King, Jr., by shopping secret tape transcripts of King cheating on his wife to various reporters in Washington. Not a single journalist took the bait, even those who were no fans of King. But imagine, as Kovach and Rosenstiel do, what would have happened in the current media climate. "Would rumor of King's extramarital activities be 'Issue One' on *The McLaughlin Group*? Or ferried into a debate on talk radio or *Crossfire*?"[22] The reputation of one of the most influential Americans of our time would have been dragged through the mud. How might history have been affected?

And of course, there is the omnipresent and intensified commercial pressure that pushes news outlets to new extremes in an attempt to woo or thrill the public — a public with more choices, and perhaps less incentive, for tuning in to the news in the post–Cold War world. Who cares if readers, listeners, or watchers are disgusted by the messenger; they are naturally titillated by filth. Aren't we all?

What are some of the results of the new news environment?

First, as the number of cable television stations has exploded, so has the need for round-the-clock news to fill the endless cycle — a need that is being fed by talking heads and government spinners. We're even seeing spinners spiral straight to broadcast celebrity, with former White House spokesman George Stephanopoulos now a commentator on ABC News. But a twenty-four-hour news cycle puts a strain on serious reporting. Stagecraft and shouting are superseding substance to serve the god of entertainment.

Second is what David Ignatius aptly describes as "sequential hysteria," in which each story gets its fifteen minutes of fame and is then nearly forgotten. As Ignatius writes, "Nothing is done about a problem until it reaches this critical 'meltdown' state — and then, for a few brief days or weeks, too much is done. Then it's back to normal inattention. It's like a dinner party where there's only one conversation going on at any given time — a screaming, hysterical conversation at that."[23]

Third is the diminishing amount of time and space accorded to international news. A survey by Claude Moisy for Harvard University's Joan Shorenstein Center found that the time devoted to foreign news on U.S. networks dropped from 45 percent in the 1970s to 13.5 percent by 1995.[24] NBC's *Nightly News* focused only 609 minutes on international news stories in the entire year of 1997. What time the media does spend on the world, it tends to concentrate on a few key stories, leaving much global news uncovered.

Fourth, we see fewer media resources devoted to the weighty, but unglamorous, issues that actually affect our lives. When Princess Diana died, TV anchors and correspondents were hastily put on planes to London and Paris. Newspapers and magazines included special sections or editions. The funeral was broadcast in full. But much of international affairs does not make for a sexy story — especially economic news, which is hard to tell with pictures. And yet, as discussed above, financial crisis in Brazil can have a much greater impact on my life or yours than can a war in the Balkans, much less the death of a member of the British royal family.

On the positive side, the expansion of cable TV and the Internet means that those with a serious interest or need can keep close tabs on specific foreign news. Bloomberg monitors a twenty-four-hour stock market for traders. There are specialty newsletters on energy, emerging markets, the environment, and more. But this also underscores the growing gap between the electronically enfranchised and the rest of the American public, between the elite and the uninterested.

Over time, we could see the final death of the general news industry as it is supplanted by the specialty news outlets on the Web and cable TV, with "prime-time news" giving way to pure entertainment. This, in turn, will strike another blow at what we proclaim as our most basic principle: an inclusive, active democracy of and by and for the people. All the people.

THE PUBLIC

Ironically, studies show not only increasing public distaste for politicians, the press, and what the press does to our political leaders. They also show that the press and political leaders underestimate the public when it comes to the substance of our foreign policies. The press tends to focus its coverage of candidates on controversies and slip-ups rather than the content of this or that speech. And just as the public peers at Washington across the great democratic divide, so in Washington, officials are undemocratically skeptical of the ability of the public to decide what is or is not in its interest.

Consider the astonishing results of an April 1998 Pew Research Center survey of top government officials:

> Among members of Congress, just 31% think Americans know enough about issues to make wise decisions about public policy. Even fewer political appointees (13%) and senior civil servants (14%) feel this way. Those in the executive branch also have far less confidence than members of Congress in the public's decision making on Election Day. Just 34% of presidential appointees and career civil servants express a great deal of confidence in this regard, compared to 64% of those in Congress.[25]

Polls also show that the public is more committed to American global engagement than its leaders seem to believe. A 1999 survey by the Chicago Council on Foreign Relations (CFR) found that 61 percent of Americans favor an active part for the United States in world affairs. Among those who say that globalization is "mostly good" for the United States, the number is even higher at 72 percent.

The public also is more favorable toward the United Nations than Washington's behavior would suggest. The Chicago CFR poll found that 57 percent favor U.S. participation in UN peacekeeping forces. A plurality of the public (45 percent) supports strengthening the United Nations as a very important foreign-policy goal and more believe the United States should pay its UN dues.

For the first time since 1978, the Chicago poll indicates, there is more public support for expanding defense spending than for reducing it, though a plurality of Americans would like it to stay the same.[26] Surveys also show that the American public is willing to accept more casualties for a good cause than most in Washington believe. For example, a May 1999 study by the Program on International Policy Attitudes found that if NATO undertook a more extensive operation in Kosovo and American troops were killed, only a minority would want to end the operation, while most would want to persist and would even favor "beefing up forces or striking back hard."[27]

Yet elected officials in Washington persist in misreading the public will, and using what they perceive as the public's neo-isolationism to justify attempts to roll back America's global role. As Steven Kull and I. M. Destler suggest in their 1999 book, *Misreading the Public: The Myth of a New Isolationism*, policy practitioners tend to equate the public's dissatisfaction with America's burden's as a desire for disengagement, when in fact the public simply desires more international burden sharing. Similarly, practitioners take public criticism of foreign-aid spending levels as opposition to programs in principle, when in fact the criticism generally reflects an exaggerated view of the spending. Indeed, "when asked to distribute resources, most Americans assign more to foreign aid than is currently allocated."[28]

This communication gap between practitioners and the public can have specific and damaging consequences. It led us to be extraordinarily hesitant in taking on Senator Helms and others who opposed paying back what we owed the United Nations. Why wasn't the Administration more forceful, when poll after poll shows the majority of Americans strongly support the United Nations and America's participation in it, favor strengthening the United Nations, do not fear it is eroding our sovereignty, wanted to pay the money we owed, and greatly prefer using military force through the UN than shouldering all the costs and risks ourselves? Perhaps because of a fear that the chairman would vent his wrath by holding up nominations and making trouble on other issues, supported always by the Senate leadership. This had to be weighed, of course. But giving in to hostage taking under any circumstance can simply lead to more — as it did with Chairman Helms.

Washington's misperception of public attitudes also contributed to unnecessary caution in contemplating the use of ground troops in Kosovo to put muscle behind our diplomacy. On the one hand, we were talking tough, comparing Milosevic to Hitler. On the other, we wouldn't commit our ground troops to defeat him — a gap between rhetoric and reality that our European allies resented, and that may have given Milosevic confidence to continue his assault.

The mistaken sense that the public will not tolerate even very limited American casualties in combat has implications for how we design our military strategies — and even force structure itself. There is also the danger that our adversaries will be encouraged to exploit our sensitivity to combat casualties, believing that a few widely publicized, and hopefully humiliating, American deaths will cause us to turn tail and run. While our military has performed brilliantly in mission after mission of "immaculate coercion" through the air, we have to accept that war fighting is a dangerous, deadly business. Sooner or later there will be another conflict in which we have to put our men and women on the ground, with all the risks that implies.

On this and other issues, in the end, our leaders must learn again to trust the best in our public opinion rather than, on the advice of their political consultants, to pander to the worst. To be plain: Our leaders must lead.

The Big Dog Threatened

As we left the room, I remember thinking to myself that it's great to be an American.

It was August 1995. I was in Paris with a delegation of U.S. officials to present the President's new plan for ending the fighting in Bosnia. The plan had been well received in London and Bonn. At the heart of my message there and in other European capitals was this: The United States would act with or without others. The chances of success were greatest if our allies joined us — but we *would* proceed, in any case. We were taking the lead. But leadership involved building a partnership of like-minded nations.

In the end, after my meeting in Paris, the French were to come on board, with all the others we approached. But at the meeting with the French, one particularly legalistic, argumentative official had asked how they could be so sure of American intentions. Didn't the Congress make foreign policy, not this President?

I let myself show anger, leaned across the table, told him to have no doubt about our will to act — and offered to send him a copy of our Constitution if he questioned the President's authority. He subsided as Jean-David Levitte, my French counterpart and an extraordinarily sensible and skilled diplomat, assured me that the French took us at our word.

As we left, I reflected that it was hardly my skill that was moving the allies behind us. This was an exercise of American influence; the U.S. officials traveling with me called it the big dog barking as we flew from stop to stop — and it was a great feeling to be speaking for America. The exercise of American power would move others and, we hoped, even the mountain of Bosnia.

These *are* great times to be an American. We won the Cold War. At the beginning of a new century, we are prosperous and at peace. The darkest clouds of nuclear holocaust have been lifted. If you are an American reading this book, you live in the most powerful nation in human history.

Not only is our military power overwhelming. America's economic strength is the envy of the world. We have the lowest combined rates of unemployment and inflation in three decades. Employment rose by 2.9 million in 1998 alone — an average rate of 242,000 new jobs every month. At the same time, the federal government recorded its first unified budget surplus since 1969.[1] Abroad, American capital is financing much of the revolution in information technology and growth of the Internet. At least at the turn of the century, most electronic roads lead to the United States.

Diplomatically, whether we like it or not, the road to resolution for almost every major problem, no matter where on the globe it occurs, runs through Washington, D.C. Israeli president Rabin and Palestinian chairman Arafat chose the White House lawn for their historic handshake of peace. Determined American diplomacy, backed by U.S.-led air strikes, brought Bosnia's Serbs to the negotiating table and paved the way to the Dayton Accords. Even when America doesn't sit in the driver's seat, our support is fundamental. In 1996, as Canada put together a stand-by humanitarian mission for Eastern Zaire, they counted on us for close support — because only America had the intelligence, lift, and logistics capabilities to get the mission on its feet.

The ideals on which America was founded are ascendant around the world, and as democracy and open societies spread, the magnetic pull of American culture grows more powerful than ever. Emphasizing individuality, it fits well with the ways in which new technologies — most notably the personal computer — empower the individual. You can find Kentucky Fried Chicken in Moscow and Burger King in Seoul. Young Chinese frequent Internet cafes and sport Michael Jordan T-shirts. In South Korea, when President Kim Dae-Jung was running for office, his advisors suggested a photo opportunity of the candidate connecting with real people. So Kim went out to join some laborers in their daily work — wearing a Los Angeles Dodgers baseball cap. Can you imagine an American politician stumping for votes with a foreign logo?

But we should beware of hubris in accepting the new conventional wisdom: that contemporary America is the model for all the world. A decade ago, the conventional wisdom held Japan as the model for the future. We, like the world, are a work in progress. It cannot be otherwise when one in five American children lives in a family receiving food stamps. One in six has no health insurance. And in 1997 alone, 4,205 children and teens lost their lives to gunfire — the equivalent of one child every two hours.[2]

Complacency can lead us to policies of merely reacting to events rather than trying to shape them, to thinking tactically rather than strategically. It is all too easy, and sometimes all too tempting, to let emergencies dictate the agenda. Crises inevitably crowd the headlines. They must be dealt with as they arise. In government, business, or daily life, we find that the urgent tends to obscure the important.

Every Administration inherits tough problems. The Clinton Administration was no different. In 1993, our in-boxes spilled over with immediate crises, like Haiti, Bosnia, Iraq, Somalia, and North Korea. By the end of 1996, while none of these matters had disappeared, they were close to under control.

No one should argue that we handled all these matters perfectly. Of course, we did not. But in four years' time, we transformed these issues from all-consuming crises to more manageable problems. This created the possibility to concentrate on the longer-term, strategic threats and problems facing us in the post–Cold War world. During 1993–96 we made a start on a number of strategic fronts, and progress in those areas has continued. We have drawn up the blueprints, laid the cornerstones, and even built the ground floors of some key new foreign-policy structures.

In Europe, we established the Partnership for Peace and led the way to open NATO's doors to new democracies. This could and should be a central strand in an effort to create, over the next generation, a peaceful, undivided, democratic Europe — including Russia. In Asia, we worked for a new stability by establishing a strategic dialogue with the People's Republic of China while making clear that any attack on Taiwan would have grave consequences. We updated our security relations with Japan while working with the South Koreans on an initiative for lasting peace on the peninsula. We addressed the threat of weapons of mass destruction, including extending indefinitely the Non-Proliferation Treaty to stop the spread of nuclear weapons and signing the Comprehensive Test Ban Treaty to end nuclear testing for all time. President Clinton led the most dramatic changes in the world trading system since the end of World War II, through more than two hundred trade agreements — including GATT,

NAFTA, APEC, and the Summit of the Americas — to bring down barriers to American products.

Perhaps most important, the President set as the central strategic objective of the United States the promotion of democracy and open markets abroad. This is not mere rhetoric. We have a tremendous interest in the success of the democratic revolution that has helped to define our era. It is by no means assured. For example, new democracies bear a necessary but terrible burden when trying to carry out the economic reforms necessary to build their economies. Those reforms, especially as often dictated by the International Monetary Fund, can hurt the poor while advantaging the rich (including any local kleptocracy that feeds on the opportunities for corruption that accompany such reforms). This can lead to widespread disillusion not only with the reforms, but about the new democracy as well. "I voted," many may ask, "and now where are the benefits the candidates promised?" The first elected President in a nation's history, approaching reelection, may be more than tempted either to cut back on the economic reforms or even to tamper with the electoral process. This is one of the central challenges facing the international community, and the United States as its leader: how to make economic reforms politically sustainable. Cushioning their impact on the poor is both a great moral and a great strategic issue.

There is another reason why we mustn't simply relax and enjoy ourselves in these relatively good times. Even if we try to act strategically, the many threats we face abroad cannot be addressed if we think only along traditional lines in our national security discussions — or if we assume that our power will allow us to seek unilateral solutions to multinational problems. In an age of globalization, this is a recipe for disaster.

Going Global

Globalization is a simple catchword for an overarching phenomenon: the linkage, even fusion, around the world of communications and financial systems. This has enabled exponential growth in exchanges of goods, services, capital, and ideas across international borders. You see its evidence every day, from the food on your table to the car you drive, the ATM machine on the corner, or the satellite dish on your roof.

Some would argue, accurately, that none of these phenomena is really new. Economic interdependence has been a fact of life since the Phoenicians traded across the Mediterranean thousands of years ago. What *is* new are the pace and scope of change, driven by a technology revolution. A stunning fact: Traders, buyers, and investors move well over a trillion dollars around the world every day.[3] The daily turnover on the currency markets is greater than the entire global stock of official foreign-exchange reserves.[4]

Or take the Internet. In 1990, only a few people, mostly academics, had even heard of it. By 1998, the Net linked more than 150 million users around the world. From the mid-1980s to the late 1990s, the number of people logging onto the Internet doubled every year. Predictions are that by early in this century, more than 300 million people will be on-line.[5] That's more than the entire population of the United States of America. (This is a huge number, but only a fraction of the world's population — and the electronically disenfranchised are at a real competitive disadvantage. The hope is that the Internet and new technologies like "streaming video" can be used to bring electronic classrooms to poorer regions and nations, thus helping them to catch up to their better-trained, more productive competitors.)

The benefits are extraordinary for small or rural entrepreneurs. Imagine you run a business from home, far from a city center.

With a laptop computer and a $100 modem, you can put up a Web page for less than the cost of renting a billboard — and potentially catch the eye of millions of consumers cruising the information superhighway. You can sell to customers halfway around the world and put foreign supplies at your fingertips — without the transactional costs and barriers that might have kept you out of trade until now. Such opportunities were unthinkable only a decade ago.

With opportunity comes danger. I have already addressed some of the most dramatic. If you are not convinced, consider also this more mundane example: With some two million people crossing an international border every day — and 115.5 million visitors to the United States in 1996 alone — it is harder to shield and sequester ourselves from dangerous infectious diseases. Anytime, anywhere that anyone travels, invisible germs tag along. AIDS, which originated in Africa, became the number-one killer of American men aged fifteen to forty-five. Mosquitoes capable of carrying dengue fever, viral encephalitis, and yellow fever journeyed to the United States in 1985 on tires imported from Asia.[6] "Airport malaria" has entered the annals of public-health problems, as travelers pick up and take home diseases like gift shop souvenirs. Infectious disease expert Laurie Garrett points out, "Even before commercial air travel, swine flu in 1918–19 managed to circumnavigate the planet five times in 18 months, killing 22 million people, 500,000 in the United States."[7] Imagine how many lives a virulent flu could claim today, with airlines carrying well over a billion passengers each year.[8]

Such dangers menace us not only as individuals, but as a nation. The fact is that every day, in many different ways, the forces of globalization are eroding our national sovereignty, our democratic ability to manage our own affairs. Consider:

- The shift to electronic transactions provides a challenge to our tax regulation. It could lead to reduced tax bases or an increasing burden on individuals and technologically challenged companies.

- Trade used to be negotiated among sovereign governments. Now, a large and growing percentage of international trade occurs not between national entities but within single transnational corporations. This gives the corporate sector, and individual firms, unprecedented influence in setting the agenda on international trade-and-finance negotiations. Power is shifting from the seat of our government to the seats at the boardroom table. About half the world's one hundred largest economies are corporations, not nations. General Motors' sales are larger than the GNP of Denmark, Microsoft's still larger.

- A foreign corporation, beyond the reach of any government, can decide to open its latest plant in Anytown USA. This action will generate employment for some Americans, but it also could drive local firms out of business, costing other workers their jobs. And when that plant decides to relocate in search of cheaper labor, cutting off in one fell swoop a major source of community income, who in City Hall or on Capitol Hill will be able to make it stay?

- Fifteen years ago, high-resolution satellite photography was under exclusive government control. Even the fact that our satellites took such photos was a highly (but badly) guarded secret. Today, if you have the money to pay, satellite photos with one-meter resolution can be had on the open market — available even to potential military enemies.

- For good or ill, with new information empowering ordinary citizens to judge our government's performance more keenly, technology enabling local groups to forge vast alliances across borders, and a global economy enhancing the importance and influence of firms, a whole host of new actors is challenging, confronting, and sometimes competing with governments on turf that was once their exclusive domain. The international campaign on land mines, coordinated through computer links from a house in Vermont, forced an issue on many governments that would rather have avoided it.

- Most fundamentally, globalization has constricted not only national economic policies but the nature of democratic politics as well. As Asia learned in the mid-1990s, the global market imposes its discipline on nations little less than national markets do on states and provinces. This narrows the range of economic policies any government can pursue over any length of time if they are not to tempt disaster. The political corollary: The range of relevant, mainstream political debate has narrowed as well. You could see this in the elections of the mid- and late 1990s not only in the United States but in the United Kingdom, France, Germany, Japan, and South Korea as well.
- Complicating the task of democratic governance in our own and other nations is the fact that through expanding global communications, elites around the world are developing ties to each other that rival their bonds to the disadvantaged in their own societies.

To save our sovereignty, to retain our capacity to decide our future, we have to accept the fact that the dangerous effects of globalization, as outlined in this book, can only be addressed in concert with other nations. Yet here in Washington, mainstream political figures on both the right and the left, and in both our political parties, are putting our power and our future at risk. Some are "America First" nationalists. Some are chest-thumping unilateralists. Many of them are back-door isolationists who mouth the rhetoric of international leadership but refuse to appropriate the resources that leadership demands.

You can see it in the fight they wage every year against funding for foreign affairs — as if it were a back-breaking taxpayer burden, instead of about 1 percent of our total national budget. You can see it in their resistance to America's role in military coalitions — as if it were cheaper in blood and treasure to tackle each mission alone. You can see it in their refusal to pay all that we owe the United Nations — an organization America was instrumental in creating. Imperfect as it is, the UN serves our interests.

Those obsessed with saving America's sovereignty from the clutches of international institutions are missing the fundamental point about the new world. America's sovereignty *is* being lost. To some degree, it is lost to the UN and other international bodies. But to a far greater degree, America's sovereignty is being lost to the forces of globalization. The unilateralists can try to build all the walls and barriers they want. They can insist that America act alone or not at all. But many of the threats we face today, such as currency crises, international crime, drug flows, terrorism, AIDS, and pollution, cannot be defeated single-handedly or shut out at the border. Turning our backs will not turn back the clock. It will only leave us more vulnerable.

If we want to protect the safety and well-being of our people — the ultimate test of any nation's sovereignty — the wisest course is to join our strength with others who share our goals. For the simple truth is this: If we don't give up some of our sovereignty through positive cooperation with others, we will give up far more to the unregulated global forces that are already eroding our borders and shaping our lives.

What do I mean by such cooperation? For example:

Modern transnational criminals work together more closely than ever; governments should as well. To combat cybercrime, we need international agreements to assist "transborder searches" for the computers used in intrusions here and to ensure that evidence is not destroyed in such cases. At the very least, governments should share more information on criminal gangs on a regular, day-to-day basis. Mayor Rudolph Giuliani has required New York police precincts to exchange information daily, and to use computers and telecommunications to track and interpret criminal trends. Why can't governments do so internationally?

To address the spread of dangerous nuclear, chemical, and biological materials,we should toughen international nonproliferation regimes and give them teeth where necessary. For example, as written, the Chemical Weapons Convention and the Biological Weapons Convention apply to states, not to individuals. Harvard's Matthew Meselson and a number of colleagues from the United States and other nations have developed a draft convention that would make violations of the Chemical and Biological Weapons Conventions crimes under international law — as aircraft hijacking is now. Surely, development or possession of these weapons is far the more serious offense. The Biological Weapons Convention also needs better enforcement provisions — in particular, on-site inspections.

Of course, adopting and adhering to common regimes, from weapons conventions to extradition treaties, requires individual nations to adapt their domestic laws. This may be hard for the United States, as our laws typically are freer than most. The fight against international crime can raise real questions of sovereignty and civil liberties concerns. But ask yourself which loss of sovereignty you prefer — small concessions to law enforcement or sweeping surrenders to criminals.

America must also do its part in peacekeeping operations, working whenever possible through the United Nations. If we do not, our interests suffer, our leadership diminishes, and innocent people die. And I know from experience that while peacekeeping operations take up only a small fraction of the Pentagon's budget, the issues they are designed to address (the Bosnias, Somalias, Haitis, Kosovos) take up a very large fraction of a President's time and worry.

Our leadership is vital to such operations. No other nation can provide the experience and capacities we can. America's willingness to do its part can make or break a mission. This is especially true with regard to logistics and intelligence support, where our resources and capabilities are unparalleled. Even when other nations are prepared to commit troops, they may need the United States to fly them in.

Yet despite our extraordinary military might and proven expertise, the United States provides only about 4 percent of personnel for UN peacekeeping operations. We rank behind Fiji, Ireland, and Nepal in overall troop contributions and have taken part in fewer missions than Pakistan, Poland, and Ghana. What accounts for this hesitancy? The fact is, peacekeeping operations are extremely controversial. Some argue against risking American lives when no vital interests are at stake. Others allege that peacekeeping missions so sap resources or compromise readiness as to weaken our national defenses beyond repair. And still others fear that missions of peace undermine the warrior ethos: "Can Peacekeepers Make War?" asked a skeptical *US News and World Report* in January 1998. And even if they can, is peacekeeping a sensible use of their time and talent?

Concern over U.S. participation in peacekeeping is not a new phenomenon. While the United States sent aircraft, military observers, pilots, radio operators, and mediators to the first UN observer mission in Palestine in 1948, we did not contribute that many military officials to a UN mission again until the early 1990s.[9] Under President Reagan, U.S. support for the United

Nations, much less American participation in UN peacekeeping operations, dwindled. No new UN peace operations were approved from 1978 to 1988. (Even Ronald Reagan, however, called for "a standing UN force, an army of conscience — that is fully equipped and prepared to carve out humanitarian sanctuaries through force if necessary."[10]) President Bush clearly saw the United Nations' potential to advance American interests. In addition to pledging to "explore new ways to ensure adequate American financial support for UN peacekeeping," his Administration supported the start of twelve new peace operations, and Bush sent a large U.S. field hospital unit to Croatia and observers to Cambodia, Kuwait, and Western Sahara.[11]

Indeed, the scope of peacekeeping operations has accelerated dramatically since the Cold War's end. Of the forty-nine UN peace operations since 1948, thirty-six were created between 1988 and 1998. As of December 1999, there were seventeen UN peacekeeping operations around the world, as well as the Multinational Force in the Sinai, the NATO mission in Bosnia, the West African force in Sierra Leone, and the Australians and others in East Timor.

Presidents Bush and Clinton both have recognized that peacekeeping efforts serve our interests and respond to the best instincts of the American people. Future Presidents are very likely to reach the same conclusion. They are also likely to recognize that peacekeeping through the United Nations is a cost-effective investment. For every dollar that all governments spent on military activities in 1997, less than a quarter of a cent went to UN peacekeeping. And the American share of UN peacekeeping in 1999 was less than $1.22 per U.S. citizen — about the cost of a cup of coffee at Starbucks.[12] That is why even our allies have been so frustrated by the American delays in paying our bills at the United Nations.

In the mid-1990s, during a conversation with my counterpart in London, he suddenly launched into a denunciation of our indebtedness at the UN. He concluded with such a good line that I asked him, as the friend he was, not to repeat it. He agreed, and did not. But later, when Prime Minister Major addressed the United Nations, *he* did. Looking at the American delegation, he said pointedly: "It is not suitable for member states to enjoy representation without taxation."

This bit of ironic British humor contained a broad, central truth. No matter how powerful we may be, we cannot force our way on every issue, especially at a cut-rate price. So the challenge before Washington is twofold: both to move beyond its present petty partisanship and also to lead a powerful America into the kinds of foreign partnerships that can help preserve our national sovereignty.

From "Gotcha" Back to Governing

In December 1999, angry demonstrators ranging from anarchists to steelworkers overran Seattle in protest against the World Trade Organization, which was holding its annual conference. While most protesters were peaceful, some — apparently, in accordance with long-held plans — smashed shop fronts and looted stores, prompting police to resort to pepper spray and tear gas. Nightly footage of rampaging protesters confronting police garbed, as one observer put it, like Ninja Turtles, was an embarrassment for Seattle and America as a whole. The WTO opening ceremonies were canceled because numerous delegates, including members of the U.S. team, were unable to leave their hotels.

The meeting ended earlier than intended without making any progress on setting the agenda for the next round of global trade talks. It represented a setback to American leadership not only on market opening but also on the development of further rules governing trade and related matters — including labor standards and the environment, among the very issues of greatest concern to the demonstrators.

Domestic politics had a hand in the Seattle debacle, in particular the reluctance of the White House to offend either organized labor or environmental activists in the midst of the Gore presidential campaign. But in a larger sense Seattle was an indication of how partisanship in Washington has distracted both parties from the crucial issues before us. Here was an organization, the WTO, whose goals enjoy a broad (if by no means universal) adherence from both parties. Yet where was the bipartisan alliance that could have driven the more destructive voices of protest to the margins, where they belong? Of course there are lively disputes to be had about the nature of our participation in international trade negotiations, including the necessary role for labor and environmental concerns. In a world of politics whose purpose is policy making, they would be the subject of serious dialogue among our elected leaders, and thoughtful discussion in the press. Instead, the American people were treated to a debate whose most prominent members were masked vandals and riot-control police.

It is ironic that so many of the demonstrators were seeking an end to an international institution that can regulate the trade they fear. Trade will continue, with less rather than more regulation thanks to the delays Seattle brought about. Fewer rules will mean more power to the already powerful, at the expense of poorer nations. But chanting "Hey hey, ho ho, the WTO has got to go," these unilateralists of the left are caught in a dangerous time warp. As one protester said, "We have succeeded in turning back the invasion of the WTO into domestic policy decisions."[13] Jesse Helms couldn't have put it better in one of his statements opposing the flow of textiles into the United States — a flow that greatly benefits our consumers. In fact, unilateralists and nationalists on the right and left are cut from the same cloth. If they prevail, the effect will not be to make America stronger, richer, or more secure, as they intend. Indeed, none of the major challenges we face today can be entirely met on our own.

We cannot prevent rogue nations or terrorists from endangering our people without the cooperation of like-minded nations to help us keep dangerous weapons and materials from falling into the wrong hands, to share information about suspicious activities, to sanction unacceptable behavior, to extradite wanted criminals, and to ensure that international terrorists have nowhere to run or hide.

We cannot meet the danger of cybercrime alone, when an attack on America's heartland can be launched from a laptop halfway around the world, passing through five or six other countries before it reaches its U.S. target.

We cannot single-handedly solve every conflict or save every child in the world — much as we might like to. While we must and will always be prepared to act alone to defend our vital interests, there are many cases when a multinational response is a better way to achieve our goals without shouldering all the burdens and footing all the bills. Otherwise, every time a conflict or human tragedy strikes, we will face the unacceptable choice of tackling it alone or turning our backs and walking away.

We cannot solve our nation's drug problem without the support of supplier nations — to help stem the flow of illegal narcotics entering our country, and put drug traffickers behind bars and their operations out of business.

We must find ways to help new democracies carry out necessary economic reforms without so damaging the poor that the reforms — or democracy itself — are lost in the resulting backlash.

We do not, on our own, have the resources to help every fledgling market democracy deliver for its people, or to turn weak nations into strong, reliable partners by waving some magic wand. Yet, if the remarkable tide of democracy is reversed, our interests will surely suffer. We need the cooperation of other nations and international institutions like the United Nations, the World Bank, and the International Monetary Fund to help make sure economic and democratic reform keep advancing hand in hand.

We cannot sustain our own remarkable prosperity unless other nations around the world continue to take down barriers to our products and to generate consumers with the cash on hand to buy them. As President Clinton so often points out, we have only 4 percent of the world's population. We need the other 96 percent to buy our exports if we want our nation's economy to continue to grow.

Our friends abroad, conservative and liberal, understand their stake, and ours, in policies of international engagement. As *The Economist* observes,

A passive America, even massively armour-plated, is not much use either to others, or to itself. In order to impose stability on a chaotic, constantly surprising world, America needs to work with allies. When Saddam Hussein threatened America's oil supplies, the biggest alliance ever seen was put together at America's behest. When outlaw states such as North Korea or Iraq threaten the peace with nuclear or biological weapons, international cooperation is needed to try to contain them. Such cooperation is not created out of thin air. It needs a constant process of negotiation, communication, and mutual help that may involve (as Mr. Clinton, for all his faults, has understood) the putting of money and manpower into places where, on the face of it, America has no interest.[14]

Moreover, the more that we insist on acting alone, the more, perversely, we undermine our own authority and influence. Put simply, America cannot lead if we don't have any partners.

Time is of the essence. If we don't use these years of relatively good and peaceful times to deal with our future nightmares, we will pay a terrible price down the road. Yet we will only succeed in doing so if we restore in Washington some measure of seriousness, some ability of the two parties to work together for the common good, and a change in our political culture. Washington must go back to governing, rather than letting the political games of "gotcha" consume its energies. We can only hope the next Administration can break the vicious circles in relations with the press, Congress, and the public. And we should hope, as well, that the same technologies that have given such power over our politics to media consultants and spin doctors will also provide a positive boost to popular participation. Candidates' use of Web sites to inform as well as spin; AOL's running campaign forum; CNN and C-SPAN coverage of debates: such can be tremendous democratic devices.

The problem is not in the institutions of our democracy. We cannot fix what is wrong through our courts or only through our laws. The health of any democracy depends, in the end, on the customs of its political culture, the glue that holds together Emerson's "resounding tumult" of an open, healthy society. The greatest nightmare of all could be the further erosion of the democratic compact that has brought us through far greater crises in our past than those we face now.

What is at stake is not only our ability to act in our own interest in a rapidly changing world. It is the future of our democracy itself, the source of our greatest strength. Because there is no stronger nation than that of a free people bound in the habits of civility.

NOTES

INTRODUCTION

1. Lawrence J. Korb, "Our Overstuffed Armed Forces," *Foreign Affairs*, Nov.–Dec. 1995, p. 23.

CHAPTER ONE

1. Jonathan B. Tucker, "Chemical/Biological Terrorism: Coping with a New Threat," *Politics and the Life Sciences*, Sept. 1996, p. 173.
2. Naomi Freundlich, "Countering 'The Poor Man's Nuclear Weapons,'" *Business Week*, Dec. 16, 1996, p. 130; and Christopher Dickey, "Plagues in the Making," *Newsweek*, Oct. 9, 1995, pp. 50–51.
3. U.S. Department of State, "Patterns of Global Terrorism: 1999," Apr. 2000.
4. DCI Counterterrorist Center, "International Terrorism in 1997: A Statistical View," Mar. 1998, www.odci.gov/cia/di/products/terrorism; and U.S. Department of State, "Patterns of Global Terrorism 1999," Apr. 2000.
5. Roberto Suro, "U.S. Lacking in Terrorism Defenses: Study Cites a Need to Share Intelligence," *Washington Post*, Apr. 24, 1998, p. A1.
6. Tim Weiner, "Sophisticated Terrorists Pose Daunting Obstacle," *New York Times*, Aug. 13, 1998.
7. Quoted in "Kaczynski's Only Aim Was to Kill, Memo Says," *USA Today*, Apr. 29, 1998.
8. Brian M. Jenkins, "Understanding the Link Between Motives and Methods," in *Terrorism with Chemical and Biological Weapons*, ed. Brad Roberts (Alexandria, Va.: Chemical and Biological Arms Control Institute, 1997), p. 48.
9. Meggie, "Can a Christian Hate?," www4.stormfront.org/posterity/ci/hate.html.
10. Karl Lowe, "Analyzing Technical Constraints on Bio-Terrorism: Are They Still Important?," in *Terrorism with Chemical and Biological Weapons*, ed. Brad Roberts (Alexandria, Va.: Chemical and Biological Arms Control Institute, 1997), p. 55.
11. Ibid., pp. 59–60.
12. Tucker, op. cit., pp. 171–172.
13. James Adams, *The Next World War* (New York: Simon and Schuster, 1998), p. 166.

14. Tucker, op. cit., p. 171.
15. Quoted in David Hoffman, "Russian Nuclear Security Called Lax," *Washington Post,* Nov. 27, 1998, p. A1.
16. Matthew Bunn, "Loose Nukes Fears: Anecdotes of the Current Crisis," Dec. 5, 1998, Russian-American Nuclear Security Advisory Council (RANSAC) Web site (www.ransac.org). Bunn describes a number of such incidents.
17. John Ward Anderson and William Branigin, "Flood of Contraband Hard to Stop," *Washington Post,* Nov. 2, 1997, A1.
18. Tucker, op. cit. p. 167; and John F. Sopko, "The Changing Proliferation Threat," Foreign Policy, winter 1996, p. 12.
19. William J. Broad, Judith Miller, and Sheryl WuDunn, "How Japan Germ Terror Alerted World," *New York Times,* May 26, 1998.
20. Tucker, op. cit., p. 169.
21. Quoted in Sopko, op. cit., p. 14.
22. Ibid., p. 5.
23. Ibid.
24. Tucker, op. cit., p. 169.
25. Sopko, op. cit., p. 6.
26. Ibid.
27. Percy Preston, "The Bioweaponeers," *New Yorker,* Mar. 9, 1998, p. 60.
28. David Hoffman, "A Puzzle of Epidemic Proportions: Source of 1979 Anthrax Outbreak in Russia Still Clouded," *Washington Post,* Dec. 16, 1998, p. A1; and Jessica Stern, *The Ultimate Terrorists* (Cambridge, Mass.: Harvard University Press, 1999), p. 43.
29. Graham Allison, et al., *Avoiding Nuclear Anarchy* (Cambridge Mass.: MIT Press, 1996), p. 11.
30. David Hoffman, "Chemical Dumps Expose Russia to Big Health Risks," and "Soviets Reportedly Built Chemical Weapon Despite Pact with U.S.," *Washington Post,* Aug. 16, 1998, pp. A1 and A36.
31. Jeffrey R. Smith, "Poison, Germ Weapons Would Not Be Direct Targets," *Washington Post,* Feb. 22, 1998, p. A28.
32. William J. Broad and Judith Miller, "Germs, Atoms and Poison Gas: The Iraqi Shell Game," *New York Times,* Dec. 20, 1998; and Nicholas Rufford, "Saddam Has Hidden Anthrax Arsenal," *Sunday Times* (London), Dec. 20, 1998.
33. Quoted in Robert Taylor, "All Fall Down," *New Scientist,* May 11, 1996.

CHAPTER TWO

1. James Adams, *The Next World War* (New York: Simon and Schuster, 1998), pp. 156–158.
2. Kevin Soo Hoo, Seymour Goodman, and Lawrence Greenberg, "Information Technology and the Terrorist Threat," *Survival* 39 (3 [autumn 1997]): p. 153.

Notes

3. John H. Peterson, "Info Wars," *U.S. Naval Institute Proceedings,* May 1993, p. 89, cited in Dan Caldwell, "Power, Information and War," occasional paper, Emirates Center for Strategic Studies and Research, Abu Dhabi, UAE, 1998.
4. Adams, op. cit., pp. 169–170.
5. "Critical Foundations: Protecting America's Infrastructures," report of the President's Commission on Critical Infrastructure Protection, Oct. 1997, p. 18.
6. John T. Correll, "War in Cyberspace," *Air Force Magazine,* Jan. 1998.
7. Ibid.
8. Ibid.
9. Quoted in Bradley Graham, "U.S. Studies New Threat: Cyber Attack," *Washington Post,* May 24, 1998, p. A1; and Adams, op. cit., pp. 187–188.
10. Graham, op. cit.; and Julie Moffett, "United States: Survey Shows Attacks on Computer Systems Increasing," Radio Free Europe/Radio Liberty, Mar. 11, 1998.
11. Moffett, op. cit.; and Louise Kehoe, "Hackers Target NASA and Others Through Windows," *Financial Times,* Mar. 5, 1998.
12. Quoted in David Stout, "Pentagon Acknowledges Hacker Intrusion into a Computer System," *New York Times,* Apr. 22, 1998.
13. "Presidential Commission to Prepare for 'Electronic Pearl Harbors,'" *Telecom and Network Security Review,* Aug. 1996.
14. 1998 CSI/FBI Computer Crime and Security Survey, www.gocsi.com.
15. M. J. Zuckerman, "Security On Trial in Case of On-Line Citibank Heist," *USA Today,* Sept. 19, 1997.
16. Sharon Walsh and Robert O'Harrow, Jr., "Trying to Keep a Lock on Company Secrets," *Washington Post,* Feb. 17, 1998, p. D1; and Udo Flohr, "Bank Robbers Go Electronic," *BYTE* (www.byte.com/art/9511/sec3/aart11.htm), Nov. 1995.
17. Roy Godson and W. J. Olson, *International Organized Crime: Emerging Threat to U.S. Security,* National Strategy Information Center, 1993, pp. 36, 38.
18. Phil Williams, "Transnational Criminal Organizations: Strategic Alliances," *The Washington Quarterly,* winter 1998, pp. 64–65.
19. Jessica Stern, *The Ultimate Terrorists* (Cambridge, Mass.: Harvard University Press, 1999), p. 65.
20. John Kerry, *The Web of Crime That Threatens America's Security: The New War* (New York: Simon and Schuster, 1997), p. 31.
21. Godson and Olson, op. cit., pp. 11–12.
22. Fredric Dannen and Ira Silverman, "The Supernote," *The New Yorker,* Oct. 23, 1995, pp. 50–55; and Ron Moreau and Russell Watson, "Is It Real, or Super K?," *Newsweek,* June 10, 1996, p. 42.
23. Claire Sterling, *Thieves' World: The Threat of the New Global Network of Organized Crime* (New York: Simon and Schuster, 1994), p. 244.

24. Thomas L. Friedman, "Angry, Wired and Deadly," *New York Times*, Aug. 22, 1998.

25. Fred Bayles, "Anti-Terrorism Plans Falling Short," *USA Today*, Oct. 13, 1998.

26. Patrick Clawson et al., "What Do the Sudan/Afghanistan Strikes Harbinger?," *PolicyWatch* (Washington Institute for Near East Policy) 337 (Aug. 21, 1998).

27. "How Do Free Trade and Globalization Impinge on U.S. Security and How Does Defense Policy Affect U.S. Economic Welfare?," remarks by Dr. John Hamre at the Council on Foreign Relations, June 5, 1998.

28. Thomas W. Lippman, "Albright Chides Afghan Rulers," *Washington Post*, Aug. 19, 1998, p. A24.

29. M. J. Zuckerman, "Point Man on Terrorism Knows Security Issues, *USA Today*, May 22, 1998.

30. "Remarks by the President on American Security in a Changing World" at George Washington University, Washington, D.C., Office of the Press Secretary, The White House, Aug. 5, 1996.

CHAPTER THREE

1. General John J. Sheehan, "Building the Right Military for the 21st Century," *Strategic Review* summer 1997, p. 10.

2. James Adams, *The Next World War* (New York: Simon and Schuster, 1998), pp. 88–89.

3. Eliot A. Cohen, "A Revolution in Warfare," *Foreign Affairs*, Mar.–Apr. 1996.

4. William S. Cohen and John M. Shalikashvili, "The Best Defense for the Future," *Washington Times*, June 4, 1997.

5. Quoted in Walter Pincus, "From Tiny Aircraft to Robots and Radars, Pentagon Pursues New Tools," *Washington Post*, Mar. 29, 1998, p. A2.

6. Harlan Ullman, James Wade, et al., *Shock and Awe: Achieving Rapid Dominance* (Washington, D.C.: National Defense University Press, 1996), pp. 14–15.

7. Secretary of Defense William S. Cohen, remarks as prepared for delivery, National Defense University Joint Operations Symposium B QDR Conference, Fort McNair, Washington D.C., June 23, 1997.

8. Army Training and Doctrine Command, "Force XXI Operations" (TRADOC Pamphlet 525-5), Aug. 1994, pp. 2–9.

9. Mark Thompson, "Wired for War," *Time*, Mar. 31, 1997.

10. Quoted in Joel Garreau, "Point Men for a Revolution," *Washington Post*, Mar. 6, 1999, p. A1.

11. Sheehan, op. cit., p. 10.

12. Remarks of President Clinton at Omaha Beach, Colleville-sur-Mer, France, June 6, 1994.

13. Joseph S. Nye, Jr., and William A. Owens, "America's Information Edge," *Foreign Affairs*, Mar.–Apr. 1996. See also David C. Gompert, Richard L. Kugler, and Martin C. Libicki, "Mind the Gap" (Washington, D.C.: National Defense University Press, 1999).
14. Lawrence J. Korb, "Money to Burn at the Pentagon," *New York Times*, Sept. 25, 1998.
15. Lieutenant General (ret.) Walter F. Ulmer, Joe Collins, Owen Jacobs, et al. "American Military Culture in the 21st Century," Center for Strategic and International Studies, Jan. 10, 2000.
16. Raymond Close, "Hard Target: We Can't Defeat Terrorism with Bombs and Bombast," *Washington Post*, Aug. 30, 1998, p. C1.
17. Maxwell Taylor, *The Uncertain Trumpet* (New York: Harper and Brothers, 1960), 196–197.
18. Bruce D. Berkowitz and Allan E. Goodman, "The Logic of Covert Action," *The National Interest* 51 (spring 1998).
19. Bradley Graham, "Cyberwar: A New Weapon Awaits a Set of Rules," *Washington Post*, July 8, 1998, p. A1.
20. Bill Gertz, "China Plots Winning Role in Cyberspace: Military Paper Cites Need for 'Paralyzing Internet Software,'" *Washington Times*, Nov. 17, 1999, p. 1.
21. Quoted in Graham, op. cit.

CHAPTER FOUR

1. Ivo Daalder, *Getting to Dayton: The Making of America's Bosnia Policy* (Washington, D.C.: Brookings Institution Press/Inter-American Development Bank, 2000).
2. Press Briefing by National Security Advisor Tony Lake and Director for Strategic Plans and Policy General Wesley Clark, The White House, May 5, 1994.
3. Colonel J. Michael Hardesty and Jason D. Ellis, "Training for Peace Operations: The U.S. Army Adapts to the Post–Cold War World," *Peaceworks* (United States Institute of Peace) 12 (Feb. 1997): p. vii.
4. Author interview with Lieutenant Colonel Mike Bailey, Dec. 17, 1998.
5. Remarks at Georgetown University, Dec. 12, 1991.
6. Address by Secretary General Kofi Annan upon receiving the Jit Trainor Award for Distinction in the Conduct of Diplomacy, Georgetown University, Washington, D.C., Feb. 23, 1999.
7. Remarks by General Shalikashvili to the Robert R. McCormick Tribune Foundation, George Washington University, Washington, D.C., May 4, 1995.

CHAPTER FIVE

1. Henry Kissinger, *A World Restored* (Boston: Houghton Mifflin, 1973), p. 1.
2. Zbigniew Brzezinski, *The Grand Chessboard* (New York: Basic Books, 1998), p. 33.
3. Richard Bernstein and Ross H. Munro, "The Rising Asian Hegemon," *Foreign Affairs*, Mar.–Apr. 1997.
4. Cited in Bernstein and Munro, op. cit.
5. John Pomfret, "China Ponders New Rules of 'Unrestricted War,'" *Washington Post*, Aug. 8, 1999, p. A1.
6. John W. Garver, "China as Number One," *The China Journal* 39 (Jan. 1998): p. 61.
7. Quoted in Tom Whitehouse, "Yeltsin Ups Nuclear Ante," *The Guardian* (London), Apr. 30, 1999.
8. Michael Krepon, "Invitation to Nuclear Disaster," *Washington Post*, May 25, 1999, p. A15.
9. Ibid.
10. "Poll: 71 Percent of Russians Think Government Too Dependent on West," *AP Worldstream*, May 7, 1999.
11. Quoted in Michael Wines, "Crisis in the Balkans: The Russians," *New York Times*, Apr. 12, 1999.
12. George Tenet, Director of Central Intelligence, testimony before the Senate Armed Services Committee Hearing on Current and Projected National Security Threats, Feb. 2, 1999.
13. Nicole Winfield, "North Korea Says U.S. Must Do More," *Associated Press*, Sept. 25, 1999.
14. Remarks of the Honorable Donald Rumsfeld, Center for Security Policy, Oct. 7, 1998, printed in the *Congressional Record*, Oct. 14, 1998, pp. S12568–S12570.
15. Executive summary of the report of the Commission to Assess the Ballistic Missile Threat to the United States, July 15, 1998.
16. Peter Maass, "Get Ready, Here Comes the Exoatmospheric Kill Vehicle," *New York Times Magazine*, Sept. 26, 1999.
17. Department of Defense News Release No. 018-99, Jan. 20, 1999.
18. Bates Gill and Michael O'Hanlon, "Power Plays: . . . While There's Less to the Chinese Threat Than Meets the Eye," *Washington Post*, June 20, 1999, p. B1.
19. Samuel R. Berger, "Getting the New Russia on Its Feet," *Washington Post*, Sept. 5, 1999, p. B7.
20. David Sanger, "Political Muscle: When Allies Are Fierce Competitors," *New York Times*, May 2, 1999.
21. Chrystia Freeland, "Not-so-badfellas," *The New Republic*, Oct. 12, 1998.
22. Quoted in Freeland, op. cit.

23. *CIA World Factbook,* 1999.
24. Annual Report on Military Expenditures, 1998, submitted to the Committee on Appropriations of the U.S. House of Representatives by the Department of State, Feb. 19, 1999.
25. Thomas L. Friedman, "China's Choices," *New York Times,* Mar. 23, 1999.
26. "Can China Change?," *The Economist,* Oct. 2, 1999.
27. Quoted in "Can China Change?," op. cit.
28. Trish Saywell, "On the Edge," *Far Eastern Economic Review,* Feb. 25, 1999.
29. Executive summary of the report of the Commission to Assess the Ballistic Missile Threat to the United States, July 15, 1998.
30. John Pomfret, "N. Korea's Conduit for Crime," *Washington Post,* Apr. 25, 1999, p. A21.
31. Quoted in Stan Lehman, "Brazil Bailout Aimed at Halting Spread of Crisis," *Boston Globe,* Nov. 14, 1998.
32. David Jenkins, "Tipping into Chaos," *Sydney Morning Herald,* Oct. 28, 1998 (from *World Press Review,* Feb. 1999).
33. Quoted in Mark Lander, "New Crisis Frames Even Tougher Test of Indonesia Unity," *New York Times,* Nov. 21, 1999.
34. Brzezinski, op. cit, p. 125.
35. "A Survey of Central Asia: Put Your House in Order," *The Economist,* Feb. 7, 1998.
36. Larry Rohter, "Colombia's Offer to Rebels Appears Futile," *New York Times,* May 3, 1999.
37. Quoted in Larry Rohter, "Colombia Rebels Reign in Ceded Area," *New York Times,* May 16, 1999.
38. Quoted in Douglas Farah, "U.S. Ready to Boost Aid to Troubled Colombia," *Washington Post,* Aug. 23, 1999, p. A1.
39. Lawrence K. Altman, "More African Women Have AIDS Than Men," *New York Times,* Nov. 24, 1999; and "U.N. Issues Grim Report on the 11 Million Children Orphaned by AIDS," *New York Times,* Dec. 2, 1999.
40. Quoted in Elizabeth Becker, "European Allies to Spend More on Weapons," *New York Times,* Sept. 22, 1999.

CHAPTER SIX

1. John M. Broder, "Quietly and Dexterously, Senate Republicans Set a Trap," *New York Times,* Oct. 14, 1999.
2. News conference by President Clinton, Washington, D.C., Oct. 14, 1999.
3. Quoted in Barbara Crossette, "Around the World, Dismay over Senate Vote on Treaty," *New York Times,* Oct. 15, 1999.
4. "A Damaging Arms Control Defeat," *New York Times,* Oct. 14, 1999.
5. Gerald Tomlinson, *Speaker's Treasury of Political Stories, Anecdotes and Humor* (New York: Prentice Hall, 1990), p. 89.

6. E. J. Dionne, *They Only Look Dead* (New York: Simon and Schuster, 1996), p. 20.
7. "Politics Brief: Is There a Crisis?" *The Economist*, July 17, 1999.
8. Ibid.
9. Thomas E. Patterson, *Out of Order* (New York: Vintage Books, 1994), pp. 11–15.
10. Molly Ivins, "Garbage Town," *Washington Post*, Oct. 12, 1999.
11. The Pew Research Center for the People and the Press, "Public Appetite for Government Misjudged: Washington Leaders Wary of Public Opinion," www.people-press.org/leadrpt.htm.
12. Remarks by President Clinton at the White House Correspondents' Dinner, Washington D.C., May 1, 1999.
13. Ronald Brownstein, "New Appeals for a Return to Civility," *Los Angeles Times*, Feb. 15, 1999.
14. Quoted in James Kitfield, "A Return to Isolationism," *National Journal*, Oct. 8, 1999.
15. Ibid.
16. Ibid.
17. George Stephanopoulos, *All Too Human* (New York: Little Brown, 1999), p. 328.
18. Dick Morris, *Behind the Oval Office* (New York: Random House, 1997), p. 247.
19. Ibid., p. 254.
20. Bill Kovach and Tom Rosenstiel, "Warp Speed: America in the Age of Mixed Media," The Century Fund, New York, 1999.
21. Ibid.
22. Ibid.
23. David Ignatius, "Serial Hysterics," *Washington Post*, Sept. 15, 1999, p. A25.
24. James F. Hoge, Jr., "Foreign News: Who Gives a Damn?," *Columbia Journalism Review*, Nov.–Dec. 1997.
25. The Pew Research Center for the People and the Press, op. cit.
26. For this and previous statistics see *American Public Opinion and U.S. Foreign Policy 1999*, ed. John E. Reilly (Chicago: The Chicago Council on Foreign Relations, 1999).
27. "New Kosovo Study Finds Public Shows More Tolerance of Possible Fatalities Than Assumed," Program on International Policy Attitudes press release, Washington, D.C., May 19, 1999.
28. Steven Kull and I. M. Destler, *Misreading the Public: The Myth of a New Isolationism* (Washington, D.C.: Brookings Institution Press, 1999), p. 254.

Notes

EPILOGUE

1. An Economic Report of the President transmitted to the Congress Feb. 1999.
2. Children's Defense Fund, "The State of America's Children Yearbook 2000: 25 Key Facts About American Children," www.childrensdefense.org/keyfacts.html.
3. "A Foreign Policy Agenda for the Second Term," remarks by Samuel R. Berger, Center for Strategic and International Studies, Washington D.C., Mar. 27, 1997.
4. "Markets Go Global," *The Economist* (The World Economy Survey), Sept. 20, 1997, p. 24.
5. Frances Cairncross, *The Death of Distance* (Boston, Mass.: Harvard Business School Press, 1997), p. 87; and "Over 150 Million Internet Users Worldwide at Year-End 1998," press release, Computer Industry Almanac (www.c-i-a.com), Apr. 30, 1999.
6. "Global Trade and Travel Import Health Threats, Report Warns," *Washington Post,* June 22, 1997, p. A4.
7. Laurie Garrett, "The Return of Infectious Disease," *Foreign Affairs,* Jan.–Feb. 1996.
8. "World Airline Traffic and Load Factors Highest Ever in 1997," Montreal PIO 26/27 (www.icao.int/icao/en/nr/pio9726.htm), Dec. 23, 1997.
9. Victoria Holt, "Briefing Book on Peacekeeping: The U.S. Role in United Nations Peace Operations," Council for a Livable World Education Fund, Washington D.C., Dec. 1994, p. 12.
10. John Hillen, "Picking Up UN Peacekeeping Pieces: Knowing When to Say When," *Foreign Affairs,* July–Aug. 1998.
11. Holt, op. cit., p. 13.
12. "The United Nations," U.S. Department of State fact sheet, Jan. 2000.
13. Quoted in Joseph Kahn and David E. Sanger, "Impasse on Trade Delivers a Stinging Blow to Clinton," *New York Times,* Dec. 5, 1999.
14. "America's World," *The Economist,* Oct. 23, 1999, p. 15.

ACKNOWLEDGMENTS

Writing is usually a lonely business. The writer, a blank page or screen, perhaps a muse on a good day, alone. That was not the case with this book. Whether it was with the team of government officials that traveled back and forth to Africa with me over the past two years or with the students at Georgetown University who shared their views and arguments as we examined these issues in class, I have had the pleasure of good company, of testing ideas and learning, from many others as I worked on it.

I am deeply indebted, in particular, to a number of friends and associates.

First to Vinca Showalter Lafleur, whose keen intelligence and extraordinary pen are evident throughout this book. To Dick Todd and Liz Darhansoff, whose superb guidance and editorial skills made the book both possible and better. To Sarah Crichton, whose judgment and aversion to pedantry provided friendly discipline. To Pamela Marshall, an extraordinary copyeditor. To my assistants at Georgetown, Fran Balicudiong, Victoria Buresch, Sharon Forrest, Alice Norris, and Susan Shin, for their patience in wrestling with scribbled drafts and the mysterious differences between Word and WordPerfect. To my research assistants Miguel Buckenmeyer, Laura Cooper, Denis Dragovic, and Matthew Stevens, for their skills not only at ferreting out facts, but for helping me think and for arguing with me when they thought I was wrong. To Brian Reilly, for his generous assistance in helping Casey Gates steal the credit-card numbers. To Georgetown University, a great academic institution with first-rate students and a pretty good basketball team, for all its support over the past three years. And to the many friends who read and commented on all or part of this book, including Mike Bailey, Peter Bass, Richard Clarke, Greg Cooper, Ivo Daalder, John Deutch, Roy Godson, Dotty Lynch, Michael McFaul, John Prendergast, Molly Raiser, Susan Rice, Larry Rossin, David Rothkopf, Lanny Smith, Tara Sonenshine, Jessica Stern, Joe Stiglitz, Gordon Sullivan, Strobe Talbott, and Sandy Vershbow.

It is obligatory to write that any and all mistakes are mine, not theirs. In this case, it is all too true. And to all, my deepest thanks.

INDEX

Aceh, 215, 217–218
Acheson, Dean, 179–180
Adams, Gerry, 118–128
Adams, James, 42–43
Afghanistan, 50, 101, 222
Africa: AIDS virus in, 227; economy of, 226–228; internal conflicts in, 113, 114, 115, 227–228; Organization of African Unity, 169; peacekeeping missions in, 161; U.S. embassy bombings in, 21; weaknesses in, 226–228
Agincourt, Battle of, 75
AIDS crisis, 227, 280
aircraft, unmanned, 75
Ajaria, 221
Albright, Madeleine, 58, 132, 146, 147, 148, 257
All Source Analysis Systems (ASAS), 85–86
ambiguous warfare: anonymity and, 99–106; scenario of, 66–74; terrorists and, 99–106
Ambon, 215
Ambrose, Stephen, 92
American Type Culture Collection, 29
Anarchist's Cookbook, 26
Angola, 113, 227–228
Annan, Kofi, 161–162
anonymity: ambiguous warfare and, 99–106; of terrorists, 74

anthrax, 28, 30, 31–32, 54; culturing, 8–10; dispersion of, 10–12, 13–14; effects of, 8, 12, 13
antiterrorists, 102–106
APEC, 278
Arafat, Yasir, 275
Argentina, 50
Aristide, Jean-Bertrand, 130–141
Armageddon virus, 39
armed forces. *See* military establishment
Armenia, 221
Armey, Dick, 254
arms embargo, 144–145, 147, 150
Army, U.S.: changes in command structure, 88–89; Digital Corps, 85, 86–87; Fort Hood, 85–87, 96; Land Information Warfare Activity, 104; in Somalia, 129–130. *See also* military establishment
Aryan Nation, 29
ASAS. *See* All Source Analysis Systems
ASEAN. *See* Association of Southeast Asian Nations
Asia: conflicts in, 215, 218–222; economic crisis of, 211–212, 213
Aspin, Les, 17, 130
Association of Southeast Asian Nations (ASEAN), 216
asymmetrical warfare, 98–99
Atwood, Brian, 253
Aum Shinrikyo, 27–28, 50, 55

Index

Australia, 43
Azerbaijan, 220, 221

Bacon, Kenneth, 57
Baghdad, Iraq: attack on, 18–20, 99
Bailey, Mike, 157–160
Baker, Douglas, 29
balance of power, 179–181; imbalance of weakness, 189–191; NATO and, 180–181; scenario of, 175–179
ballistic missiles, 184–187, 205
Baltic states, 232–233
Balz, Dan, 268
base funding, 96
Berger, Sandy, 17, 56, 135, 143, 146, 149, 151, 188
Berkowitz, Bruce, 101
Bernstein, Carl, 266
Beschloss, Michael, 247
Bhagwan Shree Rajneesh, 29
bin Ladin, Usama, 22, 50–51, 100
biological weapons. *See* bioweapons
Biological Weapons Convention, 284
Biopreparat, 14
bioweapons: Aum Shinrikyo's use of, 28; characteristics of, 32; defense against, 54; dispersion of, 8, 24; effects of, 13; governments' use of, 30–31; Great Britain's use of, 30; Iraq's use of, 31–32; nonproliferation efforts against, 284; production of, 24; scenario of, 1–12; Soviet Union's use of, 30–31; U.S. use of, 30
black biology, 14
black market, 27, 50
Black October (1993), 129
Blair, Tony, 241
Blaker, James, 88
border crossings, 27, 29–30, 49
Boren, David, 258
Bork, Robert, 251

Bosnia, 91, 96, 132, 174, 274, 286; coercive diplomacy in, 117, 129, 142–151; Dayton Accords and, 76, 275; internal conflict in, 113, 114; NATO in, 142, 144, 145, 151, 161; peacekeeping in, 163; United Nations in, 142, 143, 145–148
Boston, Massachusetts, 55
Bottom-Up Review, 95
botulism, 14, 28, 31–32
Bradlee, Ben, 266
Branch, Taylor, 135
Brazil, 50, 191, 213–215, 224
Broder, John M., 239–240
Brzezinski, Zbigniew, 180, 218
bubonic plague, 14, 29
Burleigh, Peter, 253
Burundi, 113
Bush, George: assassination attempt on, 16, 99; Gulf War and, 16; and Haiti, 130; nuclear test ban and, 242; Somalia and, 166; United Nations and, 286

cable television, 267, 269
Cahill, Joe, 123
Cambodia, 113, 157–160, 286
Camp Pendleton, 87
Canada, 276
Cardoso, Fernando Henrique, 213, 214
carjacking, 49
Carrillo Fuentes, Amada, 230
Carter, Jimmy, 136–141, 259
Caspian, 191, 219–220, 221–222
CD Universe, 35–37, 38
Cedras, Raoul, 130–141
celebrity candidates, 247
censorship, Internet, 62
Center for Nonproliferation Studies, 26
Central America, 113
Central Asia, 218–222
Central Intelligence Agency (CIA): Clinton and, 249–250; Counter-

306

Index

Index

Ireland, 170, 285
Irian Jaya, 215, 218
Irish Republican Army, 51, 118, 119, 120, 121, 124
Islam. *See* Muslims
Israel, 117, 275; carjacking in, 49; honest brokering and,116
Ivins, Molly, 246–247

Jakarta, 217–218
Japan, 50, 205; Aum Shinrikyo in, 27–28, 50, 55; China and, 200; economy of, 191, 210–213; exports of, 209–210; U.S. relations with, 277
Japanese Red Army, 51
Javakheti, 221
Jefferson, Thomas, 243
Jenkins, Brian, 22
Johnson, Lyndon B., 90
Johnston Atoll, 30
Joint Chiefs of Staff: command structure, 88–92; Iraqi terrorists and, 16–17
Joint Surveillance Target Attack Radar Systems (J-STARS),78, 85
The Jolly Roger Cookbook, 26
journalists. *See* media
J-STARS. *See* Joint Surveillance Target Attack Radar Systems
juche ideology, 204
Justice Department: Iraqi terrorists and, 16–17

Kaczynski, Ted, 22
Kaiser, Bob, 268
Kassebaum, Nancy, 258
Kazakhstan, 220
Kennedy, Joe, 119–120
Kennedy, John F., xv, 238
Kennedy, Ted, 118, 120, 127
Kenya, 20
Khatami, Mohammad, 188
Khmer Rouge, 158–159
Khobar Towers, 20, 57

Kiichi, Miyazawa, 200
Kim Chong-Il, 94
Kim Dae-Jung, 276
King, Martin Luther, Jr., 268
King, Peter, 118, 119, 127
Kissinger, Henry, 180, 251–252
Klima, Ivan, 247
Kosovo, 95; China and, 202; internal conflicts in, 113, 115–116; NATO in, 161, 230–231; peacekeeping in, 164, 166, 169, 285; public attitude toward, 273; Russia and, 183–184, 188, 196; Serb cyberattacks against NATO, 105
Kovach, Bill, 267, 268
Krepon, Michael, 184
Krulak, Charles, 87
Kruzel, Joe, 151
Kull, Stephen, 272
Kuwait, 16, 95, 286
Kyl, Jon, 239

Land Information Warfare Activity (LIWA), 104
land mines, 282
Land Warrior, 79
Langley Air Force Base, 43
Lavy, Thomas Lewis, 29–30
Lebanon, 51, 258
Lee, Robert E., 83, 84
Levin, Vladimir, 46
Levitte, Jean-David, 275
Liberia, 113
Lieberthal, Kenneth, 198–199
LIWA. *See* Land Information Warfare Activity
loans for shares policy, 192–193
logic bombs, 39–40, 104
long-range missiles, 184–189
loose geeks, 27
loose nukes, 27
loose spooks, 27
Lott, Trent, 239, 240, 252–253

Index

Index

National Security Council (NSC), 56;
  cooperating with National Director
  for Combating Proliferation, 60–61;
  Northern Ireland diplomacy and,
  118–128; politics and, 261–262;
  scenario of, 66–74
national sovereignty, 280–282
NATO: balance of power and, 180–181;
  Bosnia and, 142, 144,145, 151,
  161; cyberattacks against, 105;
  enlargement of, 232–233, 277;
  Kosovo and, 161, 230–231;
  peacekeeping missions and role
  of, 161–162; Russia and, 183;
  Serbia and, 184; weaknesses of,
  230–231
Navy, U.S.: changes in command
  structure, 88–89. *See also* military
  establishment
Neal, Richard, 118, 119
Nelson, Hal, 83
Nepal, 285
nerve gas, 14, 55
Netcat, 41
news programs, 267, 269
The Next World War (Adams), 42–43
Nixon, Richard, 251–252
NMD. *See* national missile defense
nonproliferation efforts, 238–243, 277, 284
Non-Proliferation Treaty, 277
North, Oliver, 60
Northern Ireland, 118–128; Good Friday
  Agreement, 126; honest brokering
  and, 116; internal conflicts in, 113
North Korea, 232; Clinton and, 185;
  counterfeiting operations of, 51;
  criminal activities of, 205; economic
  weakness of, 204–208; long-range
  missiles in, 184, 185,187, 188;
  military of, 205–207; nuclear
  weapons of, 95,141; sanctions
  against, 205
NSC. *See* National Security Council

Nuclear Test Ban Treaty, 235–243;
  scenario of, 235–238
nuclear weapons, 31; characteristics of, 32;
  Comprehensive Test Ban Treaty and,
  238–243, 277; deterrence and threat
  of, 75; of the former Soviet Union,
  26–27; in India, 55; nonproliferation
  efforts against, 238–243, 277, 284;
  in North Korea, 141; in Russia, 50,
  54, 183–184; scenario of, 235–238;
  terrorists and, 15
Nunn, Sam, 137–140, 258
Nunn-Lugar Cooperative Threat
  Reduction program, 54
Nunn-Lugar-Domenici program, 62
Nye, Joseph, 93

Objective Individual Combat Weapon, 79
O'Dowd, Niall, 120
O'Grady, Scott, 91
Oklahoma City bombing, 20, 61
Oregon, 29
Organization for Security and
  Cooperation in Europe (OSCE), 221
Organization of African Unity, 157, 161,
  169
OSCE. *See* Organization for Security and
  Cooperation in Europe
Owens, William, 78, 88, 93

packet sniffing, 41
Paisley, Ian, 122–123, 127
Pakistan, 170, 203, 205, 285; balance of
  power and, 180; nuclear test ban
  and, 242
Palestine, 285; carjacking and, 49; honest
  brokering and,116
Panama, 223–224
Panetta, Leon, 137
PAPA virus, 39
Paraguay, 50
partisanship, 288; scenario of, 235–238; in
  U.S. Congress, 254, 255, 257–258

Index

Rossin, Larry, 132, 134, 135, 136, 139–140, 145
Rubin, Robert, 211, 213–214
Rudman, Warren, 249, 258
Rumsfeld, Donald, 185
Rumsfeld Commission, 186
Russia, 219, 221, 232, 277; Aum Shinrikyo's membership in, 55; Chechnya and, 183–184, 188; chemical weapons and, 31; cooperation with Federal Bureau of Investigation, 53; economic reforms in, 191–197; Eurasian Balkans and, 221–222; exports of, 209–210; internal conflicts in, 115; Kosovo and, 183–184, 188, 196; Mafia groups in, 50; military threat of, 183–184, 188; NATO and, 183; nuclear weapons in, 54, 183–184, 242; weapons of mass destruction and, 196
Rwanda, 93, 113, 152, 174

salmonella bacteria, 29
sanctions: cost of, 100–101; in Haiti, 131, 132, 134; against North Korea, 205
Sanger, David, 189–190
San Jose, California, 55
Sarajevo, 131, 132
sarin, 14, 25, 26, 27–28
SATAN. *See* Security Administrating Tool for Analyzing Networks
satellite systems, 75, 78, 85, 281
Saudi Arabia: energy resources in, 229
Security Administrating Tool for Analyzing Networks (SATAN), 41
self-discipline, 90–92
Senate, U.S.: Comprehensive Test Ban Treaty and, 239–241; partisan politics in, 253–259
Sendero Luminoso. *See* Shining Path
Serbs, 132, 169; cyberattacks against NATO, 105; Dayton Accords, 261;

NATO and, 184; and peacekeeping efforts in Bosnia, 142–151
Shalikashvili, John, 77–78, 96, 133, 136, 137, 143, 144, 167, 226–227
shaping fires, 87
Sheehan, John J., 75–76, 88
Shevardnadze, Eduard, 220
Shining Path, 50, 224
Sierra Leone, 113, 286
Simpson, Alan, 258
Sinn Fein, 118, 120, 121, 122, 124, 126–127
smart bullets, 79
smart weapons, 75
Smith, Jean Kennedy, 123, 127
Soderberg, Nancy, 118, 119, 120, 121, 125
soldiers, 96–97
Somalia, 99, 113, 131, 152, 154, 174; peacekeeping in, 166, 285; U.S. Army in, 129–130
sound-wave weapons, 79
South Korea, 94, 205, 207, 208, 276, 277
South Ossetia, 220–221
Soviet Union: Afghanistan and, 101; internal conflicts in,113; Mafia groups in, 50; nuclear security system, 26–27; nuclear weapons and, 31; use of bioweapons, 30–31
space-based combat systems, 80–81
Spence, Floyd, 255
Srebrenica massacre, 146, 150
Sri Lanka, 45
Stanton, Edwin M., 90
steel exports, 209–210
Stephanopoulos, George, 133, 259, 269
Stephens, Kathy, 125
Sterling, Claire, 52
Sudan, 113, 115–116
Sullivan, Gordon, 78, 83–85, 97
Summit of the Americas, 278
survivalist groups, 29–30
Sverdlovsk, 30
Sweden: cyberterrorism from, 43

Index

Index

United States (*continued*)
117–174; military presence of,
94–95, 131, 138, 140, 166–169,
232; military strength of, 275,
276, 285; national missile defense,
187–188, 233; need for global
cooperation with, 288–291;
nuclear weapons and, 31;
peacekeeping missions of, 152–165,
166–169, 284–287; politics in,
239–248; response to terrorists,
53–63; Russia and, 191–197; use of
bioweapons, 30; weaknesses of
allies, 228–231
unmanned aerial vehicles (UAV), 78–79,
85
UNPROFOR, 142, 145–148
Unrestricted War (Qiao and Wang), 182
uranium, 25, 26–27, 29, 188
U-2 spy planes, 85

Venezuela, 223, 224
Vershbow, Sandy, 145–147, 149, 150
Vietnam, 166, 263; Colombia compared
to, 223, 225–226
Virginia, 43
vortex launcher, 79
voting rights, 245
VX, 14–15, 31–32

Wade, James, 80
Wahid, Abdurrahman, 218
Wang, Xiangsui, 182
warfare: ambiguous, 99–106; asymmetrical, 98–99; effect of, on
civilians, 112–113, 115
War Powers Resolution, 257–258
Washington, D.C., 55, 235–291
weapons: development of, 75, 78–82;
disintegrating bombs and missiles,
103; information warfare and, 104;
integration of technology systems,
81–83; precision-guided, 76; radio-

frequency, 79; smart, 75; sound-
wave, 79. *See also* bioweapons;
chemical weapons; nuclear
weapons; weapons of mass
destruction
weapons of mass destruction (WMD):
accessing, 24–32; Aum Shinrikyo's
use of, 27–28; on the black market,
27; globalization and, 20, 25–27;
government response to spread
of, 59–63; government's use of,
30–31; in Iran,184–187; Non-
Proliferation Treaty and, 277;
response training to, 54, 55, 62; in
Russia, 196; terrorism and, 15–16,
23, 29–32
Weiner, Tim, 21
Western Sahara, 286
Wheeler, Leroy, 29
White House: partisan politics and,
259–262; self-discipline and, 91
Why England Slept (Kennedy), xv
Wilson, Woodrow, 122
wing walking, 77
WMD. *See* weapons of mass destruction
Woodward, Bob, 265–266
Woolsey, James, 17
World Bank, 233, 290
World Trade Center bombing, 20, 25–26,
29
World Trade Organization, 200, 287–288
World War II, 75, 91–92
Wright, Jim, 252

Yekaterinaburg, 30
Yeltsin, Boris, 129, 183, 184, 193–194
Yokohama, Japan, 28
Yokosuka, Japan, 28
Yousef, Ramzi Ahmed, 25–26, 54–55

Zaire, 276
Zilinskas, Raymond, 32
Zyuganov, Gennady, 194

318